REFLI

|

DAILY PRAYER

REFLECTIONS
FOR
DAILY PRAYER

ADVENT **2014** TO
EVE OF ADVENT **2015**

GILLIAN COOPER
PETER GRAYSTONE
JOANNE GRENFELL
MALCOLM GUITE
LINCOLN HARVEY
MARK IRELAND
ROSALYN MURPHY
MARTYN PERCY
JOHN PRITCHARD
BEN QUASH
ANGELA TILBY
FRANCES WARD
JEREMY WORTHEN
LUCY WINKETT

Church House Publishing
Church House
Great Smith Street
London SW1P 3AZ

ISBN 978 0 7151 4366 7

Published 2014 by Church House Publishing
Copyright © The Archbishops' Council 2014

Liturgical editor: Peter Moger
Series editor: Hugh Hillyard-Parker
Designed and typeset by Hugh Hillyard-Parker
Copy edited by: Ros Connelly
Printed by CPI Group (UK) Ltd, Croydon, CR0 4YY

What do you think of *Reflections for Daily Prayer*?

We'd love to hear from you – simply email us at

publishing@churchofengland.org

or write to us at

Church House Publishing, Church House,
Great Smith Street, London SW1P 3AZ.

Visit **www.dailyprayer.org.uk** for more
information on the *Reflections* series, ordering
and subscriptions.

Contents

About the authors

Gillian Cooper is a writer, teacher, and Old Testament enthusiast. She has previously worked as a theological educator and a cathedral verger, among other things, and is currently an administrator for the Diocese of Lincoln. When not at work, she may be found knitting, or walking her dog on the windswept beaches of Lincolnshire and Norfolk.

Peter Graystone works for Church Army, where he oversees pioneering projects that take the Good News way beyond the walls of a church to profoundly unchurched people. One of those locations is the internet, and he edits Christianity.org.uk, which gives free, confidential, reliable information about the Christian faith. He is a *Church Times* columnist and theatre reviewer.

Joanne Grenfell is Archdeacon of Portsdown in the Diocese of Portsmouth. She is one of eight women regional representatives in the House of Bishops. Previously she was Director of Ordinands, Residentiary Canon, and Dean of Women's Ministry in Sheffield. Her interests include communications, preaching, and literature and theology.

Malcolm Guite, the Chaplain of Girton College Cambridge, is a poet and singer–songwriter, and is the author of *What do Christians Believe?* (Granta 2006), *Faith Hope and Poetry* (Ashgate 2010), *Sounding the Seasons; Seventy Sonnets for the Christian Year* (Canterbury 2012) and *The Singing Bowl* (Canterbury 2013).

Lincoln Harvey is Lecturer in Systematic Theology at St Mellitus College in London. He is also Associate Priest at St Andrew's Fulham Fields. He has written numerous books and articles, including *A Brief Theology of Sport* (SCM Press 2014).

Mark Ireland was formerly Diocesan Missioner for Lichfield and is now (as his wife puts it) a 'proper' vicar again, leading two churches in Shropshire. He is co-author of four books on mission, evangelism and worship, of which the most recent is *How to do Mission Action Planning* (SPCK). He is a member of Archbishops' Council and aspires to climb more hills this year.

Rosalyn Murphy is vicar of St Thomas' Church, located in central Blackpool. She is a writer in biblical studies, often bringing a liberation and womanist theological perspective to her research and lectures. She is an honorary Biblical Scholar with The Queen's Foundation and the Lancashire-Cumbria Theological Partnership. Dr Murphy is also a member of the Archbishops' Council.

Martyn Percy is Principal of Ripon College Cuddesdon and the Oxford Ministry Course. He is also Professor of Theological Education at King's College London, Professorial Research Fellow at Heythrop College London and an Honorary Canon of Salisbury Cathedral.

John Pritchard has recently retired as Bishop of Oxford. Prior to that he has been Bishop of Jarrow, Archdeacon of Canterbury and Warden of Cranmer Hall, Durham. His only ambition was to be a vicar, which he was in Taunton for eight happy years. He enjoys armchair sport, walking, reading, music, theatre and recovering.

Ben Quash has been Professor of Christianity and the Arts at King's College London since 2007, and is Director of the Centre for Arts and the Sacred at King's (ASK). Prior to that he was Dean and Fellow of Peterhouse, Cambridge. He runs a collaborative MA in Christianity and the Arts with the National Gallery in London, and is also Canon Theologian of both Coventry and Bradford Cathedrals.

Angela Tilby is a Canon of Christ Church, Oxford and is Continuing Ministerial Development Adviser for the Diocese of Oxford. Prior to that she has been Vice-Principal of Westcott House, Cambridge and a senior producer at the BBC, where she made several acclaimed television programmes and series.

Frances Ward has been Dean of St Edmundsbury in the county of Suffolk since 2010. Previously she was a Residentiary Canon at Bradford Cathedral, where she immersed herself in interfaith work with the Muslim population of that city. She has published books, most recently *Why Rousseau was Wrong* in 2013.

Jeremy Worthen is a priest in the Church of England and is currently the Secretary for Ecumenical Relations and Theology at the Council for Christian Unity. He previously worked in theological education and has written on a range of subjects, including Jewish–Christian relations. His most recent book is *Responding to God's Call* (Canterbury Press, 2012).

Lucy Winkett is Rector of St James's Church Piccadilly. She contributes regularly to Radio 4's *Thought for the Day* and is the author of *Our Sound is our Wound* (Continuum 2010). She combines parish ministry with chairing an educational trust and running an all-through Church of England Academy, including a project for children on the autistic spectrum. Until 2010, she was Canon Precentor of St Paul's Cathedral.

About Reflections for Daily Prayer

Based on the *Common Worship Lectionary* readings for Morning Prayer, these daily reflections are designed to refresh and inspire times of personal prayer. The aim is to provide rich, contemporary and engaging insights into Scripture.

Each page lists the Lectionary readings for the day, with the main psalms for that day highlighted in **bold**. The Collect of the day – either the *Common Worship* collect or the shorter additional Collect – is also included.

For those using this book in conjunction with a service of Morning Prayer, the following conventions apply: a psalm printed in parentheses is omitted if it has been used as the opening canticle at that office; a psalm marked with an asterisk may be shortened if desired.

A short reflection is provided on either the Old or New Testament reading. Popular writers, experienced ministers, biblical scholars and theologians will be contributing to this series. They all bring their own emphases, enthusiasms and approaches to biblical interpretation to bear.

Regular users of Morning Prayer and *Time to Pray* (from *Common Worship: Daily Prayer*) and anyone who follows the Lectionary for their regular Bible reading will benefit from the rich variety of traditions represented in these stimulating and accessible pieces.

This volume also includes both a simple form of *Common Worship: Morning Prayer* (see inside front and back covers) and a short form of Night Prayer – also known as Compline – (see pp. 324–7), particularly for the benefit of those readers who are new to the habit of the Daily Office or for any reader while travelling.

The importance of daily prayer

Daily prayer is a way of sustaining that most special of all relationships. It helps if we want to pray, but it can be sufficient to want to want to pray, or even to want to want to want to pray! The direction of the heart is what matters, not its achievements. Gradually we are shaped and changed by the practice of daily prayer. Apprentices in prayer never graduate, but we become a little bit more the people God wants us to be.

Prayer isn't a technique; it's a relationship, and it starts in the most ordinary, instinctive reactions to everyday life:

- **Gratitude**: good things are always happening to us, however small.
- **Wonder**: we often see amazing things in nature and in people but pass them by.
- **Need**: we bump into scores of needs every day.
- **Sorrow**: we mess up.

Prayer is taking those instincts and stretching them out before God. The rules then are: start small, stay natural, be honest.

Here are four ways of putting some structure around daily prayer.

1 **The Quiet Time**. This is the classic way of reading a passage of the Bible, using Bible reading reflections like those in this book, and then praying naturally about the way the passage has struck you, taking to God the questions, resolutions, hopes, fears and other responses that have arisen within you.

2 **The Daily Office**. This is a structured way of reading Scripture and psalms, and praying for individuals, the world, the day ahead, etc. It keeps us anchored in the Lectionary, the basic reading of the Church, and so ensures that we engage with the breadth of Scripture, rather than just with our favourite passages. It also puts us in living touch with countless others around the world who are doing something similar. There is a simple form of Morning Prayer on the inside front and back covers of this book, and a form of Night Prayer (Compline) on pp. 324–7. Fuller forms can be found in *Common Worship: Daily Prayer*.

3 Holy Reading. Also known as *Lectio Divina*, this is a tried and trusted way of feeding and meditating on the Bible, described more fully on pages 6–7 of this book. In essence, here is how it is done:

- *Read:* Read the passage slowly until a phrase catches your attention.
- *Reflect:* Chew the phrase carefully, drawing the goodness out of it.
- *Respond:* Pray about the thoughts and feelings that have surfaced in you.
- *Rest:* You may want to rest in silence for a while.
- *Repeat:* Carry on with the passage ...

4 Silence. In our distracted culture some people are drawn more to silence than to words. This will involve *centring* (hunkering down), *focusing* on a short biblical phrase (e.g. 'Come, Holy Spirit'), *waiting* (repeating the phrase as necessary), and *ending* (perhaps with the Lord's Prayer). The length of time is irrelevant.

There are, of course, as many ways of praying as there are people to pray. There are no right or wrong ways to pray. 'Pray as you can, not as you can't', is wise advice. The most important thing is to make sure there is sufficient structure to keep prayer going when it's a struggle as well as when it's a joy. Prayer is too important to leave to chance.

+John Pritchard

Lectio Divina – a way of reading the Bible

Lectio Divina is a contemplative way of reading the Bible. It dates back to the early centuries of the Christian Church and was established as a monastic practice by Benedict in the sixth century. It is a way of praying the Scriptures that leads us deeper into God's word. We slow down. We read a short passage more than once. We chew it over slowly and carefully. We savour it. Scripture begins to speak to us in a new way. It speaks to us personally, and aids that union we have with God through Christ, who is himself the Living Word.

Make sure you are sitting comfortably. Breathe slowly and deeply. Ask God to speak to you through the passage that you are about to read.

This way of praying starts with our silence. We often make the mistake of thinking prayer is about what we say to God. It is actually the other way round. God wants to speak to us. He will do this through the Scriptures. So don't worry about what to say. Don't worry if nothing jumps out at you at first. God is patient. He will wait for the opportunity to get in. He will give you a word and lead you to understand its meaning for you today.

First reading: Listen

As you read the passage listen for a word or phrase that attracts you. Allow it to arise from the passage as if it is God's word for you today. Sit in silence repeating the word or phrase in your head.

Then say the word or phrase aloud.

Second reading: Ponder

As you read the passage again, ask how this word or phrase speaks to your life and why it has connected with you. Ponder it carefully. Don't worry if you get distracted – it may be part of your response to offer to God. Sit in silence and then frame a single sentence that begins to say aloud what this word or phrase says to you.

Third reading: Pray

As you read the passage for the last time, ask what Christ is calling from you. What is it that you need to do or consider or relinquish or take on as a result of what God is saying to you in this word or phrase? In the silence that follows the reading, pray for the grace of the Spirit to plant this word in your heart.

If you are in a group, talk for a few minutes and pray with each other.

If you are on your own, speak your prayer to God either aloud or in the silence of your heart.

If there is time, you may even want to read the passage a fourth time, and then end with the same silence before God with which you began.

+Stephen Cottrell

Monday 1 December

Andrew the Apostle

Ezekiel 47.1-12

*'... the water was flowing down from below the south end
of the threshold of the temple' (v.1)*

Inside Jerusalem's Dome of the Rock, you can visit the drain under the rock of sacrifice, through which the blood from the endless round of temple sacrifices flowed out into the valley below the temple. As the priest Ezekiel knew it, it would have been a foul drain, full of flies and the smell of death. Yet in the vision he received in exile of a restored temple, he sees not a river of blood flowing from it but a river of life-giving water.

Ezekiel's vision has become an inspiration to many individuals and churches, especially those influenced by charismatic renewal. Sensing a fresh outpouring of the Holy Spirit drawing them in deeper and deeper until they have to let go of their footing and swim with the flow, they surrender themselves to God, whose power will bring both healing and food (fresh fruit and teeming fish) to the hungry. And yet the danger is that seeking spiritual experience can easily become self-serving.

As we read these words on the day when we remember St Andrew, we think of a man whose first action on encountering Jesus was to find his brother and bring him to Jesus. Jesus said, 'Out of the believer's heart shall flow rivers of living water' (John 7.38). At the start of Advent, let's pray that the Holy Spirit might flow through us, not so that *we* can be blessed, but so that the lost might be found, the hungry fed and the troubled healed.

COLLECT

Almighty God,
who gave such grace to your apostle Saint Andrew
that he readily obeyed the call of your Son Jesus Christ
    and brought his brother with him:
call us by your holy word,
and give us grace to follow you without delay
    and to tell the good news of your kingdom;
through Jesus Christ your Son our Lord,
who is alive and reigns with you,
in the unity of the Holy Spirit,
one God, now and for ever.

Isaiah 43.1-13

'When you pass through the waters, I will be with you' (v.2)

During 30 years in parish ministry, there have been many times when I have felt that the waters are up to my neck – sometimes when difficult pastoral situations have taken me out of my depth, sometimes because of opposition when I have challenged something that I felt was wrong, and sometimes when I have been in the wrong myself and made mistakes.

This passage in Isaiah is addressed to a people who have been through fire and water because of their disobedience to God. After the warnings of judgement in chapters 1 to 39, God speaks with great tenderness to those whom he has had to discipline and yet longs to bless. Such is his love for the exiles that he is willing to pay a hefty ransom to buy them back from the nations and bring them home (vv.3-4).

Discipline is the costly part of discipleship, and when people we are responsible for do wrong, we need to act to put things right. God demonstrates costly love, restoring Israel's vocation to be his servant (v.10), but at the cost of becoming himself the servant who would give up his life as 'a ransom for many' (Mark 10.45).

As we face the challenges of today, aware of the failures of yesterday, let's hear again God's surprising and grace-filled verdict on his wayward people as a word to us personally: '… you are precious in my sight, and honoured, and I love you' (v.4).

Almighty God,
give us grace to cast away the works of darkness
and to put on the armour of light,
now in the time of this mortal life,
in which your Son Jesus Christ came to us in great humility;
that on the last day,
when he shall come again in his glorious majesty
to judge the living and the dead,
we may rise to the life immortal;
through him who is alive and reigns with you,
in the unity of the Holy Spirit,
one God, now and for ever.

COLLECT

Wednesday 3 December

Isaiah 43.14-end

*'Do not remember the former things … I am about to do a new
thing' (vv.18-19)*

In contrast to all those verses in Exodus and Deuteronomy about the
importance of remembering, here the Lord commands his people *not*
to remember. There can be danger in remembering, if honouring what
God has done in the past restricts our ability to see the new things
which God wants to do in our own day. Instead of looking back again
to the crossing of the Red Sea, that great act of rescue from slavery, it
was time for the people to look forward to the new act of rescue God
was planning. Bringing the people of Judah back from exile in Babylon
would require a different kind of mighty act (v.19).

Do we sometimes miss out on being part of what God is planning to
do today, because we expect God to act in the same way as in the
past, because we think we know what his activity should look like?
Does this give us a clue as to why the religious people of Jesus' day
failed to recognize God's Messiah when he came?

The word 'remember' occurs a second time in this passage, in verse 25.
The God who challenges us not to remember the former things is the
one who himself promises not to remember our sins, but to blot them
out for his own sake. Back in the time of the exile, it was already in
God's heart to blot out the sins of his people through the self-sacrifice
of the cross.

COLLECT

Almighty God,
give us grace to cast away the works of darkness
and to put on the armour of light,
now in the time of this mortal life,
in which your Son Jesus Christ came to us in great humility;
that on the last day,
when he shall come again in his glorious majesty
    to judge the living and the dead,
we may rise to the life immortal;
through him who is alive and reigns with you,
in the unity of the Holy Spirit,
one God, now and for ever.

Psalms **42**, 43 *or* 14, **15**, 16
Isaiah 44.1-8
Revelation 21.9-21

Isaiah 44.1-8

'I will pour water on the thirsty land' (v.3)

In temperate countries such as Britain we complain when it rains, but when working in South Africa, I was intrigued to discover that in the local language the word for 'rain' and the word for 'blessing' are the same. In the parched lands of the Bible, rain was also seen as a blessing. In verse 3, the same verb is used of pouring water and of pouring out God's spirit. The gift of the Spirit is seen as like the coming of rain on a parched land, and the picture of a desert flowing with streams of water is a recurring image in Isaiah of God's future blessing. If the place where we serve God today feels like a desert, let us remember Jesus' sure promise that those who thirst after righteousness will be filled (Matthew 5.6).

In verse 5, the prophet speaks of believers writing the divine name on their hands as a sign that they belong to the Lord. In many Western countries tattoos are more popular than ever, and although many contain religious symbols, these are chosen not necessarily as a sign of faith. In contrast, I have been challenged by the example of Coptic Orthodox Christians in Egypt, who often choose to have the symbol of the cross tattooed on their wrist as a reminder of their baptism – even in the knowledge that when, periodically, Christians are targeted by extremists, what is written on their hand may actually become for them a matter of life and death.

Almighty God,
as your kingdom dawns,
turn us from the darkness of sin to the light of holiness,
that we may be ready to meet you
in our Lord and Saviour, Jesus Christ.

COLLECT

Psalms **25**, 26 *or* 17, **19**
Isaiah 44.9-23
Revelation 21.22 – 22.5

Isaiah 44.9-23

'The rest of it he makes into a god ...' (v.17)

Idol worship was part of Babylonian religion, and again the exiles were being tempted (as so often in their history) to make idols to represent God, notwithstanding the second commandment (Exodus 20.4). The irony and sarcasm of the prophet make these fun verses to read ... all the toil and trouble a human being expends on making something to bow down to and worship, oblivious of the fact that the rest of the block of wood might have been put on the fire to keep them warm or cook their tea!

Never having been tempted to carve an idol, I sit back and enjoy the humour, until I remember that Paul equates greed with idolatry (Colossians 3.5). I wonder, if the prophet Isaiah were to wander around my home today, what objects that I have laboured for would attract his gaze, and what things that I cherish would provoke his scorn? Living in a roomy vicarage, I had grown used to having lots of belongings around me, until one day a young Kenyan evangelist arrived to share my home and work in my parish. Seeing my world through his eyes made me ask some difficult questions about how much my security rests in the things I own, rather than in God alone.

After the entertaining diversion of verses 9-20, the voice of God is heard again in verses 21-22, reminding the people of Israel that they did not fashion or create God, but that God created them – to be his servant. Even though they had forgotten this holy calling, God calls them to return to the One who has redeemed them.

COLLECT

Almighty God,
give us grace to cast away the works of darkness
and to put on the armour of light,
now in the time of this mortal life,
in which your Son Jesus Christ came to us in great humility;
that on the last day,
when he shall come again in his glorious majesty
    to judge the living and the dead,
we may rise to the life immortal;
through him who is alive and reigns with you,
in the unity of the Holy Spirit,
one God, now and for ever.

Psalms **9**, (10) *or* 20, 21, **23**
Isaiah 44.24 – 45.13
Revelation 22.6-end

Saturday 6 December

Isaiah 44.24 – 45.13

'Thus says the Lord to his anointed, to Cyrus' (45.1)

Cyrus? God's anointed? Come off it! Here was a non-Israelite, a man who worshipped idols and represented the occupying power, and yet God affords him the title of 'messiah' (anointed one), previously given to kings in the line of David. Cyrus is also described as God's 'shepherd' (44.28), the only person apart from David to be given these two titles before Jesus himself. Yet remarkably, under God, it was Cyrus, the pagan king of Persia, who allowed the exiles to return, Jerusalem to be rebuilt and the foundation stone of the Temple to be relaid.

For the Israelite exiles, the idea that God would use an idol-worshipping pagan to rescue them provokes a storm of protest (45.9-12) – they want to be choosy about their rescuer, even though beggars can't be choosers! When in our own communities, secular agencies or individuals with unconventional lives approach us wanting to help the Church, do we react with suspicion? Or do we ponder that God might just be using them as he did Cyrus?

God was not simply the tribal god of Israel, but the one true God of all the earth – 'I am the Lord, and there is no other' (45.5). If God can use world rulers who may not even know him to be agents of his purposes, how might that inspire us to pray for the leaders of today's global powers – China, Russia, India and the United States?

Almighty God,
as your kingdom dawns,
turn us from the darkness of sin to the light of holiness,
that we may be ready to meet you
in our Lord and Saviour, Jesus Christ.

COLLECT

13

Monday 8 December

Psalms **44** *or* 27, **30**
Isaiah 45.14-end
I Thessalonians I

Isaiah 45.14-end

'Truly, you are a God who hides himself' (v.15)

Here the prophet's response to God is one that we can all echo – for there are times when God's majestic promises and the struggle and mess of our present experience just don't stack up. We read examples and promises of God's saving power in Scripture, and yet we can all point to situations of evil and wrong where God has not overruled, and where faith hangs on by a thread.

The Israelites, who had seen their temple and city destroyed, were tempted to think that the world was in chaos and that God had cleared off. However, God challenges their perception and affirms that, even while hidden from view, he has been hard at work, preparing for that day when even those who live in far-off lands will turn to the God of Israel, recognizing that he alone is Saviour of the world. Paul's great hymn in Philippians 2 was penned in a Roman dungeon, yet even from that vantage point, he was able to glimpse the fulfilment of Isaiah's vision when every knee shall bow and every tongue shall swear (v.23).

Perhaps the hiddenness of God is part of the cost of human free will. As a wise tutor put it to me, 'God must reveal himself to give us a chance; he must also conceal himself to leave us free.'

COLLECT

O Lord, raise up, we pray, your power
and come among us,
and with great might succour us;
that whereas, through our sins and wickedness
we are grievously hindered
in running the race that is set before us,
your bountiful grace and mercy
may speedily help and deliver us;
through Jesus Christ your Son our Lord,
to whom with you and the Holy Spirit,
be honour and glory, now and for ever.

Psalms **56**, 57 *or* 32, **36**
Isaiah 46
1 Thessalonians 2.1-12

Isaiah 46

'My purpose shall stand, and I will fulfil my intention' (v.10)

Two prominent Babylonian deities are mentioned by name – Bel, the chief of the gods, and Nebo, son of Marduk and patron of the royal dynasty – whose idols were carried with great ceremony from one city to another at each new-year festival. The prophet mocks this procession, pointing out that Bel and Nebo are a burden needing to be carried about on animals (v.1), in contrast to the true God, who has carried his people since their birth, and has promised to keep on carrying them to the end (vv.3-4). Once these idols are set down in place, they are powerless either to move or to respond to pleas for help – in contrast to God, whose purpose stands fast and who will fulfil his intentions, whoever he has to use to do so – even Cyrus, that 'bird of prey from the east' (v.11).

Many of the things I plan never come about, either because they fail, or I fail to follow through, or because God has other plans. But whatever God has planned, he will accomplish (v.11). It is sobering but encouraging to be reminded that we worship a God who will always have his way in the end, either with our help or without us. We have a choice, whether to be instruments he can work with or obstacles he can overcome.

Almighty God,
purify our hearts and minds,
that when your Son Jesus Christ comes again as
judge and saviour
we may be ready to receive him,
who is our Lord and our God.

COLLECT

15

Wednesday 10 December

Psalms **62**, 63 *or* **34**
Isaiah 47
I Thessalonians 2.13-end

Isaiah 47

'...these things shall come upon you in a moment, in one day' (v.9)

Those of us who can remember the dismantling of the Berlin Wall and the lifting of the Iron Curtain a generation ago saw on television just how quickly a seemingly impregnable empire can collapse. Complacent and seemingly impregnable, Babylon would soon fall to Cyrus king of Persia in 539 BC. The one who dared to parody God's unique claim, 'I am, and there is no one besides me' (v.8, cf. Isaiah 45.22) would suddenly find everything stripped away: the exalted mistress become a servant, vulnerable at the hands of others, and the enchanter become the victim of disasters that no spells could ward off.

Babylon was judged because it had failed to show mercy to the people God had put in its hands (v.6). This makes me feel uncomfortable. Knowing that God has sometimes put responsibility for other people in my hands, and particularly the opportunity to show mercy and love to those who needed it, reminds me of the many times I have failed to do what was within my power to do.

Lord, help me today not to be complacent about my position or possessions, which could so quickly be taken from me, but to trust only in your grace, who are my Redeemer, the Holy One of Israel. And help me to use the things in my hands today to show mercy to others, while I have the chance.

COLLECT

O Lord, raise up, we pray, your power
and come among us,
and with great might succour us;
that whereas, through our sins and wickedness
we are grievously hindered
in running the race that is set before us,
your bountiful grace and mercy
may speedily help and deliver us;
through Jesus Christ your Son our Lord,
to whom with you and the Holy Spirit,
be honour and glory, now and for ever.

Isaiah 48.1-11

'... so that you would not say, "My idol did them"...' (v.5)

Prophecy in Scripture is about telling forth God's will, announcing the choices facing God's people and the consequences that will flow from them. The prophets declare the purposes of God and how he will bring them to effect, particularly through the Messiah. In this passage, the prophet articulates another purpose of prophecy – to make sure that God gets the credit for what he does. Given that the Israelites were predisposed from birth to rebel (v.8) and worship the Baals, God here speaks through the prophet to remind them who is the true controller of history.

In the medieval mystical writing *The Cloud of Unknowing* (whose author is unknown), God is described as 'a jealous lover', one who is not willing to share with any other the affections of his beloved. As the prophet puts it, 'My glory I will not give to another' (v.11). If today we feel as if (like the Israelites) we are going through 'the furnace of adversity' (v.10), perhaps we can invite our wise and loving God to use this painful experience for our good, to refine our love for him and burn away all that is not holy or good in our attitudes and behaviour.

'It is not what you are nor what you have been that God looks at with his merciful eyes, but what you desire to be.' (*The Cloud of Unknowing*, chapter 75)

Almighty God,
purify our hearts and minds,
that when your Son Jesus Christ comes again as
judge and saviour
we may be ready to receive him,
who is our Lord and our God.

COLLECT

Friday 12 December

Psalms 85, **86** *or* **31**
Isaiah 48.12-end
I Thessalonians 4.1-12

Isaiah 48.12-end

'There is no peace ... for the wicked' (v.22)

This is, without doubt, one of the most quoted verses in Isaiah, yet it is only when we read it in the context of the first verse of our passage – 'Listen to me, O Jacob ...' - that we glimpse its true meaning, for the wicked in this chapter are those who do not listen to God. The sadness in the heart of God is captured in verse 18, 'O that you had paid attention to my commandments!'. Even though God will bring his people back from Babylon, this underlying issue is not resolved, and so the return to the land will not bring the fullness of blessing they had hoped for.

As a priest now in my 50s, I am trying to carve out a bit more time in a busy ministry for careful and attentive listening to God. Yet sometimes my mind just floats back to the pile of tasks on my desk. I talked this over with a wise Franciscan, telling him I felt a failure in my attempts at contemplation because of the times I seem to get nothing out of it. He laughed, and reminded me that the point of prayer is not what we get out of it, but rather 'it's about keeping the Lord company'.

These wise words have helped me to relax into my times of stillness – offering God the simple gift of my attention, without demanding anything in return. Yet, when I rise from these times of 'keeping the Lord company', somehow the rest of the day is different.

COLLECT

O Lord, raise up, we pray, your power
and come among us,
and with great might succour us;
that whereas, through our sins and wickedness
we are grievously hindered
in running the race that is set before us,
your bountiful grace and mercy
may speedily help and deliver us;
through Jesus Christ your Son our Lord,
to whom with you and the Holy Spirit,
be honour and glory, now and for ever.

Saturday 13 December

Isaiah 49.1-13

'You are my servant, Israel, in whom I will be glorified.' (v.3)

We come now to the second Servant Song, one of four distinctive passages in this part of the book of Isaiah that speak of the 'servant of the Lord' (see also 42.1-4; 50.10; 52.13–53.12). When the Ethiopian meets Philip in Acts 8.34, he is reading the fourth song and asks: who is the prophet talking about, himself or someone else? – a question that scholars (and essay-writing ordinands!) have wrestled with for generations. In verses 5-6 the servant seems to be both an individual tasked to bring Israel back to God and also the nation of Israel itself, tasked to bring light to the nations and salvation to the ends of the earth.

Looking back on these texts from this side of the incarnation, we can see only one figure great enough to be both the Saviour of Israel, and also the embodiment of the new Israel, bringing God's salvation to the whole world. In his preaching Jesus consciously identifies himself both as Messiah and as the servant, uniting in himself these two distinct strands of Old Testament prophecy.

On those difficult days when I feel 'I have laboured in vain, I have spent my strength for nothing and vanity' (v.4), it is good to know that Jesus identified himself with the writer of these verses. That knowledge gives me strength to keep going and to affirm, 'Surely my cause is with the Lord, and my reward is with my God' (v.4).

Almighty God,
purify our hearts and minds,
that when your Son Jesus Christ comes again as
judge and saviour
we may be ready to receive him,
who is our Lord and our God.

COLLECT

Monday 15 December

Psalm **40** *or* **44**
Isaiah 49.14-25
1 Thessalonians 5.1-11

Isaiah 49.14-25

'Can a woman forget her nursing-child?' (v.15)

Parents are usually utterly committed to their children, and a nursing mother is joined at the hip, or more accurately, the breast. This is the image the author uses for God's commitment to his people in exile. It would be possible to believe that they were forgotten in faraway Babylon, but not a bit of it. They are inscribed on the palm of God's hands.

It's an image open to sentimentality, but it's also deeply attractive. Whether carried *in* God's hands or inscribed *on* God's hands, the intimacy is undeniable, and in distress there's nowhere a believer would prefer to be. But let's stay with the historical context of the passage. God's promise is to a whole people languishing in a strange land and, astonishingly, Isaiah describes a situation where it's standing room only when the exiles return, such is the scale of the redemption he will effect.

I wonder if we take God's promises seriously or if we relegate most of them into the 'inspiring poetry' category? Inspiring they may be, but they also assure us that, in the long term, God's good purposes are irresistible and the kingdom really is unstoppable.

In the meantime we should probably keep calm and carry on.

COLLECT

O Lord Jesus Christ,
who at your first coming sent your messenger
to prepare your way before you:
grant that the ministers and stewards of your mysteries
may likewise so prepare and make ready your way
by turning the hearts of the disobedient to the wisdom of the just,
that at your second coming to judge the world
we may be found an acceptable people in your sight;
for you are alive and reign with the Father
in the unity of the Holy Spirit,
one God, now and for ever.

Psalms **70**, 74 *or* **48**, 52
Isaiah 50
1 Thessalonians 5.12-end

Isaiah 50

'I did not turn backwards. I gave my back to those who struck me'
(vv.5–6)

The image of innocent suffering is one of the most powerful images we ever encounter. Few who saw the film *Gandhi* will easily forget the rows of Indians stepping forward one at a time with dignity and courage to be beaten up by British forces. The local people were simply living out Gandhi's philosophy of passive resistance.

Here, the servant of the Lord did not hide his face from insult and spitting (v.6), but set his face like flint, knowing that God would help him, and his adversaries would wear out like a garment (v.9). With Christians in many different countries of the world facing violent hostility today, this is a bold message and takes a lot of trusting. (Sadly, in a few parts of the world, Christians are just as much to blame.)

What it comes down to is a very basic spiritual question: whom do you trust? If we feel bound to trust the power of our own hands, the vengeance of our own anger, then we've lost the game already. But if we're prepared for life to beat us up a bit, believing that God really does know best, and that an eye for an eye and a tooth for a tooth leaves the world blind and toothless, then we're on the royal road to freedom.

Herbert McCabe, the English priest–philosopher, was right: 'If you don't love, you're dead; and if you do, they'll kill you.' But God always has the last word, and it's 'resurrection'. How will that last word help you today?

God for whom we watch and wait,
you sent John the Baptist to prepare the way of your Son:
give us courage to speak the truth,
to hunger for justice,
and to suffer for the cause of right,
with Jesus Christ our Lord.

COLLECT

Wednesday 17 December

Psalms **75**, 96 *or* **119.57-80**
Isaiah 51.1-8
2 Thessalonians 1

Isaiah 51.1-8

'Look to the rock from which you were hewn' (v.1)

There is great merit in living in the present, but sometimes it can blind us to the messages of the past and the potential of the future. Our culture is obsessed with scraping the jar of the present, living for today and consuming everything we can from it. We see how disastrous that policy can be when we look at the way we're exhausting the raw materials of the earth and yet expect to be immune from the effects of climate change.

Isaiah had a better plan. He drew on God's faithfulness in the past – 'Look to Abraham your father and to Sarah who bore you' (v.2) – in order to face the future with radiant confidence – 'my deliverance will be for ever, and my salvation for all generations' (v.8). Here is a full time-frame in which we can rest secure. The God who holds the past also holds the future.

I've got to the age now where I notice in obituaries how old people were when they died and suck in my breath when I see they were the same age as me. So it helps me if I remember that life isn't just a succession of greedy experiences but the steady outworking of God's faithfulness in my life, past, present and future. And at rock bottom there is rock.

COLLECT

O Lord Jesus Christ,
who at your first coming sent your messenger
to prepare your way before you:
grant that the ministers and stewards of your mysteries
may likewise so prepare and make ready your way
by turning the hearts of the disobedient to the wisdom of the just,
that at your second coming to judge the world
we may be found an acceptable people in your sight;
for you are alive and reign with the Father
in the unity of the Holy Spirit,
one God, now and for ever.

Psalms **76**, 97 *or* 56, **57** (63*)
Isaiah 51.9-16
2 Thessalonians 2

Thursday 18 December

Isaiah 51.9-16

'... why then are you afraid of a mere mortal who must die?' (v.12)

If you're going to be in awe of someone, you might as well make it someone worthwhile. Invitees to an American Prayer Breakfast at which the President of the United States was to be present were encouraged in their invitation not to be in awe of the great man – but there was no mention of God! Isaiah tries to refocus our minds. Have we forgotten the Lord our maker who stretched out the heavens and laid the foundations of the earth? Point taken.

The God in whose hands we are and who has promised 'You are my people' (v.16) isn't a small-town deity struggling to keep a foothold in society or get a mention in the weekly newspaper. This is a God who has been sending light towards us from the birth of creation for 13.7 billion years at 186,000 miles per second. Think about it – that's quite a scale. And God is God of all that.

And yet, 'I am he who comforts you' (v.12). That's what finally renders me speechless, that a God of such immensity is also a comforter, understanding why I 'fear continually all day long' (v.13) and offering such support. With a God like that, who covers so much physical, emotional and spiritual space, I think I can probably face the day.

God for whom we watch and wait,
you sent John the Baptist to prepare the way of your Son:
give us courage to speak the truth,
to hunger for justice,
and to suffer for the cause of right,
with Jesus Christ our Lord.

COLLECT

23

Friday 19 December

Psalms 144, **146**
Isaiah 51.17-end
2 Thessalonians 3

Isaiah 51.17-end

'See, I have taken from your hand the cup of staggering' (v.22)

Old Testament writers weren't shy of making causal connections between human behaviour and God's judgement. Isaiah says God's people 'have drunk at the hand of the Lord the cup of his wrath' (v.17). We may be more careful in the way we express the link between human folly and God's displeasure. Nevertheless, we would be wise not to sentamentalize it away. The fact is that the world is made with a moral 'grain', and if our lives and actions run across that grain, there will inevitably be disturbing consequences. See today's newspaper for further details. In Isaiah's time the exiles were paying the price for many years of living against the grain.

In this passage we see that God has taken the 'cup of staggering' away from the exiles and put it instead into the hands of their captors and tormentors. This is good news for the exiles, but again it's important not to become too binary in our assessment of good and evil in human nature or in national life. 'All have sinned and fall short of the glory of God' (Romans 3.23). We share the human condition of dust and glory.

And today we will have countless opportunities to choose one rather than the other. Isaiah says there was no one to guide Jerusalem in their choices (v.18). Christians would say we have the privilege of the Holy Spirit for both guidance and strength. No problem, then?

COLLECT

O Lord Jesus Christ,
who at your first coming sent your messenger
to prepare your way before you:
grant that the ministers and stewards of your mysteries
may likewise so prepare and make ready your way
by turning the hearts of the disobedient to the wisdom of the just,
that at your second coming to judge the world
we may be found an acceptable people in your sight;
for you are alive and reign with the Father
in the unity of the Holy Spirit,
one God, now and for ever.

24

Saturday 20 December

Isaiah 52.1-12

'How beautiful upon the mountains are the feet of the messenger who announces peace' (v. 7)

Singing is an appropriate vehicle to mark the glorious change of atmosphere at the start of chapter 52. Indeed, the look-outs are already singing as they see the Lord returning to the holy city, and even the city ruins are breaking into song (vv.8,9). Nor will the exiles leave captivity with their tail between their legs. Isaiah says they won't make a dash for it, but will leave with dignity, the Lord at their head.

It's wonderful to be the bearer of good news. It's been said that the gospel is something that can be shouted across the street, like 'The baby's arrived!' or 'Simon's out of danger'. When we hear good news, we too probably want to shout it out. How brilliant, then, to be able to announce the good news of peace to a world so long at war. 'Peace at last!' is an authentic gospel shout.

The only problem then is that we have to justify that great announcement by the way we try to embody that peace and share it with others. But if we believe that Christ truly has made peace on the cross and reconciled all things to himself (Colossians 1.20), the least we can do is tell people about it and invite them into that reconciled space. That's quite a task, but at least it makes daily discipleship interesting.

God for whom we watch and wait,
you sent John the Baptist to prepare the way of your Son:
give us courage to speak the truth,
to hunger for justice,
and to suffer for the cause of right,
with Jesus Christ our Lord.

COLLECT

Isaiah 52.13 – 53.end

'Surely he has borne our infirmities and carried our diseases' (v.4)

This is one of the most familiar passages in the Old Testament, not least because Handel used some of these verses so effectively in his *Messiah*. The picture of the suffering servant is bleak and powerful; it stops us in our tracks no matter how often we read it. What proves especially effective is the conflation of the people of Israel into the single despised figure that Christians are used to seeing scraped over a cross. It's interesting also to see how moving is the picture of the lamb being led to the slaughter. I have stood before Zurbarán's painting 'The Lamb of God' and been reduced to silence and tears.

There's no need to enter arguments about theories of the atonement and the morality or otherwise of a substitutionary understanding of such phrases as 'upon him was the punishment that made us whole' (v.5) or 'the Lord has laid on him the iniquity of us all' (v.6). We're in the realm here of spiritual poetry, metaphors that carry a huge punch but mustn't be tested to destruction. More important is to stop and wonder. This, somehow, is all about love, a love that releases us from the dark tyrannies of moral failure and the fears that cripple our lives. A love, moreover, that embraces embittered societies and quarrelling nations.

This isn't a place for analysis but for prayer and silence.

COLLECT

God our redeemer,
who prepared the Blessed Virgin Mary
to be the mother of your Son:
grant that, as she looked for his coming as our saviour,
so we may be ready to greet him
when he comes again as our judge;
who is alive and reigns with you,
in the unity of the Holy Spirit,
one God, now and for ever.

Psalms 128, 129, **130**, 131
Isaiah 54
2 Peter 1.16 – 2.3

Isaiah 54

'... my covenant of peace shall not be removed' (v.10)

There are some startling assertions in this passage. It's not unexpected that the Lord would be Israel's maker and redeemer, but here he is also her husband (v.5). The Lord abandoned her (no reason given), but now has moved back in with an everlasting love. 'Everlasting' is exactly what it is. Mountains may depart and hills be removed but 'my covenant of peace shall not be removed'. Ever. It's like Noah over again; the angry waters will never return.

These eschatological promises are wonderful to read but they set up a dangerous dichotomy in our minds. Do we believe this, in spite of the evidence, or do we put it into the 'delightful fantasy' bin? A third approach is more promising. This peaceable kingdom is the gift we have in God, ready to be inhabited when we give up living in our upside-down world and start living in God's reality. We've got so used to believing that war and violence are inevitable that we can't conceive of another way of doing things. But when God shows up we see our Alice in Wonderland world for what it is. And with that 'right way up' thinking comes a mandate to be makers of that peace that is God's gift and reality. And with that making of peace comes the challenge to *be* such a person today in every difficult encounter and every tough relationship.

Are we up for it?

Eternal God,
as Mary waited for the birth of your Son,
so we wait for his coming in glory;
bring us through the birth pangs of this present age
to see, with her, our great salvation
in Jesus Christ our Lord.

COLLECT

27

Wednesday 24 December

Christmas Eve

Psalms **45**, 113
Isaiah 55
2 Peter 2.4-end

Isaiah 55

'Ho, everyone who thirsts, come to the waters' (v. 1)

I've yet to meet anyone who greets people with the word 'Ho', but I understand the sentiment. It's a call for attention, rather like a town crier's 'Oyez!'. What is on offer here is no less than abundant life, symbolized by water, wine, milk and bread. 'Delight yourselves in rich food' is the invitation (v.2). You may not understand the ways and means of God (v.9), but they are gloriously higher than human expectation, and they're on offer for the whole community, now.

It's an offer I wish our culture would recognize. I once went on a seven-day expedition across the Sinai and we were warned that we must drink large quantities of water. One of the signs that we were becoming dehydrated would be that we would become grumpy. That got me thinking. We live in a grumpy society where anger easily boils over and litigation is never far away. Could it be because we're spiritually dehydrated? We're short of the living water that Isaiah and later Jesus would offer, and which takes us into the realm of the new creation where 'the trees of the field shall clap their hands ... instead of the brier shall come up the myrtle' (vv.12,13). Paradise regained.

One of the challenges for us is to drink so fully of that living water that people recognize something that provokes, interests and attracts them – so much so that they ask what it is that we're drinking. Tomorrow gives us the answer.

COLLECT

Almighty God,
you make us glad with the yearly remembrance
of the birth of your Son Jesus Christ:
grant that, as we joyfully receive him as our redeemer,
so we may with sure confidence behold him
when he shall come to be our judge;
who is alive and reigns with you,
in the unity of the Holy Spirit,
one God, now and for ever.

Psalms **110**, 117
Isaiah 62.1-5
Matthew 1.18-end

Matthew 1.18-end

'They shall name him Emmanuel, which means "God is with us"'
(v.23)

Joseph was in a quandary. A pregnant fiancée indicated something badly amiss. He would have to call off the marriage, cancel the photographer and put up with the shame. Fortunately, an angel made a timely appearance – as angels do – and Joseph got things back on track. But still, 'he had no marital relations with her until she had borne a son; and he named him Jesus' (v.25). No more details.

But how much more do we need? The angel said the child was from the Holy Spirit and 'you are to name him Jesus, for he will save his people from their sins' (v.21). That seems quite a fanfare for a six-pound bundle of humanity. Let's never diminish the wonder of this day with the trappings of cash-till Christmas. This is the day when heaven burst into our lives, when heaven invaded earth. This is the day when heaven and earth fused in the life of a vulnerable child in a forgotten village in a backwater of the Roman Empire, a child who would transform the lives not just of individuals but of civilizations.

Today there will be feasts and tears, indulgence and memories, love and argument, delight and boredom, duty and joy. But at the heart of the day is a message that explodes throughout the world, and it's all in the name: 'God is with us'. May the world believe.

Almighty God,
you have given us your only-begotten Son
to take our nature upon him
and as at this time to be born of a pure virgin:
grant that we, who have been born again
and made your children by adoption and grace,
may daily be renewed by your Holy Spirit;
through Jesus Christ your Son our Lord,
who is alive and reigns with you,
in the unity of the Holy Spirit,
one God, now and for ever.

COLLECT

Friday 26 December

Psalms **13**, 31.1-8, 150
Jeremiah 26.12-15
Acts 6

Stephen, deacon, first martyr

Acts 6

'... they saw that his face was like the face of an angel' (v.15)

When I ordain a new batch of deacons, I tend not to mention that the first deacon was soon murdered. I've found that it's strangely discouraging. The apostles realized they needed to put first things first, and their job was to pray and preach, so they needed others to serve those in need. First in line for the new role of deacon was Stephen. He gets some wonderful descriptions in this passage. He was 'full of grace and power' (v.8) and, when he was on trial, 'his face was like the face of an angel' (v.15). How many of us would merit such generous affirmation?

What seems slightly shocking is that no sooner had he been chosen for the role than he was being arrested. It's easy to forget that the dangerous hothouse of Jerusalem was the same a few weeks after Jesus' death as before. To identify with that tragic messiah opened you to a lethal response, and Stephen got it. What we also easily forget is that there is more persecution of Christians now, in countries across the globe, than there has been since the life, death and new life of Jesus. More Christians have died for their faith in the last century than in any preceding century.

It seems that persecution is 'business as usual' for very many Christians. The question, one day after joyfully celebrating the birth of Jesus, is: 'How can we in the West show ourselves to be members of the same Body of Christ – the Little One, who also had the face of an angel'?

COLLECT

Gracious Father,
who gave the first martyr Stephen
grace to pray for those who took up stones against him:
grant that in all our sufferings for the truth
we may learn to love even our enemies
and to seek forgiveness for those who desire our hurt,
looking up to heaven to him who was crucified for us,
Jesus Christ, our mediator and advocate,
who is alive and reigns with you,
in the unity of the Holy Spirit,
one God, now and for ever.

Psalms **21**, 147.13-end
Exodus 33.12-end
1 John 2.1-11

Saturday 27 December
John, Apostle and Evangelist

1 John 2.1-11

'... whoever says "I abide in him" ought to walk just as he walked'
(v.6)

A rabbi was asked how we could be sure that night has ended. He replied: 'If you can look into the face of another human being and not see a brother or sister, then whatever time it is, it's still night.' The apostle John would have understood this. 'Whoever says "I am in the light" while hating a brother or sister, is still in the darkness' (v.9). It's a very down-to-earth test. We can be sure we are followers of Jesus if we obey his commandments, and, as this letter makes clear again and again, the overwhelming commandment is to love.

The rabbis were often spot-on in their sayings. One I particularly enjoy is the saying: 'May you be covered in the dust of your rabbi.' If you follow your rabbi through arid countryside all day, you will be pretty dusty by the end. So the hope is that you will have the privilege of following one of these much revered people and therefore, inevitably, be covered in his dust. If Jesus is our rabbi, then we will have become truly dust-covered if we are doing what he did, which is loving every human being he came across. No one is saying it's easy, but equally, we can't say we are followers ('abide in him') if we don't 'walk just as he walked' (v.6). Most of us can be sure of one thing: we won't be short of people to practise on.

Today may we be covered in the dust of love.

COLLECT

Merciful Lord,
cast your bright beams of light upon the Church:
that, being enlightened by the teaching
of your blessed apostle and evangelist Saint John,
we may so walk in the light of your truth
that we may at last attain to the light of everlasting life;
through Jesus Christ your incarnate Son our Lord,
who is alive and reigns with you,
in the unity of the Holy Spirit,
one God, now and for ever.

Monday 29 December

John 1.1-18

'... God the only Son, who is close to the Father's heart' (v. 18)

Many of us will have spent Christmas at home. Unlike a summer holiday when we might travel to more exotic places, this is a time when we often stay put. We venture out only towards that which is familiar, perhaps visiting loved ones, family, old friends. Christmas is domestic – that is one of its joys.

Yet amid our domesticity, today's reading challenges us. It presses and agitates our thinking, demanding that we face up to the almost unimaginable identity of the child born in Bethlehem. This is not any old child. Nor is this simply a saviour. He was 'in the beginning' (v.1), 'without him not one thing came into being' (v.3), and – as John the Baptist testifies – 'he was before me' (v.15). There is something irreducibly odd about Christmas. This child is our maker, the Word become flesh.

Yet for all its mind-bending re-imagining of eternity and time, this passage still paints a domestic scene. This is the Son who is close to his Father's heart (v.18). This is the Son who is close to his Father's bosom. Despite its metaphysical complexities, we are simply invited into the tender embrace that is the identity of God. Christmas really is domestic: a family in Bethlehem, a Father's Son.

COLLECT

Almighty God,
who wonderfully created us in your own image
and yet more wonderfully restored us
through your Son Jesus Christ:
grant that, as he came to share in our humanity,
so we may share the life of his divinity;
who is alive and reigns with you,
in the unity of the Holy Spirit,
one God, now and for ever.

Tuesday 30 December

John 1.19-28

'Who are you?' (v.19)

Yesterday, the domestic nature of Christmas was in view: an eternal Father's embrace, revealed through a family in Bethlehem and celebrated amid the familiar, at home, with loved ones. Yet there is nothing domestic about today's reading.

Today we are taken with the priests and Levites into the unsettling presence of John the Baptist. This exotic figure emerges from the wilderness, almost feral, untamed, now standing by the Jordan. He is questioned, probed, his credentials checked. Who does he think he is? On what grounds does he do what he does? Yet John simply points away from himself. He knows this is all about Jesus. It is *his* identity that counts.

The Christian – just like John the Baptist – can only point to Jesus. Yet the temptation is to seek our identity nearer to home: family, friends, perhaps even our ministry in church, our service to the community, the help we give our neighbours, our morning prayers. But John reminds us that none of this defines us ultimately. Standing like an exotic figure at the edge of our piety, he points beyond us, looking to Jesus, who stands in our midst, unrecognized. The question is who is he, this child born of Mary? Does he define us?

God in Trinity,
eternal unity of perfect love:
gather the nations to be one family,
and draw us into your holy life
through the birth of Emmanuel,
our Lord Jesus Christ.

COLLECT

33

Wednesday 31 December

John 1.29-34

'I saw the Spirit descending from heaven like a dove' (v.32)

Christmas is a season that is almost defined by generosity. It is a time marked with the giving and receiving of presents. Wrapping paper is torn open, and children's faces are lit up as new toys are discovered beneath the Christmas tree. Of course, this is not always the case. But neither is it unrealistic. The gift-giving scene plays out across our land.

This morning's reading again makes us question the identity of the child born of Mary. John is now pointing to the baptism of Jesus, where the heavens open and the Spirit descends like a dove. Here eternity opens up in time: this Son – who is generated from the Father's heart – is endlessly given all that his Father is, that is, the Spirit. John's testimony is therefore clear: God's life is an endless giving and receiving, his single threefold identity is love.

And the gift the Son receives, he also gives. This is the one who baptizes with the Holy Spirit (v.33). We are being invited to share in this eternal exchange, a generous space opening up within God's life for a new identity. But the child of Christmas is marked. 'Here is the Lamb of God who takes away the sin of the world!' (v.29). Just like a scene from a Christmas morning, the eternal gift is opened under the shadow of a tree. This child will save sinners.

COLLECT

Almighty God,
who wonderfully created us in your own image
and yet more wonderfully restored us
through your Son Jesus Christ:
grant that, as he came to share in our humanity,
so we may share the life of his divinity;
who is alive and reigns with you,
in the unity of the Holy Spirit,
one God, now and for ever.

Psalms **103**, 150
Genesis 17.1-13
Romans 2.17-end

Naming and Circumcision
of Jesus

Romans 2.17-end

'Such a person receives praise not from others but from God' (v.29)

Time and again this week, our readings have made us question the identity of this child born of Mary. The question of identity is again asked today. The child is to be named. The child is to be marked. This is Jesus. He is a Jew. He is inescapably identified with the people of God.

Today, Paul's writing encourages us to ask the question of identity amid the noise of religious debate, legal observance and cultic ritual. The quiet identity of this child is to disrupt our understanding because, Paul explains, the heart of the matter is just that, the heart of the matter. The identity of this One is secure because he knows he is valued from eternity, his heart is full of God's praise (v.29).

And somehow, in the heart of Jesus Christ, we see the realignment of law, circumcision and the living God. In him, we sense that the covenant is more beautiful than we could ever imagine. It is a covenant within God's own life, a decision in eternity between a Father and his Son to be God-with-his-creatures. And what God decides, God is. Hence, Jesus Christ: the identity of God established in our presence.

But – just as with yesterday – the future again disrupts the scene. The body of this child is marked, cut. This child may be the eternal covenant bearer, the person of God among his people, but blood is already shed. One day it will pour.

Almighty God,
whose blessed Son was circumcised
in obedience to the law for our sake
and given the Name that is above every name:
give us grace faithfully to bear his Name,
to worship him in the freedom of the Spirit,
and to proclaim him as the Saviour of the world;
who is alive and reigns with you,
in the unity of the Holy Spirit,
one God, now and for ever.

COLLECT

35

Friday 2 January

Psalm **18.1-30**
Isaiah 60.1-12
John 1.35-42

John 1.35-42

'He said to them, "Come and see"' (v.39)

Today, the question of identity must again be asked. But this time the tables appear to have turned. Jesus is no longer the focus of enquiry; *Peter* is here being named.

Today's short passage at first feels somewhat crowded. In just a few short verses, we encounter Jesus walking by John the Baptist as Andrew and another disciple look on, before Andrew heads off to find Peter. Yet despite the personal density of the scene, there remains a sense of roominess here. There is space for all the to-ing and fro-ing, the movement, procession, the about turn. And the space seems to centre *on* Jesus: come see where he dwells (v.39) – *that* is the place of transformation. Simon son of John is renamed *there*.

The transformative nature of indwelling captures something of what the life of Jesus will mean. A people are now being gathered around him, thereby caught up in the eternal movement that is God, himself a to-ing and fro-ing, processing, begetting, the about turn of mutual indwelling. That is why there is a sense of spaciousness in Jesus into which we are invited, transformed, renamed, a people called Church. *Our* identity is somehow established between him and his Father.

We must never lose sight of the place given to us within the un-begun, unsurpassable life of God in Jesus Christ. The good news is that we – like Peter – are being transformed through indwelling.

COLLECT

Almighty God,
who wonderfully created us in your own image
and yet more wonderfully restored us
through your Son Jesus Christ:
grant that, as he came to share in our humanity,
so we may share the life of his divinity;
who is alive and reigns with you,
in the unity of the Holy Spirit,
one God, now and for ever.

Psalms **127**, 128, 131
Isaiah 60.13-end
John 1.43-end

John 1.43-end

'Can anything good come out of Nazareth?' (v.46)

Over the last few days, our readings have invited a degree of conceptual gymnastics. Our thinking has been stretched, agitated and thrown by the story of Christmas, the story of the eternal One born in our midst. This morning's reading contains another springboard: heaven opened, an angelic exchange (v.51). Yet today's reading is in fact *grounded*. Nathanael's question helps: can anything good come out of *Nazareth*?

We could be tempted to smirk at Nathanael's naivety, positioned as we are with glorious hindsight. We now know the Saviour of the world came from Nazareth. Yet Nathanael's question remains. In fact, it is intensified. Can *God* himself emerge out of a village on the edge of beyond? Can *God* come out of a small dusty place, becoming identified with the local, unprepossessing, almost unknown? *God*?

This week we've sketched eternity in time, painting images across a huge canvas. But Nathanael's question reminds us that this vast picture fits within a small frame: the local, the particular, the unremarkable has been chosen by God. And that is good news for us. It means we can be too. So Nathanael's question should not raise a smirk. It should instead free us to smile. God is *that* local.

God in Trinity,
eternal unity of perfect love:
gather the nations to be one family,
and draw us into your holy life
through the birth of Emmanuel,
our Lord Jesus Christ.

COLLECT

Monday 5 January

Psalms 8, **48**
Isaiah 62
John 2.13-end

John 2.13-end

'... for he himself knew what was in everyone' (v.25)

Today's reading disrupts. People are driven away. Coins are scattered. Tables are overthrown. And Jesus is left standing amid the debris. He speaks calmly of death and resurrection.

For us, the twelfth night of Christmas has arrived. This is the time when the Christmas tree is stripped, and the lights and tinsel are packed away. Epiphany is approaching, a new season, a new chapter; we move on. Yet the question of identity again presses. We must question the One who stands among us, driving out our best intentions, pouring out what we value, overturning what we lean on. Who is this who has no time for the circus of religion?

Today we see that Jesus knows how fathomless our corruption is, how even our religiosity – our finest intentions – can be twisted and warped into a ridiculous bartering, a pseudo-sacrifice; Jesus *knows what's in everyone* (v.25). Nevertheless, he presses on towards what lies ahead. And therein we again see him for who he is: Jesus is *freedom*. Though there's nothing desirable in us – no magnetic virtue he can no longer resist – he remains steadfastly *for us*. He knows we deserve to be driven out, scattered, ourselves overthrown like a table, and yet he walks on towards that day when it will instead be he who is driven out of Jerusalem, turned over unto death, poured out of life into a grave. Jesus is completely free to love.

COLLECT

Almighty God,
in the birth of your Son
you have poured on us the new light of your incarnate Word,
and shown us the fullness of your love:
help us to walk in his light and dwell in his love
that we may know the fullness of his joy;
who is alive and reigns with you,
in the unity of the Holy Spirit,
one God, now and for ever.

Psalms **132**, 113
Jeremiah 31.7-14
John 1.29-34

Tuesday 6 January

Epiphany

Jeremiah 31.7-14

*'See, I am going to ... gather them from the farthest parts of
the earth ... a great company' (v.8)*

The Feast of the Epiphany is a true celebration. Now the identity of
this child is to be made manifest, he is being shown forth, presented.
And what we see in the Epiphany is that Jesus is *for people*. Be they
near or afar – distant kings, gentile Magi, or local shepherds – they
are to be gathered around him within an unveiling.

So Jeremiah strikes the right note. There is to be singing, dancing and
merriment because a great ensemble is being gathered (v.8). God has
not abandoned us into exile, nor left us in the outer darkness,
accepting separation, tolerating alienation, remaining unknown. Jesus
is God presenting himself to us in the dynamic reality of his person.
He *is* God and man – *that* is the way of God revealed in Jesus Christ,
a company in person.

So this is no private God, no hidden God, no secret God who turns
away, shows his back, remains alone. It is instead the revelation of a
God who openly keeps company, who has made it public that he's
making a *public* because, here in Christ, we see that God refuses to be
known without shepherds, Magi, a great company of people. This God
will not let us know him outside the company he keeps. We have to
be *Church* with him. There is no private Epiphany.

O God,
who by the leading of a star
manifested your only Son to the peoples of the earth:
mercifully grant that we,
who know you now by faith,
may at last behold your glory face to face;
through Jesus Christ your Son our Lord,
who is alive and reigns with you,
in the unity of the Holy Spirit,
one God, now and for ever.

COLLECT

Psalms **99**, 147.1-12 *or* **77**
Isaiah 63.7-end
1 John 3

1 John 3

'How does God's love abide in anyone who has the world's goods and sees a brother or sister in need and yet refuses help?' (v.17)

There is a terrifying simplicity about the beautiful words we've read this morning. It's as if John is addressing us directly – across time and space – to summon us to embrace fully our noble calling as the 'beloved' (v.2). The simplicity of the message is all the more alarming because it remains totally realistic. Lawless deception, murderous greed, hatred, sin, death, the children of the devil, a litany of sin can be found here. John is no idealist. Yet John's voice does not waver. Authoritatively confident, his tenor is unrelenting, unhurried and undistracted by any set of excuses we might dream up. We simply cannot avoid loving each other. There really is no other way.

And John knows there is no other way, because there is no other God. John knows this because he is speaking *out of* God, John himself mysteriously participating in the divine life. And, from this point, he can pinpoint *our* location. We too are children of the Father, abiding in Christ, enveloped by the Spirit (vv.1, 24). God has given everything to us, *himself*, and we are therefore to share his life with each other. That is why – when we see a brother or a sister in material need – we *must* help (v.17). There is to be no *Christian* excuse because there is no Christian reasoning beyond God. It really is that simple: Love.

COLLECT

O God,
who by the leading of a star
manifested your only Son to the peoples of the earth:
mercifully grant that we,
who know you now by faith,
may at last behold your glory face to face;
through Jesus Christ your Son our Lord,
who is alive and reigns with you,
in the unity of the Holy Spirit,
one God, now and for ever.

1 John 4.7-end

'Love has been perfected among us...' (v.17)

Yesterday's summons to love has echoed through into today. Of course, it will echo through into eternity, because eternity is its ground, its goal: God is love. And so the logic is inescapable: those who love God must love their brothers and sisters (v.21) – it really is that simple.

And John gives us no chance to wriggle out of it. There really is nothing outside love. We simply cannot escape *him*. Of course, we tried. We took Love himself into our hands, dragging him outside the city, nailing him to a tree, executing Jesus Christ outside Jerusalem. But it didn't work. We discovered only the gospel: that which could separate us from God – *our very killing him* – God has chosen as his life in Christ (v.10). Therefore, nothing can separate. That's what's so terrifying about judgement.

But it is also what's so terrifying about each other. Eternity will be populated with the people I dislike, those I ignore, my enemies and strangers. I will not escape the people I treat so badly, because there is no way for me to live with God *unless* I live with them (v.20). So John knows we *must* be reconciled with each other. For anything else is fear, and fear has no place in love. Therefore, this day, we are to be as he is: that is, reconciled in this world (v.17).

Creator of the heavens,
who led the Magi by a star
to worship the Christ-child:
guide and sustain us,
that we may find our journey's end
in Jesus Christ our Lord.

COLLECT

41

Friday 9 January

Psalms 2, **148** *or* **55**
Isaiah 65.1-16
1 John 5.1-12

1 John 5.1-12

*'And this is the testimony: God gave us eternal life,
and this life is in his Son' (v.11)*

Yesterday, John pressed his point firmly. Because God is *this* God, we are free to love – we must be reconciled. In today's reading, the point is intensified. God's love cannot become abstract, nor can our piety remain self-contained. Both must be resolutely Christ-shaped, because only there – in him – do we find the perfect coincidence of all John is saying. Jesus is the twofold identity of love: our brother, God, has died in our stead.

And suddenly we again sense the scandal of what's happening here. Amid our lives of love, the Spirit is God testifying to God from God, the delight of the Father and the Son. And this lively overflowing testimony is miraculously in our hearts, our lives pierced by the endless delight of the Father in his Son (vv.9-10). Somehow we are between the Father and the Son, our lives reverberating with divine testimony, resonating with the liveliness of God, identified in Christ.

To confess Christ is therefore to become the testimony of the Father, the gift of the Spirit, the unending delight in Christ. Somehow, amid the blood, the sweat, the watery tears, we *are* the Father's testimony to the love of his Son, alive in the Spirit. Our minds can only boggle at the enormity of John's claims. Nonetheless, the task remains simple: love one another.

COLLECT

O God,
who by the leading of a star
manifested your only Son to the peoples of the earth:
mercifully grant that we,
who know you now by faith,
may at last behold your glory face to face;
through Jesus Christ your Son our Lord,
who is alive and reigns with you,
in the unity of the Holy Spirit,
one God, now and for ever.

Psalms 97, **149** *or* **76**, 79
Isaiah 65.17-end
1 John 5.13-end

1 John 5.13-end

'Little children, keep yourselves from idols' (v.21)

The measured confidence with which John writes is striking. He is self-consciously bold here, yet his voice never wavers as he draws things to a close (v.14). His earlier flights had taken him way beyond the cloud-breaking peaks of human thought, yet they have not shaken him. His parting words remain unhurried, gentle, Christ-like even. They come from a steady hand.

Though John knows that what he has said is mind-boggling, he also knows he has only said what he knows. Not information, but a person; John has said Jesus. *That* is why he's so calm. This is clearly the voice of the beloved disciple, the voice of one who has rested on God's chest (cf. John 13.23). And – because he still abides there, between Jesus and his Father – John is not worried. He knows his place.

But John also knows how unacceptable all of this will sound to us. *Little children!* Protected from our world *by God* (v.18)! What an affront! Can we not instead find a foothold, somewhere, anywhere beyond what happens between Jesus and his Father? Can we not construct our own defence? Protect ourselves? Like grown-ups? Of course, John knows we will *try*. But he is clear: little children, keep yourselves from idols. This is his parting word to us.

Creator of the heavens,
who led the Magi by a star
to worship the Christ-child:
guide and sustain us,
that we may find our journey's end
in Jesus Christ our Lord.

COLLECT

Monday 12 January

Psalms **2**, 110 *or* **80**, 82
Amos 1
1 Corinthians 1.1-17

1 Corinthians 1.1-17

'... by him you were called into the fellowship of his Son' (v.9)

The establishment of a Christian community in Corinth was one of Paul's greatest achievements. Corinth was a busy, socially mobile city, proud of its entrepreneurs and new wealth. Since his mission there, Paul had received bad news from 'Chloe's people' that the Church he had founded was now riven with factions. Those with high social status had become over-dominant. They were displaying an arrogance that was causing mayhem. To Paul, this was intolerable. Disunity, rivalry and quarrels undermine the very nature of the Church, which is not just a local, visible reality; the Corinthians belong to the same organism as those in every place who call on Christ. At the heart of this letter is a plea for unity, based on fellowship in Christ. The behaviour reported to Paul shows that the Corinthians have not yet truly understood the implications of the gospel.

This letter speaks to us because we, like them, live in a highly competitive society, which rewards the ambitious and often plays on our insecurities. It is easy for the Church to manifest similar characteristics – to over-value the opinionated and confident. In our own context we might ask: what are we doing to maintain the fellowship of Jesus Christ and the equal dignity of the weaker and stronger members? What would we have to offer a fractured Christian community?

COLLECT

Eternal Father,
who at the baptism of Jesus
revealed him to be your Son,
anointing him with the Holy Spirit:
grant to us, who are born again by water and the Spirit,
that we may be faithful to our calling as your adopted children;
through Jesus Christ your Son our Lord,
who is alive and reigns with you,
in the unity of the Holy Spirit,
one God, now and for ever.

Tuesday 13 January

1 Corinthians 1.18-end

'... we proclaim Christ crucified' (v.23)

The bitterness of the quarrels going on in Corinth drives Paul back to fundamentals. The cross is the antithesis of success, the end of ambition, the enemy of human pride. Those enmeshed in quarrels have not understood the power of God, which subverts the way a so-called vibrant and successful society actually works. No one who promotes their own agendas to the detriment of unity in the Church has really grasped what God has revealed in the cross. The 'wisdom' that was current in Corinthian society is empty from the point of view of the gospel. Where so much depended on charm, money and social status, God works by subverting all pretension. No one could be impressed by the cross. It is sheer 'folly', representing to 'the wise' nothing but failure and degradation. But the truth is that the cross reveals both the power and wisdom of God. The Corinthians would come closer to recognizing this if they reflected on their own social origins. Few of them came from privileged backgrounds, or wielded power or influence. Yet God chose them for a purpose: to shame those who rely on such things to manipulate others.

Today, as much as in Paul's time, Church communities are all too human. Perhaps we should consider how far we use our Church commitment to advance our own agendas or to give ourselves a status that we would not otherwise possess?

Heavenly Father,
at the Jordan you revealed Jesus as your Son:
may we recognize him as our Lord
and know ourselves to be your beloved children;
through Jesus Christ our Saviour.

COLLECT

45

Wednesday 14 January

Psalms 19, **20** *or* **119.105-128**
Amos 3
1 Corinthians 2

1 Corinthians 2

'Those who are spiritual discern all things' (v.15)

To make his point about God's subversive folly, Paul calls on his own experience as the apostle to the Corinthians, claiming that, when he first preached to the Corinthians, he resisted the clever rhetorical games that might have given him greater plausibility. Instead, he followed his crucified Lord, not concealing his limitations. What happened as a result was a miracle, a manifestation of God's power to change the human heart. There is a divine wisdom for those who accept God's way of foolishness, but it is secret, revealed only to those who have grasped the subversive significance of the cross.

The 'rulers of the age' (v.6) – those in power not only on earth but also in the supernatural world – can never understand this. Their failure of judgement was manifest by their involvement in Christ's crucifixion. So Paul links those 'wise' members of the community who are causing strife with the ignorant powers of the age who conspired to put Jesus to death. Those who think of themselves as most spiritual are, in fact, unspiritual. But there is a true spirituality that comes from God's Spirit and enables those who receive his gifts to discern the way God truly works. Paul's astonishing claim that 'we have the mind of Christ' (v.16) is a call to reality that is as shocking to us as it would have been to his original recipients.

COLLECT

Eternal Father,
who at the baptism of Jesus
revealed him to be your Son,
anointing him with the Holy Spirit:
grant to us, who are born again by water and the Spirit,
that we may be faithful to our calling as your adopted children;
through Jesus Christ your Son our Lord,
who is alive and reigns with you,
in the unity of the Holy Spirit,
one God, now and for ever.

Psalms **21**, 24 *or* 90, **92**
Amos 4
1 Corinthians 3

1 Corinthians 3

'... you belong to Christ, and Christ belongs to God' (v.23)

The leaders of the Corinthian Church regarded themselves as mature, but here Paul cuts them down to size. The health of the Church is shown by growth, not so much of numbers, but rather of virtue. Christian life is an organic reality in which all grow together, a holy temple to the Lord. Unless God is at the centre of things, the community is no more than any other human institution.

The Church is, of course, a human institution as well as a divine reality. Growth is uneven; the truly mature and the immature rub along together. Paul is aware that a number of individuals have contributed to the life of the Church in Corinth; some for good and some for ill. All come under God's judgement. Most at fault are those who have no insight into their own motivation; who assume that the strength of their opinions and their readiness to state them marks them out as leaders. The truth is that only those who are foolish enough to learn wisdom from God understand the upside-down logic of the cross. 'All things are yours' (v.21). The true leaders are not those who make others say 'I belong to Paul' but those whose life says 'Paul belongs to you'. Leadership is a sacred trust.

Are we ready to be called to account for the responsibilities we bear within the Christian community?

Heavenly Father,
at the Jordan you revealed Jesus as your Son:
may we recognize him as our Lord
and know ourselves to be your beloved children;
through Jesus Christ our Saviour.

COLLECT

47

Friday 16 January

1 Corinthians 4

'... stewards of God's mysteries' (v.1)

Paul is in a dilemma. He has insisted that all leaders are accountable as stewards and knows this also applies to him. He is prepared to be open to God's judgement but not to be written off by the Corinthians. He knows that, in this divided Church, he is seen by some as a divisive figure. He also knows that his verbal lashing is not going to heal the quarrels unless they lead to a change of heart. But at this point in his letter, he cannot hold back and his anger and disappointment burst out in sarcastic rhetoric. The Corinthians have everything; they are rich, strong, wise and powerful, while he is weak and vulnerable and often hungry and homeless for the sake of the gospel. Yet he has a claim on their hearts that other leaders do not have. He is the one who generated faith in them; he can claim spiritual fatherhood. This not only gives him moral authority, it also demonstrates what high-flown rhetoric cannot demonstrate: the power of the kingdom of God.

Paul's emotional outpouring may be off-putting in our context, where it could be judged as manipulative. But we cannot fault his honesty. He challenges his critics to look beyond his words and remember the consistency of his life. We, too, can sometimes be carried away by our feelings, but the faithfulness of our discipleship is where the power of the gospel is shown.

COLLECT

Eternal Father,
who at the baptism of Jesus
revealed him to be your Son,
anointing him with the Holy Spirit:
grant to us, who are born again by water and the Spirit,
that we may be faithful to our calling as your adopted children;
through Jesus Christ your Son our Lord,
who is alive and reigns with you,
in the unity of the Holy Spirit,
one God, now and for ever.

Psalms 29, **33** *or* 96, **97**, 100
Amos 5.18-end
1 Corinthians 5

Saturday 17 January

1 Corinthians 5

'Clean out the old yeast' (v. 7)

Now we come to what for Paul must have been the most shocking thing he has heard about the Corinthian Church. There is a case of incest: a man living with his mother-in-law. This is forbidden even in pagan society. Yet the Church has tolerated it, perhaps even affirming the couple for their courageous assertion of Christian freedom. This is not only wrong in itself; it brings scandal and potentially makes the Church a target for persecution.

Paul responds in two ways to this. The first is to build on his claim to spiritual fatherhood and assert that his judgement of this case is valid even though he is absent. Second, he calls the community back to the Easter faith. Christ's resurrection is a Passover, celebrated with unleavened bread. Just as the Jews at Passover removed the yeast from their homes to remember their liberation from captivity, so the Christian community must turn out the old yeast with its sinful associations.

Paul's response may seem harsh in our age, where there is much more tolerance of sexual behaviour once considered deviant. In our own time, we have seen how a casual or even permissive attitude by the Church towards the breaking of sexual boundaries scandalizes not only the faithful, but the rest of society, causing real harm to the gospel of Christ.

Heavenly Father,
at the Jordan you revealed Jesus as your Son:
may we recognize him as our Lord
and know ourselves to be your beloved children;
through Jesus Christ our Saviour.

COLLECT

49

Monday 19 January

Psalms 145, **146** *or* **98**, 99, 101
Amos 6
1 Corinthians 6.1-11

1 Corinthians 6.1-11

'Why not rather be wronged?' (v.7)

On top of the scandal of sexual impropriety comes another issue. Members of the Church are pursuing lawsuits with one another. It sounds as though there has been a case of financial dishonesty, and the wronged party has taken for granted his right to pursue this in court. Paul is horrified. It is proof that this quarrelsome community has not learnt the first thing about the implications of the gospel. It is a defeat of the gospel for a member of the Church to defraud a brother or sister. For the wronged party to take his Christian brother to court to get back what he has lost simply reinforces the defeat. Instead, why not simply be defrauded?

The radical challenge for us is to recognize that our relationships within the Church community are potentially graced. Our common baptism brings us salvation; we are washed, sanctified and justified. There are resources of grace available for us to help and not harm one another. Before the situation got out of hand why were the 'wise' of the community not intervening? Did they shrug their shoulders and say, 'Oh well, you know what people are like?' That, says Paul, is not good enough. Christian faith involves a change of orientation from self to Christ and to others. If this is not manifest in our dealings with one another, we have missed the point.

COLLECT

Almighty God,
in Christ you make all things new:
transform the poverty of our nature by the riches of your grace,
and in the renewal of our lives
make known your heavenly glory;
through Jesus Christ your Son our Lord,
who is alive and reigns with you,
in the unity of the Holy Spirit,
one God, now and for ever.

Psalms **132**, 147.1-12
or **106*** (*or* 103)
Amos 7
1 Corinthians 6.12-end

1 Corinthians 6.12-end

'... your bodies are members of Christ' (v. 15)

Those members of the community involved in fraud and sexual immorality have not truly realized that they are members of Christ. Christianity is not dualistic; there should be no split between mind and body. On the contrary, our human bodies are expressions of our true selves, and Christians live in the grace of Christ's resurrection. Just as he was raised by God's power, so our bodies contain the seeds of our own resurrection. Christian life should bring us freedom from the bodily compulsions that can damage our integrity, but it is not a freedom to do anything. Food is for the stomach, and the stomach for food. Our bodies have boundaries. Those who might be tempted to claim that they are free to have sex with prostitutes have failed to recognize that the body is the expression of the self saved in Christ and ripe for resurrection with him. The Christian life can never be reduced to mere intellectual assent, nor is it a form of private spirituality. What we do and refrain from doing in the body manifests our Christian integrity, or otherwise. 'I am no longer my own but yours', as the Methodist Covenant prayer puts it. We are bought with a price.

How, today, will your life manifest the dignity of the body? Your own and other people's?

COLLECT

Eternal Lord,
our beginning and our end:
bring us with the whole creation
to your glory, hidden through past ages
and made known
in Jesus Christ our Lord.

Psalms **81**, 147.13-end
or 110, **111**, 112
Amos 8
1 Corinthians 7.1-24

1 Corinthians 7.1-24

'... do not become slaves of human masters' (v.23)

The dignity of the self in Christ informs Paul's teaching about marriage. Within the body of Christ, all have rights and responsibilities. Paul's radical vision of what the Church should be brings him to the revolutionary teaching that women and men have equal sexual rights within marriage. Neither is to be used by the other. Both are to give generously, respecting the uniqueness of the other.

The logic of Paul's beliefs about the body leads to his equally radical view that an unbelieving partner is not to be divorced unless he or she desires it; they are made holy by their relationship with a believer. The Church community cannot be healthy unless the individuals in it are living their Christian lives with dignity and freedom. Whether or not to marry is a matter of personal vocation and gift. Christianity cannot be reduced to individualism, but respect for individual dignity is a crucial part of Christian life. We should not seek to control others or be controlled by our circumstances. We should take our personal history seriously, not trying to deny our past but being responsive to God in the present, now. Faithfulness is where true freedom is found. 'You were bought with a price', verse 23 repeats from 6.20. How do our lives express gratitude for the freedom and dignity of Christian vocation?

COLLECT

Almighty God,
in Christ you make all things new:
transform the poverty of our nature by the riches of your grace,
and in the renewal of our lives
make known your heavenly glory;
through Jesus Christ your Son our Lord,
who is alive and reigns with you,
in the unity of the Holy Spirit,
one God, now and for ever.

Psalms **76**, 148 *or* 113, **115**
Amos 9
1 Corinthians 7.25-end

Thursday 22 January

1 Corinthians 7.25-end

'... I too have the Spirit of God' (v.40)

There are ascetics in the Corinthian Church urging men and women not to marry. Paul's instinct is to sympathize with them; after all, he is unmarried himself and can see the practical advantages in being free in the service of the gospel. He believes that the time is short before the Lord's return and that it is good for Christians to be detached from worldly worries.

On the other hand, he knows that attempting to compel people not to marry is an example of the kind of arrogance to which some in the community are so prone. So he seeks a balance. The unmarried are free to marry, but the unmarried should consider the advantages in staying as they are.

The balance is not wholly satisfactory. It would be hard for those who were naturally sensitive to dissent from Paul's opinion. In matters of personal vocation, it is always wise to listen to the views of those we respect. But in the end we must take responsibility before God for the life choices we make. It is not only Paul who has the Spirit of God! Every baptized Christian receives the Spirit of discernment and can call on God's guidance in the confidence that mistakes are not the end of the world. How do our life choices reflect the freedom to which we are called?

Eternal Lord,
our beginning and our end:
bring us with the whole creation
to your glory, hidden through past ages
and made known
in Jesus Christ our Lord.

COLLECT

53

Friday 23 January

Psalms **27**, 149 *or* **139**
Hosea 1.1 – 2.1
1 Corinthians 8

1 Corinthians 8

'... anyone who loves God is known by him' (v.3)

Paul returns to withering criticism to attack the dinner party behaviour of some of his flock. Some of those who pride themselves on their superior knowledge and status have been attending social functions and eating whatever is offered. In Paul's world meat was not always readily available, and when it was, it usually came from animals killed for sacrifice in temples and butchered in close proximity to them.

Theologically, this is unimportant as idols are empty; everything comes from the true God. But knowing this does not mean that taking part in such feasts is right. Those who do so may argue that it is part of their Christian freedom. They are right in theory, but wrong in practice. To believers from a pagan background who still retain a residual belief in idols, eating such meat could be a cause of temptation. Christian freedom must never be interpreted in such a way as to cause harm to the faith of others. It is wrong for those who claim freedom in Christ to behave in ways that could lead others to compromise their consciences. This is not only unkind; it is to lead others into sin and thus to wound Christ himself as they are members of his body. What matters is not our superior knowledge of the ways of God, but our love for God and his knowledge of us.

COLLECT

Almighty God,
in Christ you make all things new:
transform the poverty of our nature by the riches of your grace,
and in the renewal of our lives
make known your heavenly glory;
through Jesus Christ your Son our Lord,
who is alive and reigns with you,
in the unity of the Holy Spirit,
one God, now and for ever.

1 Corinthians 9.1-14

'Am I not free? Am I not an apostle?' (v. 1)

Paul now addresses a major question that has been raised against him. Is he a true apostle? Does he have genuine authority? In earlier chapters, Paul has explained why, on his original mission, he did not exercise a clever, articulate leadership style that might have flattered his audience. Now he makes a different point. Unlike other leaders of churches, he has not asked the community for material support. He has a right to do so, but he has refrained from exercising this right. This in itself has caused some to doubt his authority. In Corinth, it seems, you pay for what you get. Paul here simply makes the point that he needs no other authority than that conveyed by the vision of Jesus he had at his conversion. He is free to claim or not to claim the support he is due.

We don't know exactly why Paul did not ask for material support from the Corinthian Church. Perhaps it was simply that in such a materialist society, he wanted to model a kind of freedom and availability that would unsettle some assumptions. His generosity in this instance questioned the materialist values of those who were attacking him.

Are there occasions when we are called to serve the gospel by refraining from our rights rather than insisting on them?

Eternal Lord,
our beginning and our end:
bring us with the whole creation
to your glory, hidden through past ages
and made known
in Jesus Christ our Lord.

COLLECT

Monday 26 January

Psalms 40, **108**
or 123, 124, 125, **126**
Hosea 2.18 – 3.end
I Corinthians 9.15-end

1 Corinthians 9.15-end

'... that I might be partaker thereof with you' (v.23, AV)

Imagine a culture where people are fixated on their rights, on making sure they receive everything they are entitled to. Imagine a culture where competition is celebrated as the great driver for human achievement, symbolized by sporting events that command huge audiences and extravagant expenditure. How can the gospel be shared and discipleship fostered in such a culture? It is a question we might ask today, and a question with which Paul was grappling 2,000 years ago as he wrote to the Christians in Corinth.

In responding to the specific issues on which they had asked for his opinion, Paul is also seeking to reshape their attitudes. While it is not always easy to track his thinking in this chapter, it seems clear enough that verse 23 summarizes his overriding point: 'And this I do for the gospel's sake, that I might be partaker thereof with you' (AV). Paul wants the Corinthians to understand that life in Christ means living for the sake of the gospel, and the gospel is not something I can possess as an object or achievement for myself. Rather, I can only have it by participating in it – by letting it become part of me, and letting my whole life become part of it – and I can only do that by sharing it with others, by giving it away. Here is the real prize, but to win it means learning to let go of the need to demand, compare and compete, and instead following the servant of all.

COLLECT

Almighty God,
whose Son revealed in signs and miracles
the wonder of your saving presence:
renew your people with your heavenly grace,
and in all our weakness
sustain us by your mighty power;
through Jesus Christ your Son our Lord,
who is alive and reigns with you,
in the unity of the Holy Spirit,
one God, now and for ever.

Psalms 34, **36** *or* **132**, 133
Hosea 4.1-16
1 Corinthians 10.1-13

1 Corinthians 10.1-13

'... our ancestors were all under the cloud' (v. 1)

Who do you think you are? Where do you come from? Television programmes where celebrities explore their family trees – sometimes with surprising results – have become very popular. At this point in 1 Corinthians, Paul wants to remind his readers who they are by talking about their family, their 'ancestors'.

This may have come as something of a surprise to the gentiles among them – probably the majority. If they had been asked to describe their family tree, they might not have thought beyond biology. Paul's point, however, is that neither biological family, nor geographical and social location, define who we are in Christ. We are part of another family, another city, another history: the response to God's calling.

Advent encouraged us to identify with some of the great figures from Israel's past, especially the prophets preaching justice and announcing hope. It may come as a surprise to us to discover that our ancestors include the faithless as well as the faithful, those consumed by resentment and disappointment as well as those who walked in trust and gratitude. All were under the cloud – and Paul repeats the word 'all' four times. All received God's grace in astonishing ways, yet not all were able to keep the gift. For us too 'on whom the ends of the ages have come' (v. 11), the gift opens out onto a journey, marked by testing as God leads us deeper into faith in divine faithfulness. Knowing who we are will help keep our feet on the ground – and keep us moving forwards.

God of all mercy,
your Son proclaimed good news to the poor,
release to the captives,
and freedom to the oppressed:
anoint us with your Holy Spirit
and set all your people free
to praise you in Christ our Lord.

COLLECT

57

Wednesday 28 January

Psalms 45, **46** *or* **119.153-end**
Hosea 5.1-7
1 Corinthians 10.14 – 11.1

1 Corinthians 10.14 – 11.1

'I do not want you to be partners with demons' (10.20)

Talk about demons tends to divide Christians today. For some, it belongs to a bygone age unless it is self-consciously metaphorical. For others, it is absolutely necessary to describe the realities of the life of faith.

This is the only place in Paul's surviving letters where he writes about demons. Those who live in Christ should not, it seems, be constantly worried about demonic presences and powers. Rather, they should imitate Paul in trying to 'please everyone in everything I do, not seeking my own advantage, but that of many, so that they may be saved' (10.33). Such missional ethics mean practising an empathetic awareness of others, and that is where our attention normally needs to go.

So why does he mention demons now? The key is his concern about idolatry: he wants to spell out that there is fearful danger here. This is not because idols have any reality, but because in the worship of idols, people willingly and consciously put themselves into the real orbit of dehumanizing forces that can only pull away from the God in whose image we are made. Is this a danger that we can happily consign to the past? If such forces remain at work, it also remains possible to expose ourselves deliberately to their energy. To think this is a small matter, or a step from which we can easily retreat, would be a serious mistake. Hence Paul pleads with his 'dear friends' (literally, 'my beloved ones'): 'flee from the worship of idols' (10.14).

COLLECT

Almighty God,
whose Son revealed in signs and miracles
the wonder of your saving presence:
renew your people with your heavenly grace,
and in all our weakness
sustain us by your mighty power;
through Jesus Christ your Son our Lord,
who is alive and reigns with you,
in the unity of the Holy Spirit,
one God, now and for ever.

Psalms **47**, 48 *or* **143**, 146
Hosea 5.8 – 6.6
1 Corinthians 11.2-16

1 Corinthians 11.2-16

'... we have no such custom' (v. 16)

Christ 'brought all newness in bringing himself,' wrote St Irenaeus of Lyons in the second century. When the Body of Christ comes together, something new is unfolding, because in Christ, God has done something powerfully, wonderfully and inexhaustibly new. Our life together – our activities together – should express that, should celebrate and explore it.

That may or may not sound like our Sunday morning worship, or indeed the average parochial church council meeting. The Corinthian Christians were evidently revelling in the new horizons that Paul's preaching of the gospel had opened up for them. In this passage, however, Paul is trying to engage them in some careful, theological discernment about that. Radical transformation of relationships and behaviour through Christ is not the same thing as evocation of the psychic charge that follows from temporarily stepping outside normal boundaries and codes. It is easy to mistake the latter for the former – then and now.

Commentators have long puzzled over just what the specific issue really is here, and how exactly Paul's argument works (or indeed doesn't). More recently, scholarship has intersected with sometimes bitter debates about gender roles in the life of the Church, though it is far from clear whether this text has any direct relevance to all that. But it does ask us to judge for ourselves (v. 13) about how, in the decisions we take or assume about customs, we make space for the true newness of the gospel to shine out in our midst.

God of all mercy,
your Son proclaimed good news to the poor,
release to the captives,
and freedom to the oppressed:
anoint us with your Holy Spirit
and set all your people free
to praise you in Christ our Lord.

COLLECT

Friday 30 January

1 Corinthians 11.17-end

'Examine yourselves' (v.28)

We may feel relieved finally to be on familiar ground as we move to the second half of chapter 11. The situation Paul writes about here looks instantly recognisable to us from Church life today: 'the Lord's supper' – Holy Communion, the Eucharist, the mass; and a pot-luck supper – though we may be more used to a bring-and-share lunch.

What will be much less familiar is the idea that these two activities should be intertwined. Somehow they came to be separated in the century or so after Paul wrote to the Corinthian believers. One outcome is that our own celebrations of the Lord's supper are less likely to dramatize overtly the divisions among us, but they may also have less power to enact the union we share in the body of Christ. In fact, it may be much easier for us to 'eat and drink without discerning the body' (v.29) when the relationship between the body on which we feed and the body to which we are joined by that feeding can appear so remote, so attenuated. We too, in very different circumstances, are tempted to believe we can go ahead and meet Christ in our 'own supper' without needing to share his presence with and in the flesh and blood of those around us. But we cannot partake of his Eucharistic body without participating in his ecclesial body. The more deeply we enter and love the one, the more deeply we will enter and love the other.

COLLECT

Almighty God,
whose Son revealed in signs and miracles
the wonder of your saving presence:
renew your people with your heavenly grace,
and in all our weakness
sustain us by your mighty power;
through Jesus Christ your Son our Lord,
who is alive and reigns with you,
in the unity of the Holy Spirit,
one God, now and for ever.

Psalm **68** *or* **147**
Hosea 8
1 Corinthians 12.1-11

1 Corinthians 12.1-11

'... the manifestation of the Spirit for the common good' (v. 7)

Some of the Corinthians, at least, liked to think of themselves as 'spiritual'. Paul is not so sure, as he made clear earlier in the letter (3.1-4). Now he comes back to the question of 'spiritual realities', perhaps the translation that best conveys the open meaning of the Greek term in verse 1 here.

Paul's readers came from a culture that was keen on comparison, achievement and competition, and the language of the 'spiritual' could easily be inflected by that. Those of the spirit liked to look down on those 'of the flesh' (1 Corinthians 3.3). Paul's starting point, by contrast, is that being spiritual is about being in 'the Spirit of God': it is a relationship with God, not certain qualities or powers that we can acquire for ourselves. Moreover, this relationship is now found 'in Christ', and therefore all our talk about spirit, spiritual things and spirituality needs to be reframed in that light. As he proceeds to explain over the next three chapters, to be spiritual is to be someone who receives gifts from the Spirit and offers them 'for the common good'. And the Spirit of God is endlessly generous: verses 4 to 11 are not intended to be a comprehensive list or definitive categorization, but rather an affirmation of the amazing diversity of ways in which the Spirit works in the Church to create a symphony of grace. For God's grace (*charis* in Greek) is the meaning of every gift (*charisma*) we may offer.

God of all mercy,
your Son proclaimed good news to the poor,
release to the captives,
and freedom to the oppressed:
anoint us with your Holy Spirit
and set all your people free
to praise you in Christ our Lord.

COLLECT

Monday 2 February

Presentation of Christ in the Temple

Psalms **48**, 146
Exodus 13.1-16
Romans 12.1-5

Romans 12.1-5

'... present your bodies as a living sacrifice' (v. 1)

Who wants to be sacrificed? Who wants to be a sacrifice? It might seem like an ugly, disconcerting question. Distrust of the demand for sacrifice is one of the deepest characteristics of modernity. No being should have to suffer so that another can walk free.

There are particular reasons too why it can and should be a disconcerting question for the Christian. Jesus does not, like other priests at other times, offer sacrifices daily for sin, but 'this he did once for all when he offered himself' (Hebrews 7.27). His self-offering on the cross is prefigured on this feast, which has gone by different names through the centuries but which we now call the Presentation of Christ. His parents 'brought him up to Jerusalem to present him to the Lord' (Luke 2.22). 'Present your bodies as a living sacrifice': it is the same verb in both passages, and in both passages it points to sacrifice.

The offering of the first-born was a reminder for Israel of the mercy of God in their deliverance from Egypt: an offering that left the beloved son alive. The offering of the beloved Son of God for the salvation of the whole world creates new life, unending life. And to share in this life, we must share also in the sacrifice: but as a 'living sacrifice' – not destroyed, not consumed in the offering, but transformed, exalted and healed, so that our many separated and broken bodies become 'one body in Christ' (v.5).

COLLECT

Almighty and ever-living God,
clothed in majesty,
whose beloved Son was this day presented in the Temple,
in substance of our flesh:
grant that we may be presented to you
with pure and clean hearts,
by your Son Jesus Christ our Lord,
who is alive and reigns with you,
in the unity of the Holy Spirit,
one God, now and for ever.

Psalms **5**, 6 (8)
Hosea 10
1 Corinthians 13

1 Corinthians 13

'... then I will know fully' (v.12)

Knowledge mattered to the Corinthians. It is one of the repeating themes of this letter, highlighted in Paul's introductory words (1 Corinthians 1.5). There is something deeply flawed in their attitude, however, and it is to do with the separation of knowledge from love; such knowledge 'puffs up' the person who would wield it, but love 'builds up' the temple of God, the body of Christ (1 Corinthians 8.1).

Now Paul tells them that knowledge, even the knowledge that comes as a gift from God, 'will come to an end' (v.8). Yet when he tries to describe the fullness of life that lies ahead for us in Christ, he still reaches for the language of knowing: 'then I will know fully, even as I have been fully known' (v.12). What begins now and lasts forever – the depth of the present and the invitation of the future – is not knowledge as a thing we hold, but knowing God and being known by God. Such knowing is also loving, and such being known is also being loved – and it never ends.

Knowledge also matters to people today. Knowledge promises power: power to influence environments and organizations; power to shape our unruly hearts and their elusive attachments. Even at its best, however, such knowledge is only for a season. Our true life rests in the knowing that is also loving the One whose loving and knowing of us are beyond comprehension, and it overflows in ordinary, costly acts of love day by day.

Almighty God,
by whose grace alone we are accepted
and called to your service:
strengthen us by your Holy Spirit
and make us worthy of our calling;
through Jesus Christ your Son our Lord,
who is alive and reigns with you,
in the unity of the Holy Spirit,
one God, now and for ever.

COLLECT

Wednesday 4 February

Psalm **119.1-32**
Hosea 11.1-11
1 Corinthians 14.1-19

1 Corinthians 14.1-19

'... strive to excel in them for building up the church' (v.12)

Why do we come to church? What are we hoping for as the service begins? Spiritual refreshment, theological enlightenment, strength and guidance for the challenges of daily life?

Paul here turns back to the subject of 'spiritual gifts' that he had introduced in chapter 12, but from the sharpened perspective of chapter 13, applying the primacy of love to the specific practices of church life: all must be done 'for building up the church' (v.12). Paul is absolutely clear that speaking in tongues is a gift from God's Spirit releasing our spirit for prayer and praise, but also that it is given for the benefit of the recipient. However, everything we do 'in church' (v.19) should be done to help the whole Church grow and not for our own spiritual gain.

Whether or not our church services regularly feature speaking in tongues and prophecy, what might it mean for us to apply Paul's imperative of love to our practices and our attitudes in public worship – his strict testing of what we may most treasure against the criterion of 'building up the church'? There may be different challenges here for those who lead worship and those who see themselves as responding and receiving. But what would it look like if all of us came to church unconcerned about how we might build up ourselves (v.4), but instead came ready to participate in an exchange of gifts from the Holy Spirit that will draw us further together into the purposes of God?

COLLECT

Almighty God,
by whose grace alone we are accepted and called to your service:
strengthen us by your Holy Spirit
and make us worthy of our calling;
through Jesus Christ your Son our Lord,
who is alive and reigns with you,
in the unity of the Holy Spirit,
one God, now and for ever.

Psalms 14, **15**, 16
Hosea 11.12 – end of 12
1 Corinthians 14.20-end

Thursday 5 February

1 Corinthians 14.20-end

'God is a God not of disorder but of peace' (v.33)

'No one likes surprises in worship,' declared my liturgy tutor when I was an ordinand. His words came back to me many years later when I was in a pre-service prayer meeting with someone pleading earnestly for 'chaos to break out this morning'. I found it hard to say 'Amen', and not just because I would be leading.

Paul might have also hesitated to join such a prayer, though he would surely have found the axiom of my old tutor incomprehensible too. There was no written order of service for when 'the whole church comes together' in Corinth (v.23), no set sequence and no knowing in advance what would happen. Moreover, there does not appear to have been a 'leader' of any sort either; Paul addresses everyone as having a shared responsibility to control what unfolds when they meet. So he assumes there will be surprises, but he is also clear about the need for some control to be exercised, 'for God is a God not of disorder but of peace' (v.33).

You do not need to be an expert in psychology to understand that startling differences in approach to worship across the Christian Churches have something to do with our emotional make-up, personal preferences and embedded coping mechanisms, as well as theological positions and spiritual traditions. All our worship, however, should speak somehow of God's peace: the divine spaciousness in which we find both security and freedom, a place to belong and a never-ending adventure of new horizons.

God of our salvation,
help us to turn away from those habits which harm our bodies
and poison our minds
and to choose again your gift of life,
revealed to us in Jesus Christ our Lord.

COLLECT

65

Friday 6 February

Psalms 17, **19**
Hosea 13.1-14
1 Corinthians 16.1-9

1 Corinthians 16.1-9

'Now concerning the collection for the saints...' (v. 1)

Perhaps one needs to be of a certain age to remember the maps of 'Paul's missionary journeys' that used to adorn church halls and were found in smaller format at the back of Sunday-school Bibles. Paul's travels were certainly motivated by the desire to bring the gospel to new places, but he was also guided by concern to connect these new churches with one another and with the old churches too, above all the church in Jerusalem. Week by week, the Corinthian Christians are to remember 'the saints' who are there.

Today, we might use the theological vocabulary of local and universal to express this: each local church is the Church, yet to be the Church is always to be in relation with other local churches and thereby the universal Church, a relation that can be characterized as 'communion'. All well and good, perhaps, but such communion can seem mostly intangible, compared to the vivid realities of life in 'our' church; occasionally it can seem tiresome, when consultation with other denominations or other provinces holds us back.

Paul travelled in part because the inherent theological relation between different churches needed to be expressed in face-to-face, personal relationships between those who could represent them. He travelled because there can be no new church that is not in communion with every church, beginning with the very first; he travelled too because that communion needs to be sustained in the face of the complacency, conflicts and divisions that have always marred its holy beauty.

COLLECT

Almighty God,
by whose grace alone we are accepted and called to your
    service:
strengthen us by your Holy Spirit
and make us worthy of our calling;
through Jesus Christ your Son our Lord,
who is alive and reigns with you,
in the unity of the Holy Spirit,
one God, now and for ever.

1 Corinthians 16.10-end

'My love be with all of you in Christ Jesus' (v.24)

It is evident from this closing passage that all is not well between Paul and the Church in Corinth. Why does he have to ask them to make sure his companion Timothy 'has nothing to fear among you' (v.10)? Are his closing comments about Apollos and the household of Stephanas attempts at some kind of mediation in the face of the 'quarrels' he had heard about from 'Chloe's people' (1 Corinthians 1.11)? And why does he interrupt his final greeting with a curse (v.22) – an extraordinary intrusion into the normal conventions of letter-writing in Paul's context, as it would be in our own?

There is something else more or less unique about the final greeting in this letter: 'My love be with all of you in Christ Jesus' (v.24). Paul knows there is serious trouble within the community, including deep antagonism towards him and those associated with him. He has desperately grave concerns about currents dragging people away from 'love for the Lord' and leaving them exposed to divine judgement (v.22). Yet he ends by pledging his abiding love not for those who are on his side, not for those who affirm true doctrine, but for 'all of you'. This cannot have been easy, but perhaps the origins of the amazing passage we know as 1 Corinthians 13 lie in what Paul needed to hear himself in this situation. At any rate, he ends by showing he is determined to keep walking the 'still more excellent way' (1 Corinthians 12.31).

God of our salvation,
help us to turn away from those habits which harm our bodies
and poison our minds
and to choose again your gift of life,
revealed to us in Jesus Christ our Lord.

COLLECT

Psalms 27, **30**
2 Chronicles 9.1-12
John 19.1-16

2 Chronicles 9.1-12

'Blessed be the Lord your God, who has delighted in you' (v.8)

The Queen of Sheba has heard of the greatness of Solomon's wisdom; his reputation is international. It is probable that Sheba was in the Yemen, so she travelled a great distance to see for herself and to test out his renown. What she experiences exceeds her expectations; here is opulence beyond measure. Even when she has given Solomon of her riches, he is able to fulfil her every desire. The host outdoes the generosity of the guest.

The material wealth is symbolic, though, of the wisdom of Solomon, and Solomon is only wise because of his faithfulness and obedience to God. As Israel rebuilds the temple destroyed by the Babylonians, the Chronicler looks back to the golden age of David and Solomon. As Israel rediscovers itself, God's blessing will rest upon those who, like Solomon, fulfil the will of God. It took a foreign dignity to recognize God's blessing on Israel, and exclaim: 'Blessed be the Lord your God, who has delighted in you!' (v.8).

The close link of prosperity – and wisdom – with faithfulness is a strong theme in Chronicles; a link decisively challenged by the fate of Job. The Chronicler portrays Solomon as too wise to depend on his wealth; his dependence remains on God, and this makes him great. For us today, what rich gifts do we receive for faithfulness and obedience to God?

COLLECT

Almighty God,
you have created the heavens and the earth
and made us in your own image:
teach us to discern your hand in all your works
and your likeness in all your children;
through Jesus Christ your Son our Lord,
who with you and the Holy Spirit reigns supreme over all things,
now and for ever.

2 Chronicles 10.1 – 11.4

'...he rejected the advice that the older men gave him' (10.8)

After Solomon dies, the golden age of God's blessing gives way to the all-too-human realities of disobedience, hardship and calamity. The reign of Rehoboam sees Israel divided, north against south. This is not a wise king. He is led astray by poor counsel; he takes time, but does not arrive at the right course of action.

As we read of the reign of Rehoboam, we continue the long passages of 2 Chronicles that will occupy us during this week. For many people they are not the most riveting of reads, and the Chronicler's message is straightforward and simple. Whereas with David and Solomon the Chronicler was at pains to gloss over their failings, now he uses the shortcomings of kings to explain the sufferings and struggles of Israel. When they repent, however, God waits for them and offers reconciliation. This is his tune, which he plays, with occasional variation, as we read on.

The best way through is to read 2 Chronicles as an exercise in discipline. Just as the kings of early Israel needed to knuckle down and be obedient, so too, perhaps, do we. When faced with boring bits of the Bible, is it up to us to choose to engage or not? Is faith about picking and choosing? Who am I to decide? Rehoboam thought he knew. He would not have bothered to read 2 Chronicles.

Almighty God,
give us reverence for all creation
and respect for every person,
that we may mirror your likeness
in Jesus Christ our Lord.

COLLECT

Wednesday 11 February

2 Chronicles 12

'You abandoned me, so I have abandoned you' (v.5)

Solomon's shields of gold were taken in the Egyptian raid led by Egypt's pharaoh. Shishak's invasion is one of the few events that have extra-biblical corroboration: Shishak was actually Sheshonq I, who conducted a military campaign throughout Palestine, though the Chronicler makes Jerusalem the focus to rub in the message of Rehoboam's unfaithfulness. The loss of the shields of Solomon is further evidence that this is a bad king; his replacement bronze shields are a poor substitute for the real thing. Rehoboam 'did evil, for he did not set his heart to seek the Lord' (v.14).

Rehoboam offers the second best, and perhaps that's the challenge to be mined from this passage today. Because often that's what we offer – God, each other, ourselves even. We are late for our daily time of prayer because we must just finish that task. We don't listen with heart and mind as someone tells us something important. We short-change ourselves and don't prepare enough for that event up ahead.

It's easy to go light on our relationship with God. We justify our slippages, let ourselves off the hook. It's not that holding to a discipline will earn us a place in heaven. But it will enable us to be that much more receptive to the grace of God that breaks through into life in mysterious ways, at unexpected times. If we let the gold go, and present the bronze instead, we will be the poorer.

COLLECT

Almighty God,
you have created the heavens and the earth
and made us in your own image:
teach us to discern your hand in all your works
and your likeness in all your children;
through Jesus Christ your Son our Lord,
who with you and the Holy Spirit reigns supreme over all things,
now and for ever.

Psalm **37***
2 Chronicles 13.1 – 14.1
John 20.1-10

2 Chronicles 13.1 – 14.1

'the people of Judah prevailed, because they relied on the Lord'
(v. 18)

The battle continues between the southern and northern kingdoms, and the Chronicler's account of Abijah's victory over Jeroboam reinstates the hegemony of the house of David. Jeroboam's ambush was a clever ploy that backfired. Abijah's victory is due to God's blessing, as is his long life and his many wives and children. But it is at a cost, for many lives have been lost in this civil war, and indeed the divisions continue between Judah and Israel. Only the repentance of Israel, the northern kingdom, will bring unity to the people of God.

It's the perennial sin: the division into two or more warring camps. Tribalism belongs here, when the identities of kin, or kingdom, or nation become the greatest loyalty, undermining the prime loyalty and identity in the Lord God. Civil war is, arguably, the worst sort. The terrible cost of war when neighbour turns against neighbour is the result of intense hatred that becomes inflamed and can take long years to forget.

'Do not think that I have come to bring peace to the earth,' said Jesus. 'I have come to set a man against his father, and a daughter against her mother' (Matthew 10.34ff). What Christ offers instead is an identity in him that transcends our tribal loyalties. For in him, there is neither Jew nor Greek, slave nor free (Galatians 3.28).

Almighty God,
give us reverence for all creation
and respect for every person,
that we may mirror your likeness
in Jesus Christ our Lord.

COLLECT

71

Friday 13 February

Psalm **31**
2 Chronicles 14.2-end
John 20.11-18

2 Chronicles 14.2-end

'Help us, O Lord our God, for we rely on you' (v.11)

Now it's the turn of the southern kingdom, Judah, to fall foul of the Lord. The kingdom has 'rest' (vv.1,5), because Asa purifies the land of the idol worship that distracted the people from Jerusalem, and the land prospers. Judah is commanded to 'seek the Lord, the God of their ancestors' (v.4). His faithfulness to God bears fruit: there is peace, a gift from God. There is building, and the cities are fortified. Asa is able to build a large army, all mighty warriors.

But his obedience to God is soon tested, this time by an enormous Ethiopian force, which proves easily overcome despite its size. This is a story that supports the Chronicler's purpose. Faith and obedience are rewarded; success ensues, even when the odds against are overwhelming.

If only it were always so! Churches would be full. Following God in Christ is altogether more difficult, especially if we think we've fulfilled all righteousness and still things go pear-shaped. In times of real desperation, there's often nowhere else to go but God, whatever the outcome. Sometimes, it's only in retrospect – sometimes far distant retrospect – the blessing of God becomes apparent. Otherwise, we need those times when we know we are dependent on God to remind us of God's blessing and to prevent us from the temptation to be self-sufficient.

COLLECT

Almighty God,
you have created the heavens and the earth
and made us in your own image:
teach us to discern your hand in all your works
and your likeness in all your children;
through Jesus Christ your Son our Lord,
who with you and the Holy Spirit reigns supreme over all things,
now and for ever.

Psalms 41, **42**, 43
2 Chronicles 15.1-15
John 20.19-end

2 Chronicles 15.1-15

*'If you seek him, he will be found by you, but if you abandon him,
he will abandon you' (v.2)*

Asa continues his exemplary reign, as the Chronicler presents it. He is
a king who seeks God, and God does not abandon him. He continues
to purify the land of abominable idols, and repairs the altar of the Lord.
His piety is attractive, and many from the northern kingdom of Israel
desert to join him. Asa leads the people to renew the covenant to the
Lord, to seek him with their whole desire. To seek God with their whole
desire is to find themselves a nation once more.

To respond to God is to shape our desires in a particular way and
direction – to focus beyond ourselves to the source of life and love.
There is a unity to be found here. When those who differ stop to recall
their shared desire for God, then those differences can be transcended,
if only for long enough to draw breath before the negotiations begin
again.

There's a unity to be found in ourselves too, when we centre our
desires and focus them in one direction. It becomes possible to
recognize the stuff of our lives that pulls us off down different avenues
or into cul-de-sacs, so we become dissipated and broken, like the
nations of old. It's worth spending a few moments each day gathering
our thoughts and focusing our desires on God.

Almighty God,
give us reverence for all creation
and respect for every person,
that we may mirror your likeness
in Jesus Christ our Lord.

COLLECT

73

Jeremiah 1

'... I am only a boy' (v.6)

Jeremiah's response to God is one we know. How can I speak into this situation? What authority do I have? Will people listen? Will I find the words? It's not easy when you need to speak out on a principle; when you propose the unpopular but right way forward; when you are questioned, contradicted, and find yourself a lone voice. Jeremiah's commission to be a prophet to the nations came with the warning at the end of the chapter that 'They will fight against you …' (v.19).

How do we discern the will of God? By looking and listening, by interpreting the signs of the times. Jeremiah saw almond branches and boiling pots, and saw the will of God in such things. But where do we look? How do we discern what's the right thing to say or do? It should take time to make up our minds. Luther said 'Here I stand: I can do no other' only after long consideration and prayer.

We're not all called to be Jeremiahs, or Luthers, but every so often our response to the truth of the matter requires us to speak out, regardless of the consequences. If we don't, it can be hard to live with the regret. Claiming that we're too young, or 'slow of speech and slow of tongue' as Moses did (Exodus 4.10), won't wash.

'Do not worry about how you are to speak or what you are to say; for what you are to say will be given to you at that time; for it is not you who speak, but the Spirit of your Father speaking through you.' (Matthew 10.19-20)

Almighty Father,
whose Son was revealed in majesty
before he suffered death upon the cross:
give us grace to perceive his glory,
that we may be strengthened to suffer with him
and be changed into his likeness, from glory to glory;
who is alive and reigns with you,
in the unity of the Holy Spirit,
one God, now and for ever.

Jeremiah 2.1-13

'... you followed me in the wilderness' (v.2)

Jesus said it, often: 'Follow me'. The image here, in Jeremiah, is an ancient Near Eastern one, of the bride who would follow her new husband from her home to his, and so God wants such desire and faithfulness. The people had followed the Lord through the wastes and desolation of the wilderness, but now that times are more fruitful, they go after other things.

To follow your heart's desire – it's worth pondering what that means. In today's world, one's heart's desire can lead in any number of directions – towards excessive wealth, consumer satisfaction, one partner after another. Ultimately of course, such desires do not fulfil; they prove to be gods that are not gods, cracked cisterns that can hold no water. These are the empty promises of worldly desire.

'For where your treasure is, there your heart will be also' (Matthew 6.21). Like R. S. Thomas, who saw the sun break through to illuminate a small field and saw it to be the pearl of great price, so the wilderness of the world requires bright and occasional illumination – or, to change the metaphor, drops of living water that catch the light, living water that gushes up to eternal life (John 4.14). During the arid time of Lent, a glass of fresh water can remind us of the sweet taste of Jesus that lingers and stirs our desire for solid joys and lasting treasure.

Holy God,
you know the disorder of our sinful lives:
set straight our crooked hearts,
and bend our wills to love your goodness
and your glory
in Jesus Christ our Lord.

COLLECT

75

Wednesday 18 February

Ash Wednesday

Psalm **38**
Daniel 9.3-6, 17-19
I Timothy 6.6-19

Daniel 9.3-6, 17-19

'For your own sake, O my God' (v. 19)

Daniel's cry is one of real desperation. As if not only he, but the whole city of God, is sinking in quicksand. Floundering is of no avail; no good to clutch at the straws of human righteousness and self-justification. The imperatives tumble over each other. Listen! Let your face shine upon us! Incline your ear! Open your eyes! Forgive! Do not delay! This is an urgent, wholehearted appeal to the mercy of God to save the city and people who bear God's name.

Anyone who suffers stress, or anxiety, or panic attacks knows the reality of this – how you feel like the foundations of life are no longer there. The more you try to find a secure foothold, the more shaky your hold on your life becomes. When the foundations are undermined, there seems nowhere to turn to escape. The more you struggle, the deeper you go.

It is Ash Wednesday today – a day on which to take seriously the reality of our utter dependence upon God. A day on which to remember how lost we are when we rely upon our own merit and virtue – how quickly things turn to dust and ashes in our hands without the grace of God sustaining and leading us. Let us pray today for a deepened sense of God's grace throughout the days of Lent ahead, so we come to know more clearly and dearly, and nearly, that sustaining love. Without it, we are already the dust to which we shall return. But not yet, for God's sake.

COLLECT

Almighty and everlasting God,
you hate nothing that you have made
and forgive the sins of all those who are penitent:
create and make in us new and contrite hearts
that we, worthily lamenting our sins
and acknowledging our wretchedness,
may receive from you, the God of all mercy,
perfect remission and forgiveness;
through Jesus Christ your Son our Lord,
who is alive and reigns with you,
in the unity of the Holy Spirit,
one God, now and for ever.

Thursday 19 February

Jeremiah 2.14-32

'We are free, we will come to you no more' (v.31)

Freedom is largely understood today as freedom from constraint. This is freedom towards self-actualization, self-realization. When I'm unconstrained by any commitment to others, I can flourish, fulfil my potential, become what I am – so the mantra goes. The Lord God says: 'For long ago you broke your yoke and burst your bonds, and you said, "I will not serve!"' (v.20). This idea of freedom is obviously as old as the hills, for here it is, alive and kicking, among Jeremiah's contemporaries.

Such freedom, though, leads only to slavery. The sarcasm of the Lord is deftly directed towards a people that has already been rescued from slavery and oppression. And here they are, squandering the gift of freedom and exchanging it for another slavery, this time to lusts and passions, to self-indulgence. No freedom here.

St Augustine reminds us that we find perfect freedom in service. Service – that word turns up in so many contexts in today's world: in a game of tennis, in animal mating, in the armed forces, in actions done to benefit others, in the worship offered to God. However it is used, it's a relational word: service is something offered *by* one *to* another. No room here for that freefall away from responsibility that Jeremiah rails against! Perfect freedom comes when we tie ourselves in to the society of others, the society of God.

Holy God,
our lives are laid open before you:
rescue us from the chaos of sin
and through the death of your Son
bring us healing and make us whole
in Jesus Christ our Lord.

COLLECT

Friday 20 February

Psalms **3**, 7 *or* **51**, 54
Jeremiah 3.6-22
John 4.27-42

Jeremiah 3.6-22

'And I thought you would call me, My Father' (v.19)

The description of the people swings back and forth between the faithless whore and the children, continuing the lament of God at the betrayal of Israel. There is real tenderness here: a parent calling out for the lost child, hearing the plaintive weeping on the bare heights. There is also a yearning for reconciliation, for a coming-together of those who are estranged.

The Lord God is revealed as 'My Father', crying out for restored relationship: a Father who shows love with all the pain and loss of the rejected, who expresses the intimacy of the closest of any human relationship. Tender are the words; for though God has every right to wrath, yet what is here is the poignant calling for the acknowledgement of guilt so forgiveness can freely flow.

It's hard to forgive when we are wronged, when others betray us. The brilliance of C. S. Lewis' allegorical tale *The Great Divorce* lies in his description of those people who are trapped in their inability to forgive, who cannot be free of bitterness and recrimination, or of the selfish desire to control others and to manipulate. Hell is turning away from God into ever more distant solipsistic atomism where such faithlessness becomes habitual. 'My Father' waits as any parent waits through the night for the return of the adolescent. The parent who says, again and again, 'I thought you would call me'.

COLLECT

Almighty and everlasting God,
you hate nothing that you have made
and forgive the sins of all those who are penitent:
create and make in us new and contrite hearts
that we, worthily lamenting our sins
and acknowledging our wretchedness,
may receive from you, the God of all mercy,
perfect remission and forgiveness;
through Jesus Christ your Son our Lord,
who is alive and reigns with you,
in the unity of the Holy Spirit,
one God, now and for ever.

Psalm **71** *or* **68**
Jeremiah 4.1-18
John 4.43-end

Jeremiah 4.1-18

'O Jerusalem, wash your heart clean of wickedness' (v.14)

'Almighty God, unto whom all hearts be open, all desires known.' So begins the Collect for Purity in the Anglican liturgy. To come before God in worship requires open hearts, pure of any distraction or corruption, ready to receive the God of light and love. A heart that is filled with anger or bitterness, or is preoccupied with pornographic imagers and dirty secrets – such a heart needs to be transformed.

Or perhaps the heart is troubled and struggling, broken perhaps by loss. Perhaps it is beating irregularly – too quickly, too slowly. Full of disease or ill at ease through stress. Experiencing palpitations. Expressing with physical symptoms things that might be wrong in life.

John Donne talked, in one of his poems written at Montgomery Castle, of a 'naked thinking heart' – a heart open and undefended, a heart active in thought and feeling. Psalm 51 talks of 'a broken and contrite heart', which God will not despise (Psalm 51.17). Throughout the ages, the heart has symbolized the centre of life, of motivation, of response and responsibility.

Hardness of heart brings its own reward. For the city of Jerusalem it was the threat of war from the North, the boiling pot spilling over, bringing destruction, cleansing the heart of its wickedness, whether it liked it or not. How much better a heart responsive to God's love – a heart of flesh, not of stone.

COLLECT

Holy God,
our lives are laid open before you:
rescue us from the chaos of sin
and through the death of your Son
bring us healing and make us whole
in Jesus Christ our Lord.

Monday 23 February

Jeremiah 4.19-end

'I looked … there was no one at all' (v.25)

The pictures we have of prophets in our minds are very often a bit of a stereotype: an old man with a beard, a venerable figure with a powerful pen and ascetic lifestyle. Jeremiah, however, is young and, as we read later in this book, he has the word of God like 'a burning fire shut up in my bones' (Jeremiah 20.9). Over the next few days we will be seared by these flames: Jeremiah is unsparing, uncompromising and makes for difficult reading. Here, his anguish is plain because he anticipates the invading army moving towards beloved Jerusalem. The political is personal as Jeremiah feels personally the fear and desperation of approaching disaster. The intimacy of Jeremiah's metaphors is striking and moving: death is close, as close as an invading soldier drawing back the drapes of his bedroom (v.20). Death is certain and imminent.

For us at these centuries' distance, it might be hard to engage with this heightened language and energetic desperation. But Jeremiah teaches us a depth of personal involvement that is characteristic of him and leaves us with the question: what impact do broader political realities have on our own faith? Many of us receive information through the news while sitting in our own living rooms, alone or in small groups. One possible exercise is to take one news story and engage with it ourselves even if it is sending a letter or giving some money.

COLLECT

Almighty God,
whose Son Jesus Christ fasted forty days in the wilderness,
and was tempted as we are, yet without sin:
give us grace to discipline ourselves in obedience to your Spirit;
and, as you know our weakness,
so may we know your power to save;
through Jesus Christ your Son our Lord,
who is alive and reigns with you,
in the unity of the Holy Spirit,
one God, now and for ever.

Psalm **44** *or* **73**
Jeremiah 5.1-19
John 5.19-29

Tuesday 24 February

Jeremiah 5.1-19

'How can I pardon you?' (v.7)

Throughout this week, the lament for Jerusalem and the impending destruction is the theme. It's worth noting the ways that Jeremiah tries to communicate the urgency of all this; to have this kind of desperation and depth of agony written into the Scriptures is a theological reflection in itself. Jeremiah is employing every ounce of his linguistic capability in the service of convincing his readers that this situation is serious, and it is getting worse by the hour.

The poetic theme in this passage is that of a lawsuit. There are two indictments: first against the poor themselves, and then against the powerful. There are echoes of Genesis here, where the search was for enough righteous people so that Sodom would be saved. Here, the threshold is lower; Jeremiah is called to search for just one person, not ten as Abraham did (Genesis 18.32). These are the depths to which Jerusalem has fallen. And the completeness of the condemnation is alarming; not one person among the poor or the powerful is found, and so pardon is simply not possible.

The problem is not degeneracy per se, but what Jeremiah calls stubbornness, cynicism and self-sufficiency. In modern terms, this could be described as a sort of 'functional atheism', an assumption that if things are going to change (even in Church communities) then it is up to us alone to make this happen. We often live and work as if God didn't exist, even while praying, meeting and planning the future.

Heavenly Father,
your Son battled with the powers of darkness,
and grew closer to you in the desert:
help us to use these days to grow in wisdom and prayer
that we may witness to your saving love
in Jesus Christ our Lord.

COLLECT

Wednesday 25 February

Psalms **6**, 17 *or* **77**
Jeremiah 5.20-end
John 5.30-end

Jeremiah 5.20-end

'... though the waves toss, they cannot prevail' (v.22)

After the indictments of yesterday, now come the poetic motifs of judgement and sentence. Jeremiah is still in his metaphorical law court. The indictments are clear: stubbornness and self-reliance. There is a beauty here, though, despite the strong condemnatory language. Jeremiah combines the dismissal of the people (they have turned aside and gone away) with a tender and evocative description of what God has done, how God has created the world, freely given to the people who have rejected their God. The rather delicate way in which he points out that the sand is a barrier for the sea to protect the people (v.22) – a barrier 'perpetual' so that however stormy the sea, the people will be sheltered – is moving.

In verse 29, God is hurt by the contrast between all the kindnesses of nature heaped upon the people and the way in which they simply don't see or hear with what gifts they are surrounded. This is powerful and arguably recognisable in a contemporary discussion about ecological disaster and the hubris of humanity who believe that whatever they do, the natural world will always be there. Jeremiah is pointing his readers to notice, to experience, to understand that they are living in a context of gifts. For his audience, as for us today, this surely means nothing less than accepting the gifted context in which we live and, in response, living less self-centredly and more thankfully for everything we receive.

COLLECT

Almighty God,
whose Son Jesus Christ fasted forty days in the wilderness,
and was tempted as we are, yet without sin:
give us grace to discipline ourselves in obedience to your Spirit;
and, as you know our weakness,
so may we know your power to save;
through Jesus Christ your Son our Lord,
who is alive and reigns with you,
in the unity of the Holy Spirit,
one God, now and for ever.

Jeremiah 6.9-21

'... ancient paths, where the good way lies' (v.16)

The main metaphor employed by Jeremiah to illustrate the stubbornness of people is to say that they can't hear or are not listening. There is a sense of people living their lives while wilfully ignoring the presence of God around and among them. Again the structure of indictment–judgement–sentence is used by Jeremiah to try to show the consequences of their actions. There is a completeness again in his description of the population; old and young together (v.11) are all living as if God is not there, not trying to communicate with the people. And this time, there is an invitation to the people so that they know what they have to do (from verse 16 onwards).

For modern readers, we shouldn't mistake this invitation. The 'ancient paths' are not synonymous with 'the good old days'. The ancient paths are, he says, where the 'good way lies', reviving a radical and dangerous memory of the time where God's justice and mercy infused human society and all complacency was challenged.

In the final few verses Jeremiah plays with the symbols of paths, crossroads and stumbling blocks, the ancient words whose echoes we hear centuries later when Paul uses the same language to describe Jesus himself (e.g. 1 Corinthians 1.23). It seems that the people are on a journey, walking towards the crossroads where the choices will be hard and the perils of falling more and more evident.

Heavenly Father,
your Son battled with the powers of darkness,
and grew closer to you in the desert:
help us to use these days to grow in wisdom and prayer
that we may witness to your saving love
in Jesus Christ our Lord.

COLLECT

Friday 27 February

Psalm **22** *or* **55**
Jeremiah 6.22-end
John 6.16-27

Jeremiah 6.22-end

'... a refiner among my people' (v.27)

Vivid and noisy metaphors make this tumultuous passage all the more powerful in its announcement of doom for Jerusalem. The roaring sea, the thundering of horses' hooves, the clashing of military equipment leads Jeremiah to say that 'we have heard news of them' (v.24). Unlike the stubborn-hearted people who can't hear God, what they can hear now are the noises of impending destruction. And their response is one of despair, anguish, helplessness.

Within this helpless and hopeless situation, the people react by lamenting. The depth of their despair is as strong as if their only child had been killed. And in the midst of all this, Jeremiah makes a comment about his own place, his own vocation: he is a tester and a refiner. However, the action he is taking – of refining – is futile, 'for the wicked are not removed' (v.29). Yet still he speaks out; still he calls for lament and repentance.

This is another instance of Jeremiah's mixing of the personal and political. The portentous public events – the impending invasion and destruction of Jerusalem – are intimate to Jeremiah and his own purpose and vocation. Even though he identifies the uselessness of his witness, it is still his calling somehow to continue to find ways to say what he has to say. The irony is that even what he identified as futile words finds meaning and power for us today, centuries later. There seems therefore to be meaning in raising our own voices against injustice even when it seems hopeless or purposeless. There seems to be meaning in the protest itself, in the very act of speaking out, regardless of perceived successes or failures in achieving change in our lifetime.

COLLECT

Almighty God,
whose Son Jesus Christ fasted forty days in the wilderness,
and was tempted as we are, yet without sin:
give us grace to discipline ourselves in obedience to your Spirit;
and, as you know our weakness,
so may we know your power to save;
through Jesus Christ your Son our Lord,
who is alive and reigns with you,
in the unity of the Holy Spirit,
one God, now and for ever.

Lent

Psalms 59, **63** *or* **76**, 79
Jeremiah 7.1-20
John 6.27-40

Saturday 28 February

Jeremiah 7.1-20

'I will not hear you ...' (v.16)

At the beginning of chapter seven, we start reading what is known as Jeremiah's 'temple sermon'. It is a strongly worded statement of the main themes of Jeremiah's prophecy, which brings him into dispute with the temple ideology on which the state relied. What is striking is that Jeremiah is called to proclaim this challenge 'in the gate of the Lord's house' (v.2) – in the very temple itself. Jeremiah mocks the repetition of temple theology with its assumption of preservation of the status quo. He challenges any unthinking reliance on repetitious and banal liturgy (v.4).

This is strong teaching for us too. Jeremiah is excoriating about those who ignore the link between prayer and action. Turning up for worship while acting unjustly during the rest of the week is a hypocrisy too far for this prophet, and his critique is without qualification. In his own day, it was the oppression of orphans and widows (those most economically and socially disadvantaged) that delegitimized the repetitious prayers. For contemporary Christians, there will be a thousand examples of wasteful or competitive living that is dissonant with the freely given, grace-filled love of God in Christ. Even worse, Jeremiah claims, there is no shame among the people for the gap between their liturgy and their ethics. The searing question of verse 11, to Christian ears, will be familiar as Jesus of Nazareth raged centuries later in the spirit of Jeremiah, accusing the temple of harbouring those who would act unjustly towards the poor.

From verse 16, Jeremiah reveals what God is saying to him personally, instructing him not to pray for this people or to raise his voice in support of them. The condemnation is complete. The utterness of the oracle is overwhelming. Jeremiah is truly a voice for all those who despair at the world in which we live.

Heavenly Father,
your Son battled with the powers of darkness,
and grew closer to you in the desert:
help us to use these days to grow in wisdom and prayer
that we may witness to your saving love
in Jesus Christ our Lord.

COLLECT

Lent

Monday 2 March

Psalms 26, **32** *or* **80**, 82
Jeremiah 7.21-end
John 6.41-51

Jeremiah 7.21-end

'... the days are surely coming' (v.32)

The temple sermon continues, and Jeremiah moves from criticizing the repetitive words of the liturgy to the gap he sees between liturgical action and the ethics of everyday life. Not only are the words empty and futile when they are not matched up with the actions of the people; now the ritual action and sacrifices are not authentic either.

There is a ruthlessness about Jeremiah's determination to leave nothing unsaid, nothing unscrutinized. Again all that is required of the people is that they listen, but this seems to be impossible for the ones who have 'stiffened their necks' (v.26). In typical Jeremiah style, it is not just hearing that he advocates, but listening, which implies an attentiveness, a willingness to be addressed by God, an openness to being shaped by the will of God that is more than simply hearing what is said.

The contrast is clear and is as contemporary as it is ancient. The opposite of attentiveness to God is living under the delusion of autonomy and self-sufficiency. Perhaps it is simply part of the human condition to live with the tension between a proper self-confidence as a child of God and the recognition that we are utterly dependent too: our willingness to be ready to be 'unmade' by God. Somehow cultivating in ourselves the courage even to ask for this is what Jeremiah is describing; nothing less will do.

COLLECT

Almighty God,
you show to those who are in error the light of your truth,
that they may return to the way of righteousness:
grant to all those who are admitted
    into the fellowship of Christ's religion,
that they may reject those things
    that are contrary to their profession,
and follow all such things as are agreeable to the same;
through our Lord Jesus Christ,
who is alive and reigns with you,
in the unity of the Holy Spirit,
one God, now and for ever.

Jeremiah 8.1-15

'... saying "Peace, peace", when there is no peace' (v.11)

While we might have got used to the extreme nature of some of Jeremiah's language and images, this chapter begins with something pretty shocking. Having condemned without qualification the ritual words and practices in the temple and having described the terror about to befall the people in the imminent invasion and destruction of the city by marauding troops, now Jeremiah says that not only is the present and the future subject to God's judgement, but the past is too. Those bones that have been laid to rest with honour, ritual and respect in the past will themselves now be dishonoured. Even the past acts of decency are now jeopardized by the present refusal of the people to be attentive to God.

Jeremiah is making a challenging point about time here: it is as if there is no time, or at least no progression in time, when it comes to considering the presence of God in relationship with the people. This is a profound reflection for today. It is a version of the reflection Jesus makes when he implores the crowd not to worry about tomorrow or yesterday because today has enough worries of its own. It's as if *now* is what there is and so now, today, is what matters. It won't stop us reflecting on the past or planning for the future, but the urgency of Jeremiah tells us that the time when it's even possible to be as deeply attentive to God as we should is right now, here where we are today.

Almighty God,
by the prayer and discipline of Lent
may we enter into the mystery of Christ's sufferings,
and by following in his Way
come to share in his glory;
through Jesus Christ our Lord.

COLLECT

87

Wednesday 4 March

Psalm **35** *or* **119.105-128**
Jeremiah 8.18 – 9.11
John 6.60-end

Jeremiah 8.18 – 9.11

'... no balm in Gilead' (8.22)

The tone moves in this passage from the legal indictments, judgements and sentences of the previous chapters to a more tragic vocabulary of illness, pain, grief and death. These verses contain a lament – not only Jeremiah's lament but the lament of the Lord. The insertion of the phrase 'says the Lord' (8.17) ensures that we, as readers, understand this is not just Jeremiah who weeps for the people; we are witnessing the grief of God. It is grief such as that of a parent for a sick child; somehow the pain of the child becomes the pain of the parent (8.21). All that both can do is watch the disease take hold and do its worst on the body of the beloved child. We are told here of the Lord's rage, grief and despair; somehow the refusal of the people to repent has removed the power of God to save them. There are simply no more options left. The restatement of 'they do not know me' (9.3) highlights the isolation and desolation of God, pleading with the people to return to the one who has loved them from the beginning.

As with much of Jeremiah's prophecy, although it will have been said in a specific circumstance, the general underlying themes are universal and applicable to different situations in different centuries. We are left wondering what our lives look like to this pleading God, grief-stricken at the state of the world we have helped to create.

COLLECT

Almighty God,
you show to those who are in error the light of your truth,
that they may return to the way of righteousness:
grant to all those who are admitted
    into the fellowship of Christ's religion,
that they may reject those things
    that are contrary to their profession,
and follow all such things as are agreeable to the same;
through our Lord Jesus Christ,
who is alive and reigns with you,
in the unity of the Holy Spirit,
one God, now and for ever.

Jeremiah 9.12-24

'... send for the skilled women to come' (v.17)

It might be something of a relief to find some verses in this passage that are not quite so emotive, not quite so freighted with fury and despair. It may be that these verses, as other passages, are written by a different writer, enlarging on and deepening the themes of the more passionate prophetic writer who has gone before. The themes of wisdom, understanding, interpretation of the law, are all here. Thoroughly contemporary instructions are found from verse 23, where the wealthy, the wise and the strong are directed not to boast about their accomplishments. There is only one way to deepen our delight, and that is to trust in God knowing that love, justice and righteousness are worth more than might and money.

The middle section calling on women to lament follows a profound tradition of female mourners, musicians, singers, asking the women to give voice to the uncomforted people and their uncomforted God. It gives something of a response to the perennial question of suffering in the world. Impossible to explain or understand, perhaps what we can do in the face of terrible cruelty is lament, raise our voices in protest, give expression to the wordless pain evoked in us by what we see sometimes on the news. It is a way of combating compassion fatigue, a way of remembering our deep connectedness as human beings with other people whose names we may never know, but whose distress we see.

Almighty God,
by the prayer and discipline of Lent
may we enter into the mystery of Christ's sufferings,
and by following in his Way
come to share in his glory;
through Jesus Christ our Lord.

COLLECT

Friday 6 March

Psalms 40, **41** *or* **88** (95)
Jeremiah 10.1-16
John 7.14-24

Jeremiah 10.1-16

'... scarecrows in a cucumber field' (v.5)

The outpouring of contrasts continues between life lived by the people now and life as it could be lived if the people were close to the heart of God. The detail of how idols are constructed and built is compelling; we can almost hear the axe working on the trunk of the tree, and the decoration of the wood with precious metals fastened with hammer and nails. The most wonderful picture of a scarecrow in a cucumber field is perhaps the most derisory image Jeremiah can think of for the 'false gods' so beloved of the people. The scarecrow is a static, lifeless form that has to be carried about because it can't even walk, guarding cucumber crops, in contrast to the grieving heart of God, who, we are about to be reminded again, put the stars in the heavens and made the rivers and the mountains. The disparity couldn't be starker.

The critical faith issue for Jeremiah – as arguably for us today – is not atheism but idolatry. Jeremiah uses the Hebrew word *hebel* (vv.3,8,15) to describe these idols, meaning 'nothingness'. But the idols are not only lifeless and vacuous, they are economically valuable. They have some worth in worldly terms, but none before God. Food for thought for a contemporary culture that values wealth, and continues to spend money on building and decorating idols.

COLLECT

Almighty God,
you show to those who are in error the light of your truth,
that they may return to the way of righteousness:
grant to all those who are admitted
    into the fellowship of Christ's religion,
that they may reject those things
    that are contrary to their profession,
and follow all such things as are agreeable to the same;
through our Lord Jesus Christ,
who is alive and reigns with you,
in the unity of the Holy Spirit,
one God, now and for ever.

Psalms 3, **25** *or* 96, **97**, 100
Jeremiah 10.17-24
John 7.25-36

Jeremiah 10.17-24

'Correct me, O Lord ...' (v.24)

Once again Jeremiah moves back to his reflections on the relationship between public calamity and private grief in the face of this calamity. The people are told to gather their possessions, to be ready, packed, to go into exile. It is an act of imagination; by describing the impending disaster in practical and personal terms of tents, children, forced journeys, the prophet is inviting the listening audience to imagine how they will feel when the political situation becomes real in their own lives.

Jeremiah identifies a failure of leadership as the main problem. The 'shepherds' (the kings) have failed their people, and what will inevitably follow is the exile of the people. The final two verses of this excerpt form a prayer that could easily be prayed as a personal prayer today. Jeremiah invites us to affirm what we suspect is true, although we don't live by it, that in the end, we human beings don't control our own lives; that the direction of our lives is determined by any number of things, and certainly not only by our decisions or by trying to align things and people to our will.

It is a dangerous prayer to ask for correction, but the theme of Jeremiah's teaching is about little else. The call is to attentiveness right now, in this present moment, because in a very real sense, there is nothing else. The call is to dare to ask to be shaped by God's love and correction, to learn to lament along with God over the stubbornness of our own hearts and the suffering of the people; and to live as if on tiptoe, to live as if the future is already here.

Almighty God,
by the prayer and discipline of Lent
may we enter into the mystery of Christ's sufferings,
and by following in his Way
come to share in his glory;
through Jesus Christ our Lord.

COLLECT

Monday 9 March

Psalms **5**, 7 *or* **98**, 99, 101
Jeremiah 11.1-17
John 7.37-52

Jeremiah 11.1-17

'... your gods have become as many as your towns' (v. 13)

There is a strong tendency in human nature to homogenize things: to suppress difference. There is also a strong tendency to dissipate things: to over-accentuate difference.

Egypt, as this passage recalls, was an 'iron-smelter'. Just as a furnace reduces particular objects with their various shapes to one malleable liquid, so Egypt sought to crush the particular loves, commitments and beliefs of its subjects by asserting one great monolithic vision of what the empire stood for. No wonder that the brave and rebellious Hebrews learnt to prize particularity.

But, lifetimes later, in Jeremiah's day, their descendants in Judah risk going the other way, and losing all sense of the divine unity that makes and holds difference together. They have gods for every corner of life, every place. These gods are merely the expression of needs; they are idols that mirror the multiple human interests that generate them. Taken together they are incoherent and amount to nothing. There is no sum to the parts.

Jeremiah calls his people back to the one true God who neither suppresses difference nor is himself just one more differential among many. This God made the universe, with all its differences. He defends them from the smelter, but requires his people never to forget their ultimate source.

COLLECT

Almighty God,
whose most dear Son went not up to joy but first he suffered pain,
and entered not into glory before he was crucified:
mercifully grant that we, walking in the way of the cross,
may find it none other than the way of life and peace;
through Jesus Christ your Son our Lord,
who is alive and reigns with you,
in the unity of the Holy Spirit,
one God, now and for ever.

Jeremiah 11.18 – 12.6

'Why does the way of the guilty prosper?' (12.1)

This is one of the great questions of the Bible. It is echoed in the book of Job, and again in some of the Psalms. In Psalm 73, for example, the wicked initially appear invulnerable: 'All in vain I have kept my heart clean and washed my hands in innocence', says the Psalmist (Psalm 73.13). The wicked, meanwhile, simply 'increase in riches' (Psalm 73.12).

Here, in one of what are sometimes called Jeremiah's 'confessions', we see his human vulnerability and the personal burden of the prophetic task. He is attacked by those near to him, and he cannot see any evidence of God's judgement doing what it is meant to do in his situation. This sensitive and often isolated prophet, whose task fell to him so young, has what in Christian terms we might see as a Gethsemane experience.

The loneliness and endurance of the prophet are a challenge but may also be an encouragement in a world where there seems much unjust prosperity, and it is hard to speak out against it. The Psalmist in Psalm 73 learnt to see deeper only when he 'went into the sanctuary of God' (Psalm 73.17); there, he learnt to see that the wicked are in fact set in 'slippery places' (Psalm 73.18).

Like Jeremiah, who manages to stay in the way of faithfulness even when he is close to despair, Christians have found that it is in the worship of God that the real 'ends' of things are disclosed.

Eternal God,
give us insight
to discern your will for us,
to give up what harms us,
and to seek the perfection we are promised
in Jesus Christ our Lord.

COLLECT

Jeremiah 13.1-11

'... the loincloth was ruined' (v.7)

The High Priest of the Jerusalem temple had two sets of priestly vestments: the so-called 'Golden Garments' that were worn often throughout the year, and a set of four, unembroidered linen garments that were worn on one day in the year only, when he entered the Holy of Holies on the Day of Atonement. Their purity was to be uncompromised, so a new set was used every year.

Jeremiah, who was from a priestly family, would have known the symbolic significance of the loincloth he was asked to buy and wear. It was something that could have a holy purpose – something that could express the greatest purity, and the greatest intimacy with God (as the linen undergarment touched the very skin of the priest).

At God's instruction, he wears this garment – never washing it – until it is soiled, and thus tells the story of his people's failures in responding to their call to be pure. Soiled as they are, they will then be put away to moulder – in a terrible warning of exile yet to come.

Like Adam and Eve hiding from God, or the seed in Jesus' parable that falls on rocky ground, this mouldering loincloth is a summons to all God's people to seek again the relationship with God in which we realize our highest calling: clinging to God.

And the first step in this clinging is to *listen*.

COLLECT

Almighty God,
whose most dear Son went not up to joy but first he suffered pain,
and entered not into glory before he was crucified:
mercifully grant that we, walking in the way of the cross,
may find it none other than the way of life and peace;
through Jesus Christ your Son our Lord,
who is alive and reigns with you,
in the unity of the Holy Spirit,
one God, now and for ever.

Lent

Psalms **56**, 57 *or* 113, **115**
Jeremiah 14
John 8.31-47

Thursday 12 March

Jeremiah 14

*'Because there has been no rain on the land the farmers are
dismayed; they cover their heads' (v.4)*

Why do the farmers adopt gestures of shame and penitence when faced
with drought? Our supposedly sophisticated technological world looks
askance at what – in most human cultures and epochs – has been the
majority view, namely that the human, natural and spiritual realms are
all interconnected. When something is 'out of joint' with one of them,
then all three are affected – and sometimes disastrously. Shakespeare's
characters often suggest that dark deeds are afoot, and the heavens
displeased, by referring to unnatural occurrences and omens in the
animal and plant kingdoms – as in *Macbeth*, when the horses eat one
another on the night that King Duncan is assassinated.

Our confident, rational accounts of the world may do us service when
they dispel superstition and unwarranted fear – and we may rightly be
suspicious of claims that 'unnatural births', or lightning strikes, are signs
of God's anger at our iniquity. But they can also be used to disguise from
us some of the complex and culpable effects of what we do at the
human level on the non-human world around us. And this is more a
challenge than ever when the rapaciousness and automation of our
agricultural, industrial and economic systems have their worst effects
on places a long way away.

We do not easily perceive what ought often to make us cover our heads.
Jeremiah's farmers and nobles may have a lesson to teach us, both in
their sin, and also in their repentance.

Eternal God,
give us insight
to discern your will for us,
to give up what harms us,
and to seek the perfection we are promised
in Jesus Christ our Lord.

COLLECT

Friday 13 March

Jeremiah 15.10-end

'Why is ... my wound incurable, refusing to be healed?' (v.18)

Jeremiah accuses God in the strongest terms here. 'Truly, you are to me like a deceitful brook, like waters that fail' (v.18). This is the voice of one who feels desperately abandoned.

The prophet at this low point recalls for me the figure of Philoctetes from Greek legend – a Greek warrior-hero and the inheritor of Heracles' bow and arrows. Philoctetes receives an incurable wound from a snake bite. It festers and stinks so much that his former comrades set him ashore on the island of Lemnos, where he is left utterly alone. Like Jeremiah, all his memories of the joys and delights of earlier times turn to ashes in his mouth.

Philoctetes will one day be saved by the utilitarian calculations of the Greek army in their war against Troy. After some years they have to return to Lemnos because they need the bow and arrows in their war effort – and after some debate (and the intercession of one man more compassionate than the others), Philoctetes is taken too, and healed, and returned to the fellowship of his people.

Jeremiah does not have to wait for his hope of salvation; it is neither delayed nor utilitarian. Assurance comes quickly from the God he is accusing, 'I am with you to save you and deliver you'. Not because God wants something he has, but because God wants *him*.

COLLECT

Almighty God,
whose most dear Son went not up to joy but first he suffered pain,
and entered not into glory before he was crucified:
mercifully grant that we, walking in the way of the cross,
may find it none other than the way of life and peace;
through Jesus Christ your Son our Lord,
who is alive and reigns with you,
in the unity of the Holy Spirit,
one God, now and for ever.

Jeremiah 16.10 – 17.4

'Your wealth and all your treasures I will give for spoil as the price of your sin' (17.3)

Sin has a price – every time. There is no sin without cost, and (as Dietrich Bonhoeffer reminded us), even if grace is offered to us for free, it is not cheap. This is because Christ bought it with his own blood.

The people of Judah, like Esau at the time of the patriarchs, are willing by their own act to lose the heritage that God gave them. This heritage will go to others, because – even if it was only momentarily (like Esau) – they cared more for something lesser.

Esau sold his birthright for a bowl of lentil stew, and he and his twin brother became sworn enemies as a consequence. But years later, Esau found new opportunities and new resources, and he and his brother would one day find a way back to one another and be reconciled.

God's fierce words of judgement against Judah for its worship of false gods are held in this passage within a greater promise that there will once again be a way back. The eyes of God that see the people's iniquity are the same eyes that watch over them when they are scattered. God will send hunters to rocky crevices in order to gather his beloved. Likewise (in a way that anticipates what Jesus will one day promise), he will send fishers to the deeps to draw his children back to him. The people's sin has a terrible cost, but the cost will not be the loss of God's regard for them.

Eternal God,
give us insight
to discern your will for us,
to give up what harms us,
and to seek the perfection we are promised
in Jesus Christ our Lord.

COLLECT

Lent

Monday 16 March

Psalms 70, **77** *or* 123, 124, 125, **126**
Jeremiah 17.5-18
John 9.18-end

Jeremiah 17.5-18

'Like the partridge hatching what it did not lay, so are all who amass wealth unjustly' (v.11)

Jeremiah's words speak into a situation of acute anxiety about what he calls 'the fatal day'. He wrestles with a feeling that his destiny could go either way, that so much is poised in the balance. The unjust are powerful. In the closing verses of this excerpt, Jeremiah reveals that he longs for healing, salvation, and refuge, but that he fears terror, shame, and disaster.

In situations of anxiety, Jeremiah's strategy is to think big. He sets the immediate sequence of events in the context of a far bigger story of ultimate origins and ultimate ends, for there is reason to hope that what was there right at the very beginning of time – God's 'glorious throne', 'shrine' of our sanctuary' (v.12) – will endure to the end as well. In the world of unjust humans, there is no such endurance. Partridges hatch what they did not lay. But God lays the egg as well as hatching it; he made the world and will not forsake it. The inconstancy of human actions is bracketed by the constancy of God. And in this bigger picture, Jeremiah can reassure himself with words very reminiscent of another 'beginning' – the beginning of the Psalter: 'Happy are those who do not follow the advice of the wicked ... they are like trees planted by streams of water ... and their leaves do not wither' (Psalm 1.1,3).

COLLECT

Merciful Lord,
absolve your people from their offences,
that through your bountiful goodness
we may all be delivered from the chains of those sins
which by our frailty we have committed;
grant this, heavenly Father,
for Jesus Christ's sake, our blessed Lord and Saviour,
who is alive and reigns with you,
in the unity of the Holy Spirit,
one God, now and for ever.

Psalms 54, **79** or **132**, 133
Jeremiah 18.1-12
John 10.1-10

Tuesday 17 March

Jeremiah 18.1-12

'... he reworked it into another vessel' (v.4)

Like the potter who will not waste the clay he was using when a pot goes wrong, God too is willing to put it to a new purpose. God is a recycling God.

The language of God's infinite resourcefulness and responsiveness can seem very apt here, and it helps us to understand that we are in a relationship with God in which there is reciprocity. The things we do – whether to repent or to resist God – have consequences for how God relates to us. God's intentions can appear to alter when we – like the pot – 'spoil'. God will devise a new strategy to deal with the failure. 'I will change my mind', says the voice of God in this passage (v.8). Another pot will be made.

But we ought not to be misled by this bold statement into thinking of God as fickle. Read the text closely, and it is clear that the apparent changeability of God is really the result of the changeability of human beings in relation to God's purposes. If we change for good, God will not enact a promised destruction, and if we change for bad, God will not deliver a promised blessing. In the realm of human action, we have room to move, and as we move it will be as though God moves with us. But the realm of human action in its entirety is nevertheless held within the divine potter's sure and unerring hands.

Merciful Lord,
you know our struggle to serve you:
when sin spoils our lives
and overshadows our hearts,
come to our aid
and turn us back to you again;
through Jesus Christ our Lord.

COLLECT

Wednesday 18 March

Psalms 63, **90** *or* **119.153-end**
Jeremiah 18.13-end
John 10.11-21

Jeremiah 18.13-end

'I will show them my back, not my face' (v.17)

These are dark words for God's people, and dark days for Jeremiah. The people here are cursed, both by God and his prophet, and, in return, the prophet is on the receiving end of the murderous hostility of the people.

Things seem too dire for even a glimmer of hope. But perhaps there is one – even in that most devastating of divine utterances, 'I will turn my back on you'. Jesus himself would speak like that to Simon Peter when he said 'Get behind me, Satan!' (Matthew 16.23). What you see from behind is the back of the one who has put you behind them. But you also see the back of one whom you *follow*. Being at someone's back can be a mark or an occasion of discipleship, and Simon Peter's discipleship most certainly did not end when Jesus turned his back on him. It was deepened.

Moses, too, was shown God's 'back', on Mount Sinai, as we hear in Exodus 33. This was not a curse – on the contrary it was a privilege. It was a means by which all the 'goodness of God' would come to him. Early Christian commentary read this episode as a sign that Moses was being made a very special sort of disciple.

Here, in Jeremiah's day, might it be that, within the curse that is being laid upon them, the people are at the same time being given another chance to follow? An invitation to change course and be changed?

COLLECT

Merciful Lord,
absolve your people from their offences,
that through your bountiful goodness
we may all be delivered from the chains of those sins
which by our frailty we have committed;
grant this, heavenly Father,
for Jesus Christ's sake, our blessed Lord and Saviour,
who is alive and reigns with you,
in the unity of the Holy Spirit,
one God, now and for ever.

Psalms 25, 147.1-12
Isaiah 11.1-10
Matthew 13.54-end

Thursday 19 March

Joseph of Nazareth

Isaiah 11.1-10

'… the lion shall eat straw' (v.7)

In a world where genetic modification becomes more and more easy, and more and more widespread, we have rightly become nervous about the many ways in which we interfere with 'wild nature'. But it's something we have done for centuries, and continue to do even without the help of the latest scientific technology. Sometimes it will be to make our dogs more dangerous, sometimes less, depending what more or less self-serving need we have for such changes. Sometimes it will be to make our leeks bigger or our roses more fragrant.

Perhaps this vision of God's holy mountain seems like a travesty of wild nature in the service of a human dream. What sort of a lion eats straw? Wouldn't such a lion have lost its 'lion-ness' to such a degree that it hardly merits the name? But this may not be a prediction of what awaits lions at the end of time, so much as a proclamation of the ultimate invincibility of the peace which passes all understanding. It passes all understanding, so we need pictures like these to help us approach a conception of it. But it's a real peace nevertheless, and it is surely coming, just as it pre-existed the creation of the world and that world's fall. For it is the peace of *God*, and we look forward to it not in a genetically modified future so much as a messianically modified one. Lions will experience it in their own proper way, according to God's plans for them, as we will experience it in ours.

God our Father,
who from the family of your servant David
raised up Joseph the carpenter
to be the guardian of your incarnate Son
and husband of the Blessed Virgin Mary:
give us grace to follow him
in faithful obedience to your commands;
through Jesus Christ your Son our Lord,
who is alive and reigns with you,
in the unity of the Holy Spirit,
one God, now and for ever.

COLLECT

Friday 20 March

Jeremiah 19.14 – 20.6

'I am making you a terror to yourself' (20.4)

It is a common phrase: we are our own worst enemies. Horror films of various kinds have dramatized this: a beleaguered group of people barricade themselves in somewhere to escape a threat from beyond, but even with every hatch, door or window sealed and guarded, they still find themselves being picked off one by one – for the enemy is within.

We can easily become 'terrors to ourselves', acting in a way that seeks to keep danger away but finding we are that danger. What Pashhur the priest does to Jeremiah the prophet is unwittingly a form of self-harm, for God's priests ought not to suppress God's prophets. Jeremiah declares that what Pashhur has done to him will be done to Pashhur and the temple and city he cares about. All will be 'put in the stocks' (20.2); all will be placed in captivity; all will have their agency removed.

Pashhur may prompt us to examine what we try to suppress or exclude because of what we want to defend or preserve. It may be that the 'priest' in us is trying to shut up the prophetic voice of God in us. If so, we are doomed to failure, and we are our own worst enemies, for this voice cannot be kept at bay.

COLLECT

Merciful Lord,
absolve your people from their offences,
that through your bountiful goodness
we may all be delivered from the chains of those sins
which by our frailty we have committed;
grant this, heavenly Father,
for Jesus Christ's sake, our blessed Lord and Saviour,
who is alive and reigns with you,
in the unity of the Holy Spirit,
one God, now and for ever.

Saturday 21 March

Jeremiah 20.7-end

'Sing to the Lord! ... Cursed be the day on which I was born!'
(vv. 13,14)

If there was ever an argument against proof texting from the Bible by citing only single verses or phrases, this is it. Within just a few verses, Jeremiah makes these two bizarrely discordant exclamations, one of praise and one of curse. What context can make sense of this discordance? Or what lesson can be learnt from it?

At one very immediate level, this conflict of two apparently incompatible feelings may work to reassure us that the Bible knows how all human beings feel a good deal of the time. We feel complicated; our feelings seem to conflict. Jeremiah gives permission to voice these conflicts to God, which is a lesson in how to pray. Prayer is not a tea party, and polite manners are not needed.

At another level, Jeremiah shows something profoundly challenging about the life of faith. We cannot live without God, but to live in obedience to him is to be tested. He experiences the paradox of a situation where he blames God for making him speak, and at the same time cannot help but speak God's words. To speak makes him suffer, and not to speak makes him suffer. T.S. Eliot in his *Four Quartets* gives the same testimony in relation to the 'dove descending': the work of God's Spirit in us (as once in the prophets). 'Consumed by either fire or fire', we're faced with the choice of one pyre or another: living with the consequences of our sin or undergoing our redemption.

Merciful Lord,
you know our struggle to serve you:
when sin spoils our lives
and overshadows our hearts,
come to our aid
and turn us back to you again;
through Jesus Christ our Lord.

COLLECT

103

Psalms. **73**, 121 *or* **1**, 2, 3
Jeremiah 21.1-10
John 11.28-44

Jeremiah 21.1-10

'... the way of life and the way of death' (v.8)

'Couldn't you just lighten it up a little, Jeremiah? Perhaps start with some good news?'

It's as well Jeremiah didn't have to get his oracles past any political spin-doctors, or even a Diocesan Press Officer! But of course he had to face something more draconian than that! We know he was imprisoned, mocked and tormented because he spoke truth to power, and even in the narrative here we can see that the king's 'enquiry' is really a loaded question, for the messenger feeds Jeremiah the answer the king wants to hear: 'perhaps the Lord will ... make him withdraw from us' (v.2).

But Jeremiah pulls no punches and delivers not just 'an inconvenient truth' but a devastating, morale-sapping broadside: the king and the city face inevitable defeat. And yet, hidden in this death-dooming Jeremiad is a tiny, paradoxical strand of hope; the Lord is offering a way of life, running beside the way of death. The path of loss and exile will prove to be life-giving; it is staying where we are that will be deadly.

As we read through Jeremiah, we must imaginatively inhabit this paradox. Defeat, the loss of the familiar, exile in a strange culture (all familiar to Christians in our culture) may be a path to life. Passiontide is a good time to remember that.

COLLECT

Most merciful God,
who by the death and resurrection of your Son Jesus Christ
delivered and saved the world:
grant that by faith in him who suffered on the cross
we may triumph in the power of his victory;
through Jesus Christ your Son our Lord,
who is alive and reigns with you,
in the unity of the Holy Spirit,
one God, now and for ever.

Psalms **35**, 123 *or* **5**, 6 (8)
Jeremiah 22.1-5, 13-19
John 11.45-end

Jeremiah 22.1-5, 13-19

'I will build myself a spacious house' (v.14)

Perhaps this text ought to be smuggled into one of London's shiniest new buildings, the Shard. People opening the blinds in its 'large upper rooms' might find verses 13-14 engraved on the windows or inscribed on the panelling. This is not to say of course that any of the business conducted in that tallest of buildings is necessarily involved in 'dishonest gain' or 'practising oppression and violence' (v.17), but Jeremiah is right I think to point out that an obsession with image, with buildings that constitute a competitive representation of prestige and power, may well be a cover for fundamental moral failure and blindness. It is not 'competing in cedar' that makes us kings, but doing justice and righteousness.

Whatever we make of his architectural critique, Jeremiah's checklist of those who need special care and attention, to be given justice by the powerful, is as pertinent to our time as to his: those who have been robbed or defrauded – that might include the customers of payday loan companies; the alien – there is a message for our politicians and border-control agencies; the orphan and the widow – that is to say, those without family back-up or social support, who cannot meet their own needs and whose needs are not being met by others. There is a reminder that some form of effective social security is essential to a just society.

Gracious Father,
you gave up your Son
out of love for the world:
lead us to ponder the mysteries of his passion,
that we may know eternal peace
through the shedding of our Saviour's blood,
Jesus Christ our Lord.

COLLECT

Wednesday 25 March

Annunciation of Our Lord
to the Blessed Virgin Mary

Psalms 111, 113
I Samuel 2.1-10
Romans 5.12-end

1 Samuel 2.1-10

'... not by might' (v.9)

'Not by might shall a man prevail' (v.9, NASV). This is the kernel of Hannah's glorious song, the first draft of the Magnificat, a flash of insight shared across the centuries between two marginalized women, a lesson which the men of the world have yet to learn.

The feast of the Annunciation is a good day to read this text, which so radically subverts the proud talk, the arrogant mouths, 'the bows of the mighty' (v.4). Not only because Mary in her humility and fruitful obedience is the exact opposite of these, but because the way God himself took, in the incarnation, his way of defeating evil, was not our way. Not by might, not from above, not by smiting, but by choosing to share our weakness, by being woven in Mary's womb, into the weakness of the changing flesh. Not by the action of a tyrant, but by the passion of a Saviour, as we learn afresh this Passiontide, God defeats the darkness and renews life and light. And if he is to fulfil Hannah's prophecy, and lift the needy from the ash heap to make them sit with princes, then the Prince of Peace must come first with us to the dust and the ash heap. Today Mary helps him begin that task; next week we shall see him do it, shall hear him say 'It is finished'.

COLLECT

We beseech you, O Lord,
pour your grace into our hearts,
that as we have known the incarnation of your Son Jesus Christ
    by the message of an angel,
so by his cross and passion
we may be brought to the glory of his resurrection;
through Jesus Christ your Son our Lord,
who is alive and reigns with you,
in the unity of the Holy Spirit,
one God, now and for ever.

Jeremiah 23.9-32

'My heart is broken within me' (v.9, RSV)

It is heart-breaking to believe in God. To believe in God in a broken world is to keep hope alive, but hope in a broken world is almost always hope deferred, and 'hope deferred makes the heart sick' (Proverbs 13.12). How much easier it is to have no expectations: is the land full of adulterers? It won't hurt as long as you don't believe in marriage. Are the prophets, the priests, the leaders in Church and nation sometimes corrupted and corrupting? Well, just give in to the cynicism and contempt of the times and you won't be disappointed.

What makes Jeremiah such compelling reading, even at his darkest, is that he won't give up or give in. He sees the corruption more clearly than anyone, but he persists in expecting better. He won't take the easy option or accept the second best: the false hopes, the lying dreams. 'My heart is broken within me and my bones shake', he tells us, but a broken heart is still a loving heart. For the same love that breaks it is the love that keeps it alive. And our Lord knows that too. 'My heart is broken and my bones shake' might be the words from the cross of one whose love for us will not be defeated by disappointment.

Friday 27 March

Psalms **22**, 126 *or* 17, **19**
Jeremiah 24
John 12.20-36*a*

Jeremiah 24

'Two baskets of figs' (v. 1)

Kenneth Anger, the American experimental filmmaker, wrote an infamous and scandalmongering book called *Hollywood Babylon,* of which the *New York Times* said, 'here is a book without one single redeeming merit'. From Anger's book, to the lyrics of Bob Marley, it has become a commonplace to associate the shallow materialism and consumerism of our times with the 'Babylon' of the Jewish exile. It is not surprising that Christians too, struggling to keep alive the radical love of the gospel and the values of the kingdom in the midst of contemporary 'me-culture', should also think of themselves as Babylonian exiles.

But if so, then Jeremiah's vision should give us pause. It is not to Jerusalem but to Babylon that the Word comes. Not in Jerusalem, but in Babylon that we are to be given a new heart to know the Lord. We think we're in the good basket, but perhaps instead of pining for our 'Jerusalem', looking back nostalgically to the 'good old days' when churches were full and the gospel got a hearing on the public stage, we should instead be looking and listening closely to the Babylon around us. Are there stirrings of hope? Rumours of angels? Signs from the Lord in the music and the films? Should we look for any good in Hollywood-Babylon? I think Jeremiah says 'Yes!'

COLLECT

Most merciful God,
who by the death and resurrection of your Son Jesus Christ
delivered and saved the world:
grant that by faith in him who suffered on the cross
we may triumph in the power of his victory;
through Jesus Christ your Son our Lord,
who is alive and reigns with you,
in the unity of the Holy Spirit,
one God, now and for ever.

Jeremiah 25.1-14

'I have spoken persistently' (v.3)

In the world of the quick fix, of instant gratification, of sound bites, of a constant stream of new acts, new faces, new slogans, persistence is in short supply. Even had he trimmed his sails to the wind, Jeremiah would have been fortunate to have lasted 23 years on any contemporary 'media outlet'. The first sign of grey hair and he would have been gone.

And perhaps that's why his persistence, and the persistence of all the Scriptures, the quiet persistence of this Lectionary, is so rewarding. Disquieting too, of course – in the case of Jeremiah, sometimes very disquieting! But as the whole of Jeremiah's persistent and consistent message proclaims, we sometimes need unsettling; we need bad news and inconvenient truths before we can grasp and ask for the good news of salvation.

The persistence of this single prophetic message, from Jeremiah to Nelson Mandela, that all is not well, that we must turn from evil and wrongdoing, the very persistence of that message is itself a sign of the patience and the grace of God. However many times we may have decided, as individuals or as a nation, that we have finished with God, the persistence of the prophets is a sign that he has not yet finished with us.

Gracious Father,
you gave up your Son
out of love for the world:
lead us to ponder the mysteries of his passion,
that we may know eternal peace
through the shedding of our Saviour's blood,
Jesus Christ our Lord.

COLLECT

Monday 30 March

Monday of Holy Week

Luke 22.1-23

'... until the kingdom of God comes' (v.18)

Holy week compresses the contrasts and contradictions of life, holding them in terrible tension. Outer action meets inner truth, private agony becomes public spectacle, our deepest yearnings and our darkest dreads coalesce in the same experience. So this passage begins with political conspiracy, foreshadows personal betrayal, and yet sets these in the midst of intimate exchange – the poignant farewell of friends. And that farewell becomes a shared meal, both ritualized and spontaneous. Jesus transforms and renews the Passover. In breaking the bread and pouring the wine, he shows that *he* will not be passed over, that he chooses instead to be the lamb whose blood saves others. Even the symbols of those dreadful things that will be done to his body and blood are transformed into gift, into signs and tokens of love, 'I have eagerly desired this,' he says, 'to share this moment, this meal, this sacrament, the heart of who I am, with you.' Here is wounded Love bidding us welcome.

As we follow the dark events of this week, we should remember that Love has 'desired' this, that through the pain, he sees the joy set before him, his joy and ours, when we shall drink the fruit of the vine, new with him. Meanwhile we still hold these contradictions in tension 'until the kingdom of God comes'.

COLLECT

Almighty and everlasting God,
who in your tender love towards the human race
    sent your Son our Saviour Jesus Christ
to take upon him our flesh
and to suffer death upon the cross:
grant that we may follow the example of his patience and humility,
and also be made partakers of his resurrection;
through Jesus Christ your Son our Lord,
who is alive and reigns with you,
in the unity of the Holy Spirit,
one God, now and for ever.

Luke 22. [24-38] 39-53

'He drew near to Jesus to kiss him' (v.47, RSV)

There is no betrayal without intimacy, no intimacy without the risk of betrayal. To love at all, to trust anyone, is to risk that undoing. If God in Christ is to take on our humanity, then he must take on this, this dreadful reversal, in which the kiss that could and should be the kiss of peace, the kiss of fellowship, becomes the kiss of treachery.

At this moment in the garden, Jesus not only takes in and experiences this worst of all the shocks that flesh is heir to, but also takes it on. He takes it on by showing that love does not have to be defeated or reversed by betrayal, that when our humanity is betrayed and abandoned by our own inhumanity, we are not abandoned by God. Peter, as we shall see tomorrow, is also a betrayer, but the Love that hangs on the cross hangs on to him, finds and restores him.

Peter remembered and hung on; Judas despaired and hanged himself. But perhaps one reason that Christ descended into hell was to find Judas and 'draw near to him', to find the Judas in us, and offer him the same chance to turn again that Peter eventually took, so that, even for Judas, the kiss of betrayal might be redeemed again by the kiss of peace.

True and humble king,
hailed by the crowd as Messiah:
grant us the faith to know you and love you,
that we may be found beside you
on the way of the cross,
which is the path of glory.

COLLECT

Psalm 102 [*or* 102.1-18]
Wisdom 1.16 – 2.1; 2.12–22
or Jeremiah 11.18-20
Luke 22.54-end

Luke 22.54-end

'Then Peter remembered' (v.61)

'Some dance to remember, some dance to forget.' That famous line from the Eagles' hit song 'Hotel California' speaks to the ambivalence of memory. We can be trapped in memories, and yet remembering can also be the key that sets us free. So it is with Peter. The cock crows and he remembers. First he remembers the prediction of his denial, the prediction he has so weakly fulfilled, and he weeps bitterly. He weeps because he remembers what high hopes and self-confidence he had; he weeps because he has failed himself and his friend; he weeps in shame and humiliation. But, thanks be to God, his memory does not stop there. If he is to have any hope, then today Peter must remember the words of Jesus we heard yesterday: 'when once you have turned back, strengthen your brothers' (Luke 22.32).

It is bitter to remember our failure, but to remember that Jesus knew and knows our failure, that he prays for us and loves us through it, that he still sees a role for us and a place in his kingdom, that he sees not only our fall but also our rising – that is to remember well, to remember deeply, to know, with Peter, what T. S. Eliot meant in the *Four Quartets* when he said: 'This is the use of memory: for liberation.'

COLLECT

Almighty and everlasting God,
who in your tender love towards the human race
    sent your Son our Saviour Jesus Christ
to take upon him our flesh
and to suffer death upon the cross:
grant that we may follow the example of his patience and humility,
and also be made partakers of his resurrection;
through Jesus Christ your Son our Lord,
who is alive and reigns with you,
in the unity of the Holy Spirit,
one God, now and for ever.

Psalms 42, 43
Leviticus 16.2-24
Luke 23.1-25

Luke 23.1-25

'Herod and Pilate became friends' (v. 12)

Evil has its own twisted fellowship, and perversity has its own perverted communion. It is ironic that on this Maundy Thursday, the day we celebrate the founding of a true communion in and through the gift of Christ's love, we should have a reading that depicts a corrupt and corrupting political alliance founded on the rejection of that love.

Herod and Pilate were indeed 'at enmity'. They represented opposed powers and races, opposed philosophies and faiths, held in an uneasy stalemate that would soon give way to the appalling violence that destroyed Jerusalem in 70 AD. But here, these two cunning politicians, with their precarious and vainglorious hold on power, find common cause, and more than common cause. They had both in their own way recognized a truth in Jesus; they both failed its test and rejected its claims on them, and then both proceeded to pervert the course of justice. Those who have done dreadful deeds crave each other's company, for some horrors are too much to bear alone; they seek a mutual entrenchment, a co-dependency, a conspiracy against the repentance that might come upon them if they were alone. We see it in death squads, drug gangs, and paedophile rings, and we see it starting here between Herod and Pilate. But in the foot-washing ceremonies that will take place in countless churches today, we celebrate its opposite and antidote, the new commandment that founds true community.

God our Father,
you have invited us to share in the supper
which your Son gave to his Church
to proclaim his death until he comes:
may he nourish us by his presence,
and unite us in his love;
who is alive and reigns with you,
in the unity of the Holy Spirit,
one God, now and for ever.

COLLECT

113

Psalm 69
Genesis 22.1-18
John 19.38-end *or* Hebrews 10.1-10

Hebrews 10.1-10

'Once for all' (vv.2,10)

The whole of Hebrews, with its radical re-interpretation of temple sacrifice, its mystical glimpses of the mysteries of heaven, is summed up in these three little words: 'once for all'. Christ's self-offering once for all, in sacrifice on the cross and in glory in the garden, is the single event that gives shape and meaning to all other events.

Christians used to worry and dispute with one another about whether every Eucharist, in which we remember Christ's sacrifice on Good Friday, is a renewal of this one event, a mere remembrance of it, or a 'vain repetition' of it. But really there is no repetition, there is only this single event, and every celebration of communion, every remembrance of his sacrifice, every moment of conversion and renewal in our personal history or the history of our Church, is a doorway out of time back into this one all-changing, all-saving event.

Just as cosmologists refer to the 'Big Bang' as a 'singularity', a one-off event from which all other events unfold, one that lies behind all the other recurring events we observe in our universe, so we might think of Jesus' death 'once for all' on the cross as a little like that: a spiritual 'singularity', a founding event that underlies and informs everything else.

Some Christians like to put others to the test, saying: 'Can you name the day on which you were saved?' There can only ever be one answer to that question: 'I was saved on Good Friday.'

COLLECT

Almighty Father,
look with mercy on this your family
for which our Lord Jesus Christ was content to be betrayed
    and given up into the hands of sinners
    and to suffer death upon the cross;
who is alive and glorified with you and the Holy Spirit,
one God, now and for ever.

Psalm 142
Hosea 6.1-6
John 2.18-22

John 2.18-22

'The temple of his body' (v.21)

On the day after its destruction, when his body lies cold in the tomb, we contemplate the holiness of the body we have broken.

It took 46 years to build the temple in Jerusalem, but if we said it had taken 33 years to make the temple of Christ's body, we should be short of the mark. These intricate, intimate, precious and perilous estates we call our bodies were longer in the making than we can imagine. That 'fearful and wonderful' making goes back beyond the glimpses we get in Psalm 139 of God at work in the womb, back through the intricate lines of inheritance from forbears and ancestors, back through the evolution of species, through the first formation of the folded strands of life itself, back to the beginning of that mysterious nexus of embodied being to which we give the little name 'cosmos'.

That these strange, beautiful bodies, with their interweaving of interdependent systems, and their billion connections of the brain, should arise and be formed from the stuff of the world, the dust of the earth, is a mystery and miracle, which not only puts us in awe, but is hallowed by God, for he tells us in this passage that the body is a temple. Ours is the body he took by grace, laid down in love, and will raise in glory.

Grant, Lord,
that we who are baptized into the death
of your Son our Saviour Jesus Christ
may continually put to death our evil desires
and be buried with him;
and that through the grave and gate of death
we may pass to our joyful resurrection;
through his merits,
who died and was buried and rose again for us,
your Son Jesus Christ our Lord.

COLLECT

Easter Season

Monday 6 April

Psalms **111**, 117, 146
Song of Solomon 1.9 – 2.7
Mark 16.1-8

Monday of Easter Week

Mark 16.1-8

'... terror and amazement' (v.8)

They missed it! The women who came to the tomb early on Sunday morning missed the resurrection. As far as we know, there were no witnesses to Jesus' resurrection – not human ones anyway. By the time the women arrived with spices, by the time the stone was rolled away, by the time the white-robed man took his place, it had already happened. Without an announcement of any kind, Jesus got on with what God alone can do, and for which he needed no help. In the dark of the night, he had quietly risen from the dead.

Crucifixion is public. It is loud, explicit and nauseating. But resurrection is not like that. It happens out of sight and unannounced. This is true of our lives. When the weight of life is brutal on our shoulders, those are the conditions that most resemble the first Easter. But personal resurrection may already have begun – life returning inside the shroud, inside the tomb.

Terror and amazement. Is that *really* a resurrection experience? Yes, actually! One day in eternity the resurrection will be complete. There will be alleluias, trumpets and triumph. But that isn't how the resurrection began. It began with three scared women who had nothing to say.

Today, twenty-four hours after the choirs have stopped exulting and the worship bands have fallen silent, some people find themselves wishing they could share their Church's jubilant certainty. There is a wonderful, godly precedent.

COLLECT

Lord of all life and power,
who through the mighty resurrection of your Son
overcame the old order of sin and death
to make all things new in him:
grant that we, being dead to sin
and alive to you in Jesus Christ,
may reign with him in glory;
to whom with you and the Holy Spirit
be praise and honour, glory and might,
now and in all eternity.

Psalms **112**, 147.1-12
Song of Solomon 2.8-end
Luke 24.1-12

Tuesday of Easter Week

Luke 24.1-12

'... he went home, amazed at what had happened' (v.12)

For the followers of Jesus, working out what had happened on the first Easter Sunday was a slow process. The women's initial reaction was confusion. Then they were frightened. Then they imprecisely recalled something Jesus had said. The men's first reaction was to dismiss what they were told out of hand. Only Peter afforded the women the dignity of going to see whether there was any substance to what they said. But he had no flash of insight, just puzzlement.

Resurrection is real, but it will not be hurried. The tragedies of our lives often come at speed – bereavement, breakdown of a relationship, pain. But the way God brings new life is measured.

When I am bereaved, resurrection begins when I look at a photograph of the person whose loss has wounded me, and the sight of it unexpectedly brings a joyful memory instead of distress.

When a relationship ends, resurrection begins when I realize for the first time that I am enjoying something because I am me, not because I am half of a couple.

When pain is intolerable, resurrection begins when I slip away from the body that has limited and disabled me, and step liberated into the presence of God. That, more than any other, is how God silently brings new life.

Today, as on that Sunday that changed everything, God reveals himself slowly. But his plan to make all things new is irrepressible.

God of glory,
by the raising of your Son
you have broken the chains of death and hell:
fill your Church with faith and hope;
for a new day has dawned
and the way to life stands open
in our Saviour Jesus Christ.

COLLECT

117

Wednesday 8 April

Wednesday of Easter Week

Psalms 113, 147.13-end
Song of Solomon 3
Matthew 28.16-end

Matthew 28.16-end

'I am with you always' (v.20)

Jesus had to leave. He simply could not have fulfilled his mission had he stayed on earth. One man could not have taken the good news to our entire world. To do that required one to multiply to eleven (v.16), eleven to multiply to three thousand (Acts 2.41), the thousands to multiply to millions, and so on.

We are among those millions charged with taking the message of Jesus and passing it on to children yet unborn and neighbours yet ungreeted. So we need some reassurances. Here are three.

You don't need to know all the answers. Even some of the eyewitnesses to Jesus' resurrection weren't sure what they were seeing (v.17). Just tell the story of what Jesus means to you. It's not the end of the world if you can't answer a tough question or get outclassed in a discussion.

Your job is to tell people about your faith, to invite people into the church community and to pass on what you have discovered about Jesus (v.19). Whether people convert is for God to worry about, so relax. It's not the end of the world if your attempts are fruitless.

At no time and in no place will you ever be alone. The Spirit of Jesus is with you (v.20). It may be invisible, but it is as real as oxygen and gravity. And that's how it will be until finally it is the end of the world.

COLLECT

Lord of all life and power,
who through the mighty resurrection of your Son
overcame the old order of sin and death
to make all things new in him:
grant that we, being dead to sin
and alive to you in Jesus Christ,
may reign with him in glory;
to whom with you and the Holy Spirit
be praise and honour, glory and might,
now and in all eternity.

Psalms **114**, 148
Song of Solomon 5.2 – 6.3
Luke 7.11-17

Thursday 9 April

Thursday of Easter Week

Luke 7.11-17

'Do not weep' (v.13)

Because we live in an age and in a country where a welfare system protects those who have nowhere else to turn, we might miss two important things about this story. The young man who had succumbed to a mortal illness was an only child. And his mother was widowed. For her, the only means of support she had in the world had been taken from her. When Jesus restored the boy to her, he was rescuing her from destitution.

What does this tell us about God? That he has come to earth so that people should not perish in poverty. As Christian people our commitment to those in need is absolute. In what we do we are God's agents to bring life.

But this was no ordinary action on behalf of the poor. Something remarkable happened in Nain that day. The crowds caught sight of something that only God can do – bring life out of death. They were all filled with awe, the Bible tells us, and they praised God.

What does that tell us about God? That he has come to earth so that death will not be the end. As Christian people our commitment to those who have not heard that eternal life awaits them is absolute. In what we say we are God's agents to bring life.

God of glory,
by the raising of your Son
you have broken the chains of death and hell:
fill your Church with faith and hope;
for a new day has dawned
and the way to life stands open
in our Saviour Jesus Christ.

COLLECT

Friday 10 April

Psalms **115**, 149
Song of Solomon 7.10 – 8.4
Luke 8.41-end

Luke 8.41-end

'Do not fear. Only believe ...' (v.50)

Two people were driven by overwhelming need to take risks.

The woman with the severe gynaecological condition would have been considered unclean by the men who oversaw village life. She would not have been allowed to worship in the synagogue. Such was her desperation to try anything, she touched Jesus. That made him ritually unclean as well. So not just one remarkable thing happened, but two. She was healed, which is wonderful. And she found the courage to explain what she'd done, which is astonishing under the circumstances. If all the private Christians in the country, worshipping but never speaking of Jesus to their neighbours, could muster the courage to do the same, the impact would be miraculous.

The reason it was so risky for her is that the person who declared her unclean was right there. It was the responsibility of the leader of the synagogue. But Jairus was taking a risk of his own. The Jewish authorities had begun to turn against Jesus. People like him tended to come to Jesus in secret; they didn't draw attention to themselves. Imagine what he felt when he got the message that because of the delay caused by the woman, it was too late to save his daughter. But amazingly he witnessed what the intervention of Jesus can do to transform a situation. Unlike the woman, Jairus was told not to speak of what had happened. Could you have kept silent?

COLLECT

Lord of all life and power,
who through the mighty resurrection of your Son
overcame the old order of sin and death
to make all things new in him:
grant that we, being dead to sin
and alive to you in Jesus Christ,
may reign with him in glory;
to whom with you and the Holy Spirit
be praise and honour, glory and might,
now and in all eternity.

Psalms **116**, 150
Song of Solomon 8.5-7
John 11.17-44

John 11.17-44

'Jesus began to weep' (v.35)

We join this story a considerable time after Jesus heard of the distress in a family for whom he had a deep affection. And that reveals something peculiar.

Earlier in the chapter, we learn that Mary and Martha sent a message to Jesus that their brother was critically ill. Jesus did nothing about it for two days (11.6). Then the news came that Lazarus had died. Jesus was unmoved. It was not until four days after the tragedy that Jesus stood in front of the tomb. And at that point he cried.

Why then and not before?

Perhaps it was at that point that Jesus realized the enormity of what he was going to do. He was going to drag Lazarus back from the peace and perfection of Paradise to this human life of pain and injustice. Only he knew the full significance.

If the Christian belief in resurrection is true, then the power of death to terrify, depress or trap us is transformed. From the joyous viewpoint of Heaven, our earthly life will seem to have been a colourless, fleeting thing. No wonder Jesus was 'greatly disturbed' at having to call Lazarus back (v.33).

We are told that the miracle gave a glimpse of 'the glory of God' (v.40). But that glimpse is as nothing compared to the glory that is the destiny of those who follow Jesus in life, through death and into resurrection.

God of glory,
by the raising of your Son
you have broken the chains of death and hell:
fill your Church with faith and hope;
for a new day has dawned
and the way to life stands open
in our Saviour Jesus Christ.

COLLECT

Monday 13 April

Psalms 2, **19** *or* **1**, 2, 3
Deuteronomy 1.3-18
John 20.1-10

John 20.1-10

'... as yet they did not understand' (v.9)

Three people who loved Jesus deeply reacted in different ways to finding his tomb empty.

Mary was up early. Perhaps an anguished night meant she hadn't slept at all. Her first thought was that enemies of Jesus had taken his body under cover of night and dumped it in the criminals' mass grave. It was most unusual for the Governor of Jerusalem to release the corpse of a man executed for treason, so to assume that fanatics had defied Pilate's ruling was quite reasonable.

Simon Peter, making up in boldness what he lacked in fitness, lurched past his companion into the tomb. Luke's Gospel also has an account of his reaction to seeing a discarded shroud – he wondered what in heaven's name was going on.

Bolstered by Peter, the other disciple followed him into the tomb. John's account tells us that what he saw caused him to believe. But what exactly did he believe at that moment?

Later on, Jesus' followers scoured the Hebrew Scriptures to try to make sense of the extraordinary events. They undoubtedly found Hosea 6.2, which speaks of godly revival on the third day. They found Psalm 16.10, in which death is not strong enough to hold God's right-hand man. They found the story of Jonah, who emerges from three days in the deep to proclaim a just and merciful God.

But on that first Sunday, all they could manage was to stumble home.

COLLECT

Almighty Father,
you have given your only Son to die for our sins
and to rise again for our justification:
grant us so to put away the leaven of malice and wickedness
that we may always serve you
in pureness of living and truth;
through the merits of your Son Jesus Christ our Lord,
who is alive and reigns with you,
in the unity of the Holy Spirit,
one God, now and for ever.

Psalms **8**, 20, 21 *or* **5**, 6 (8)
Deuteronomy 1.19-40
John 20.11-18

John 20.11-18

'... she turned round and saw Jesus' (v.14)

During the Second World War, a painting of this scene by the sixteenth-century artist Titian was London's most treasured picture. For a month in 1942 it was, by public demand, the sole painting on display in the National Gallery when thousands had been removed to Welsh slate mines for safekeeping. It was cherished because, as the bombs fell, Londoners found reassurance in this story that love is so strong that it can survive death.

The resurrection appearances of Jesus have the ring of truth about them because they are so downbeat. Hollywood film directors scripting this turning point in the whole of Western civilization would devise a scene in which superhuman hands toppled the tombstone while the enemies of Jesus staggered back aghast. But John's account could not possibly be more different. Resurrection came with the whisper of a name and a message of good news.

Jesus' first appearance after his resurrection was to Mary Magdalene. She was a woman who had lost her way through life and then found calm and purpose when she followed Jesus. She was a forgiven sinner. She was a person who, on that Sunday morning, was demoralized and in distress. And she was someone whose evidence had every likelihood of being dismissed in the male-dominated culture of the day.

You couldn't make it up!

Risen Christ,
for whom no door is locked, no entrance barred:
open the doors of our hearts,
that we may seek the good of others
and walk the joyful road of sacrifice and peace,
to the praise of God the Father.

COLLECT

Wednesday 15 April

John 20.19-end

'These are written so that you may come to believe ...' (v.31)

We live in a sceptical age. Seeing is believing. The story of Thomas reaching out to touch Jesus appeals to us because we understand why he asked for proof.

But the experience of millions of Christians is that believing leads to seeing. When you live from day to day assuming that there is a good and loving God, changes take place. You are acutely aware of a purpose in life. You become a better person because you start living for the benefit of others. Things make sense that previously didn't.

Jesus made it clear to Thomas that proof is a privilege, not a right.

Suppose we could go back two thousand years and tell Thomas about a smartphone. He would be staggered. 'I won't believe that unless I can stretch out my hand and touch it,' he would say. So you would hold it out and he would put his finger on the screen. And there would be Google, YouTube and Wikipedia – he could look himself up!

Ridiculous, of course! But because this story has been preserved, Thomas can come forward 2,000 years to us with this message: 'There is a Saviour. He is risen and he is alive. If that belief forms the basis of your life, you will discover a fuller, more secure, more meaningful way of being. And that will turn out to more compelling than proof. Reach out your hand. I did.'

COLLECT

Almighty Father,
you have given your only Son to die for our sins
and to rise again for our justification:
grant us so to put away the leaven of malice and wickedness
that we may always serve you
in pureness of living and truth;
through the merits of your Son Jesus Christ our Lord,
who is alive and reigns with you,
in the unity of the Holy Spirit,
one God, now and for ever.

John 21.1-14

'... the disciples did not know that it was Jesus' (v.4)

You cannot live the entire of your life at an intense emotional pitch. You just can't! This Bible passage is about what you do the day after your religious highlight, or one week after your honeymoon, or a month after you popped champagne corks. And what do you do? Well, you go back to work, or home-making, or volunteering, or whatever your mundane daily activity is.

It's easy to assume that, after following Jesus for three miraculous years, his disciples would be too important to go back to their old trade. But with the donations that funded Jesus' mission at an end, they still had to pay the rent. However, because they were now making their way through life with the awareness that they had a risen Saviour, some things were subtly different:

– A good day's work could be as exhilarating as a miracle (v.11).

– The one they had followed as Lord and leader was now calling them his mates (a literal translation of v.5).

– A different set of ideas was influencing their everyday behaviour. Left-handed habits were being challenged by right-handed alternatives, and the results were good (v.6).

– Something as commonplace as breakfast was enriched by God's presence even though no one mentioned him by name (v.12).

The resurrection of Jesus is a reality this very day. Those quiet transformations could be yours too.

Risen Christ,
for whom no door is locked, no entrance barred:
open the doors of our hearts,
that we may seek the good of others
and walk the joyful road of sacrifice and peace,
to the praise of God the Father.

COLLECT

Friday 17 April

Psalms 57, **61** *or* 17, **19**
Deuteronomy 4.15-31
John 21.15-19

John 21.15-19

'... do you love me?' (v.16)

Peter must have looked back on this month as the most traumatic of his life. During the night before Jesus died, he had three opportunities to stand up for his friend. Before the cock crowed, he flunked the lot. Now, after breakfast on a beach, there were three requests to declare his love for Jesus. They were public and he was a bloke, so they must have been painful.

Subsequently, he was given three demands to serve God's people. Nobody knows what he said that morning because the Bible doesn't record it. However, we know a lot about what he did in the years that followed, and it is absolutely clear that his repentance was total.

It is the business of every follower of Jesus to serve him by feeding his sheep (v.17). It might involve practical care for those who are lonely or lost. It might involve working for justice on behalf of those who are denied life in its fullness. Or, in this unequal world, it might literally involve feeding those who are hungry.

What is our motivation for doing this? Not guilt; not hope of reward; not a desire to draw attention to yourself. For Peter and for each of us, it has to proceed naturally from love for the Lord. When a person loves Jesus, these things follow as surely as a sheep follows a shepherd.

COLLECT

Almighty Father,
you have given your only Son to die for our sins
and to rise again for our justification:
grant us so to put away the leaven of malice and wickedness
that we may always serve you
in pureness of living and truth;
through the merits of your Son Jesus Christ our Lord,
who is alive and reigns with you,
in the unity of the Holy Spirit,
one God, now and for ever.

Psalms 63, **84** *or* 20, 21, **23**
Deuteronomy 4.32-40
John 21.20-end

Saturday 18 April

John 21.20-end

'Follow me!' (v.22)

In the months that followed Jesus' resurrection, his followers expected him to return triumphantly at any moment. This belief is still central to Christian faith, but it has taken much longer than the first believers anticipated.

During the years in which the New Testament was being written, the way Christians thought changed. In the letters that were written first, the message was that everyone should be urgently ready. In the words we read yesterday and today, written some decades after Jesus' resurrection, there is a more questioning attitude. Why did Peter die a hideous death before Jesus returned? Were the rumours true that John had been promised by Jesus that he would still be alive at his return? If he died after such promises, did it call into question Jesus' trustworthiness?

The end of John's gospel is a postscript that answers those questions. The very fact that the book was written shows what was decided. A new generation of children who had never met Jesus was growing. The eyewitnesses were old. A written account was vital before it was too late – a biography that also offered a theological commentary on Jesus' teaching.

We should be endlessly grateful that the Gospel writers decided this because it allows us, twenty centuries later, to have confidence in the accounts. Even so, it's disappointing that there are sayings of Jesus that could fill book after book that we will never read.

Risen Christ,
for whom no door is locked, no entrance barred:
open the doors of our hearts,
that we may seek the good of others
and walk the joyful road of sacrifice and peace,
to the praise of God the Father.

COLLECT

Psalms **96**, 97 *or* 27, **30**
Deuteronomy 5.1-22
Ephesians 1.1-14

Ephesians 1.1-14

'... an apostle of Christ Jesus by the will of God' (v. 1)

When an email drops into my inbox with elaborate salutations in the name of Jesus Christ, I'm usually being asked to send money to someone who says they are a brother or sister in the faith, but is actually a fraudster. Email scams are designed to catch out the unwary; they are no sign of authentic fellowship.

For Paul and the early Christians who followed and imitated him, Christ-centred greetings were a way of demonstrating identity, belonging and authority. The writer of Ephesians wanted to form and foster relationships across a network of churches, whose members no longer knew each other personally. The name of Jesus Christ, along with the assurance of their own place in the family of God, was the only way early leaders had of introducing themselves as his authorized representatives to an ever-growing body of believers.

Reading the early verses of Ephesians, we can know that we are part of this body of believers, marked by the Holy Spirit from the beginning of time as belonging in faith. The glorious hymn of praise that moves the letter on beyond its opening greeting summarizes the many ways in which God's blessings are known among Christ's followers. We are asked for nothing in return. Our community is defined by the praise that it offers, praise that circulates through and around us in word and action – an authentic sign of life in Christ for a growing and changing Church.

COLLECT

Almighty Father,
who in your great mercy gladdened the disciples
    with the sight of the risen Lord:
give us such knowledge of his presence with us,
that we may be strengthened and sustained by his risen life
and serve you continually in righteousness and truth;
through Jesus Christ your Son our Lord,
who is alive and reigns with you,
in the unity of the Holy Spirit,
one God, now and for ever.

Psalms **98**, 99, 100 *or* 32, **36**
Deuteronomy 5.22-end
Ephesians 1.15-end

Ephesians 1.15-end

'I do not cease to give thanks for you …' (v.16)

At the end of our last supper together, my host Pastor Johannes prayed for me and gave thanks to God for my time with his family during that Easter's school exchange visit. I had never openly been prayed for before, and I found myself silently biting back tears, overwhelmed by a sense of belonging and being loved, both by God and by my new friends.

The writer of Ephesians returns to the theme of thanksgiving that has already dominated the letter's opening verses, bringing into yet sharper focus the hope and blessings that are embodied in Christ's followers. Thanksgiving moves into encouragement, as we are enjoined to grow in our knowledge and love of God. And encouragement moves into praise, with the writer almost losing himself in the wonder of the blessings he prays for.

Though stylized, this is no mere rhetoric; the author's thankfulness for our faithfulness and his concern for our spiritual growth enable him to carry us through with him into a deeper appreciation of the power of the exalted Christ. Gratitude builds us up in faith.

To say in person, to write, to text, or to tweet our prayerful thanksgiving for those who, whether near or far, journey with us in faith, reminds us of our inheritance among the saints and of the greatness of the gift that salvation through Christ offers to each of us.

Risen Christ,
you filled your disciples with boldness and fresh hope:
strengthen us to proclaim your risen life
and fill us with your peace,
to the glory of God the Father.

COLLECT

Wednesday 22 April

Psalm **105** *or* **34**
Deuteronomy 6
Ephesians 2.1-10

Ephesians 2.1-10

'But God ...' (v.4)

I wonder whether you've ever lost your train of thought when writing a letter. Although your sentence may mislay its logic, the conviction with which you write can still surprise your reader into an unexpectedly new understanding.

'You were dead,' many versions of the second chapter of Ephesians begin. 'You being dead' would be more accurate, but such a translation would lead us down a very long sentence indeed, whose main verb couldn't be found until verse 5: 'made us alive together with Christ'. By this point the subject has slid from a 'you' into a 'we'. Where did the meaning go?

To reach new life in Christ, both author and reader need first to understand their past – their sinfulness, their bondage to evil forces, and their death – before arriving at the turning point of this passage and of their lives: 'But God ...' It's on these words (ho de theos) that the sense of the letter hinges: with a quick glance back to 'once' in verse two, a contrasting 'now' is implied, and all of humanity is caught up in the transformation.

While once we were dead, now through baptism we are brought into life with Christ. This change is possible because of God's initiative, brought about through grace alone – an act of extraordinary generosity to a wholly undeserving people. Christ is the turning point who embodies God's intervention for all his people: for you, for me, for us, for humanity.

COLLECT

Almighty Father,
who in your great mercy gladdened the disciples
    with the sight of the risen Lord:
give us such knowledge of his presence with us,
that we may be strengthened and sustained by his risen life
and serve you continually in righteousness and truth;
through Jesus Christ your Son our Lord,
who is alive and reigns with you,
in the unity of the Holy Spirit,
one God, now and for ever.

Psalms 5, 146
Joshua 1.1-9
Ephesians 6.10-20

George, martyr,
patron of England

Joshua 1.1-9

'... the Lord your God is with you wherever you go' (v.9)

Patriotic writers of the English Reformation loved the image of St George, England's patron saint, on horseback, veering neither to the left nor to the right, as he rode through what visionary poet and painter William Blake described as 'England's green and pleasant land'. A new nation was being claimed, which was to be both Protestant and prosperous. Joshua provided the type for much of this imagery, along with passages from Isaiah, Ephesians and Thessalonians.

Modern readers may struggle with some of the Scriptures' military and nationalistic imagery and may even read with misgivings Joshua's conquest of the Lebanon, recalling the current occupation of Palestine. Much violence is done in the name of God, and none of it, contemporary or historical, reflects God's will for humankind.

Although his battle tactics have been studied by politicians and army generals, Joshua is primarily a spiritual leader. As the community moves from wandering to settled, and recovers from the death of Moses, Joshua is the one who inspires trust. He has grown in the time of exile, learning from his mistakes. He has stood alongside Moses through times of battle and revelation. God's words of advice to Joshua are simple and have little to do with war: follow the law; pray the Scriptures; be courageous; know that God is with you.

Though entrusted with its stewardship, no nation, no people, no religion possesses a land. Patriotism and the science of war may bolster bravado, but righteousness, prayer, courage and faithfulness lead us to God.

God of hosts,
who so kindled the flame of love
in the heart of your servant George
that he bore witness to the risen Lord
by his life and by his death:
give us the same faith and power of love
that we who rejoice in his triumphs
may come to share with him the fullness of the resurrection;
through Jesus Christ your Son our Lord,
who is alive and reigns with you,
in the unity of the Holy Spirit,
one God, now and for ever.

COLLECT

Friday 24 April

Ephesians 3.1-13

'... fellow heirs, members of the same body, and sharers
in the promise' (v.6)

Looking back on his diocese's strategy for growth, a bishop described a mistake that had been made in its planning. Social engagement, he had thought, would be possible once the Church had grown sufficiently. He came to realize that this was the wrong way round: the Church would grow when it discovered its vocation to serve and transform society.

The author of Ephesians, writing to a Church that is growing from being a local gathering into a far-reaching network, has a very high view of what the Church can do. But being churchy is not part of his strategy. Instead, the Church is to speak the truth to the rulers and authorities of the heavenly places – to what the American biblical scholar, Walter Wink, has called 'all the tangible manifestations which power takes'.

Jesus Christ brought about a new order, which included breaking down walls and barriers between Jews and gentiles. Understanding this revelation led the early Church to grow into a community of belonging, which could reveal through its own example the mystery of God's inclusive love, present from the beginning of time, but revealed anew in Christ.

The Church will not grow now if we invite people to join us so that they may become more like us. The Church will surely grow if, like the imprisoned St Paul, we live in a way that breaks down barriers, models unity, and stands up to the powers that would take us away from God.

COLLECT

Almighty Father,
who in your great mercy gladdened the disciples
    with the sight of the risen Lord:
give us such knowledge of his presence with us,
that we may be strengthened and sustained by his risen life
and serve you continually in righteousness and truth;
through Jesus Christ your Son our Lord,
who is alive and reigns with you,
in the unity of the Holy Spirit,
one God, now and for ever.

Psalms 37.23-end, 148
Isaiah 62.6-10
or Ecclesiasticus 51.13-end
Acts 12.25 – 13.13

Saturday 25 April

Mark the Evangelist

Acts 12.25 – 13.13

'...John, whose other name was Mark' (12.25)

I wonder if you've ever been the volunteer who sets out the chairs for a church council meeting. Or the mate who turns up to carry boxes for a friend who is moving to an exciting new home and job. Or the substitute who gets to do some of the warm up, but never makes it onto the football pitch in the game itself. Maybe you're the person whose name isn't even remembered – a decent but forgettable person.

John, whose other name was Mark, was a bit of a hanger on, with Barnabas and Saul being the leading lights in a new mission from the Church in Antioch to spread the gospel across Cyprus. John Mark certainly saw dramatic moments of conversion, but history doesn't tell what he contributed. He didn't complete the trip, but went back to Jerusalem instead.

John Mark might be the Mark whose feast we celebrate today; who went on to write the Gospel of Mark, based on the sermons of Peter; and who founded the Church in Alexandria. Or he might be someone different.

Some make large contributions; others small. Some are remembered 2,000 years later for their efforts; others have their names misspelled at the foot of the third team's annual photograph.

Even the smallest, feeblest and most hesitant of efforts causes God to rejoice, if we are returning our gifts with love to the one who made us.

Almighty God,
who enlightened your holy Church
through the inspired witness of your evangelist Saint Mark:
grant that we, being firmly grounded in the truth of the gospel,
may be faithful to its teaching both in word and deed;
through Jesus Christ your Son our Lord,
who is alive and reigns with you,
in the unity of the Holy Spirit,
one God, now and for ever.

COLLECT

Monday 27 April

Psalm **103** *or* **44**
Deuteronomy 9.1-21
Ephesians 4.1-16

Ephesians 4.1-16

'... in building itself up in love' (v.16)

You may have heard the joke about the two members of the same denomination stranded alone on a desert island, who after ten years had started three congregations ... You might know that the proliferation of Pentecostal churches in Latin America is described by some as exhibiting the hallmarks of the amoeba school of Church growth. Churches multiply, growing, dividing and growing again. While this may be an effective strategy for numerical growth, it struggles to bear witness to our belief in one body, one Spirit, one hope, one Lord, one faith, one baptism, one God and Father of all.

We are already reconciled to one another and to God through Christ on the cross. Our reconciliation also goes on each day in myriad small examples of humility, gentleness and patient forbearance. Yet these virtues are sorely tested today in the disagreements that afflict so many churches about biblical authority, gender and sexuality.

We don't have to be uniform to be united: organs, limbs and ligaments are different in form and purpose, yet still contribute to the body. But a healthy body has those parts knitted together in a way that enables movement and growth.

Breaking away in disagreement can initially feel liberating, but it offers a divisive way of belonging, to communities that are already fragmented and unequal. Only by listening and attending to the different parts of our body will we become like the Christ who offers us hope.

COLLECT

Almighty God,
whose Son Jesus Christ is the resurrection and the life:
raise us, who trust in him,
from the death of sin to the life of righteousness,
that we may seek those things which are above,
where he reigns with you
in the unity of the Holy Spirit,
one God, now and for ever.

Psalms **139** *or* **48**, 52
Deuteronomy 9.23 – 10.5
Ephesians 4.17-end

Ephesians 4.17-end

'… clothe yourselves with the new self' (v.24)

I seem to spend an inordinate amount of time sewing achievement badges onto my daughter's green Cub Scout jumper. Expeditions, healthy living, knot tying: each has an award that must be earned. One day, I hope, a sewing badge will be won, and my job will disappear.

Imagine that you were being baptized, as the early Christians were, at dawn on Easter morn. You'd turn to the West and renounce the forces of darkness, before stripping off your old clothes, putting on new garments and turning to face the rising sun. Your new robes would be brilliant white, and you would never need to earn for them badges of belonging or achievement.

Becoming a Christian means putting away all bitterness, wrath, anger, wrangling, slander and malice, and stepping into a new freedom where we are clothed with kindness, tenderheartedness and forgiveness. The temptation to turn back to the old ways of darkness never goes away, but God promises the Holy Spirit to keep us focused on the light. God also gives us the assurance that we don't have to keep earning badges of grace: the new life we are given is simply a gift.

With grace, though, comes the responsibility of living in community: being members of one another. Marked in baptism by the Spirit with the seal of Christ, we risk intimacy with our fellow travellers, knowing, loving and forgiving them, as we are known, loved and forgiven by God.

Risen Christ,
faithful shepherd of your Father's sheep:
teach us to hear your voice
and to follow your command,
that all your people may be gathered into one flock,
to the glory of God the Father.

COLLECT

Wednesday 29 April

Psalm **135** *or* **119.57-80**
Deuteronomy 10.12-end
Ephesians 5.1-14

Ephesians 5.1-14

'Rise from the dead, and Christ will shine on you' (v.14)

The Ephesian community is as beloved to the author as a cherished godchild. Imagine if chapter 5 of this letter were to be written today – or perhaps emailed – to such a person. I wonder how its mixture of love and advice might be conveyed?

You are very precious to your parents, and I am honoured to be your godparent. Because of my work across the new network of emerging churches, I'm not able to see you often, but I pray for you all the time. I want you to know that you belong in the household of God, and that we cherish you.

I can't claim to be the source of all wisdom – some people think I'm an old curmudgeon – but I'd like to offer you some advice as you begin to negotiate your own way through God's complicated, joyful, painful, mixed-up world.

There are many people in the world who prefer to live in darkness. They thrive on using other people – their minds, their bodies and their lives – for cheap and selfish pleasure. They speak ill of those who do good; they want what they haven't got; they'll say or do anything to get their own way. As a young person, it might seem to you that you need to fit in with this crowd in order to belong.

But you belong in God's family: in the light, not in the darkness. You can shine a light on the things that hurt and exclude and diminish other people. Corruption, slave labour, human trafficking, pornography, racism – they diminish all human beings. Never give in to the darkness. Walk in the light.

COLLECT

Almighty God,
whose Son Jesus Christ is the resurrection and the life:
raise us, who trust in him,
from the death of sin to the life of righteousness,
that we may seek those things which are above,
where he reigns with you
in the unity of the Holy Spirit,
one God, now and for ever.

Psalms **118** *or* 56, **57** (63*)
Deuteronomy 11.8-end
Ephesians 5.15-end

Ephesians 5.15-end

'Be subject to one another out of reverence for Christ' (v.21)

Yesterday's letter continues, in encouragement and instruction.

I just heard the very good news about your engagement to C. Congratulations!

Love is a great mystery, and I'm sure it's something you will learn more about as you establish your own household together. I can imagine the two of you, one at each end of the dinner table, offering hospitality to your friends and family. I'm sure there will be good food to share, wine (in moderation), laughter, singing, and much passionate debate about how to be part of God's work in the world.

You are already a strong and confident leader, making a difference in the world. It's good that you share your commitment to justice and equality with C, and that you will allow each other to flourish in your calling. In the culture in which I grew up, roles and expectations were different, but I am glad that the respect that you show each other is such a strong witness to the presence of God in your lives.

Of course, you'll both make mistakes and find things you need to work at, but the goodness and forgiveness that you've learned in your faith and from your family will keep your relationship healthy.

Your parents will miss having you around at home, but a new chapter of your life is opening. My prayers for both of you, and for the work that you'll do together in these changing times to further the gospel.

Risen Christ,
faithful shepherd of your Father's sheep:
teach us to hear your voice
and to follow your command,
that all your people may be gathered into one flock,
to the glory of God the Father.

COLLECT

Friday I May

Philip and James, Apostles

Psalms 139, 146
Proverbs 4.10-18
James 1.1-12

Proverbs 4.10-18

'When you walk, your step will not be hampered' (v.12)

Learning about God often happens at least as much in community as it does through our private and individual relationship with God. That community doesn't need to be fixed or hand picked; it can just be where we happen to end up. Apart from both being apostles, Philip and James don't overlap much in the gospels; they only share a feast day because their relics rest in the same church in Rome. They are both often confused with other early saints who share their names. Philip is responsible for bringing his friend Nathanael to the Lord. James, son of Alphaeus, is probably not the brother of Jesus, though possibly the cousin.

As I took more and more funerals in the outer housing estate where I was a curate, I saw more and more of the same people: brothers, cousins, aunts, grandchildren, all related to each other in ways I didn't quite understand. Only a small proportion ever came to church on Sundays, and when they came, they usually brought the prayers of their extended families and neighbours. There were common spiritual concerns in the community, even if people didn't all meet up at the same time or in the same place.

It takes a community to learn to walk in Christ's footsteps, and that community needs to welcome every kind of fellow traveller. I'm grateful for a Church that walks with those who aren't certain where they are going, or whether they belong.

COLLECT

Almighty Father,
whom truly to know is eternal life:
teach us to know your Son Jesus Christ
as the way, the truth, and the life;
that we may follow the steps
    of your holy apostles Philip and James,
and walk steadfastly in the way that leads to your glory;
through Jesus Christ your Son our Lord,
who is alive and reigns with you,
in the unity of the Holy Spirit,
one God, now and for ever.

Saturday 2 May

Ephesians 6.10-end

'... the whole armour of God' (v.10)

Speeches that rally the troops are familiar in Western culture: Henry V's words before Agincourt, General Montgomery's gathering of his battalion before the decisive battle of El Alamein, General Patton's speech before D-Day. Concluding his letter to the troubled Ephesian community, and aware of the persecution of those close to him, the author of Ephesians offers a bold and impassioned peroration, summing up his argument and encouraging fellow Christians to live out the Christian life in a hostile environment.

Despite the imagery of putting on the armour of God, this is no conventional call to arms. The idioms of war are turned upside down, and truth, righteousness, peace, faith, salvation, and the Spirit become the new weapons. God will protect the faithful, but their task now is to bring in a gospel of peace where previously there has been spiritual darkness.

To take up arms for God means being rooted and grounded in love, unswayed by the world's destructive forces. The weapons of darkness can be laid down, and a transcendent and renewing light come into being.

Religious extremists and politicians continue to take up arms in the name of God. Washed in the water of baptism, Christians are dedicated to taking up a different kind of arms, and indeed to putting on the whole armour of God. Extremists for peace and love, Christians are given a new identity in Jesus Christ.

Almighty God,
whose Son Jesus Christ is the resurrection and the life:
raise us, who trust in him,
from the death of sin to the life of righteousness,
that we may seek those things which are above,
where he reigns with you
in the unity of the Holy Spirit,
one God, now and for ever.

COLLECT

Monday 4 May

Psalm **145** *or* **71**
Deuteronomy 16.1-20
I Peter 1.1-12

1 Peter 1.1-12

*'By his great mercy he has given us a new birth
into a living hope' (v.3)*

Christians live a double life. We live in this world (in Oxford or Gateshead or Taunton) and in the new world of God's re-creation where his writ runs fully and joyfully – 'an inheritance that is imperishable, undefiled, and unfading' (v.4). It's not easy having dual citizenship because we have our loyalties in both (possibly competing) places, but the unifying factor is our identity in Christ; we have been chosen and destined by God.

Does that mean some haven't been chosen and destined? No; it means some haven't realized what a privilege and opportunity they have. When I see people reported in the media, falling over themselves to deny they have such an implausible thing as belief in God, I simply grieve. I don't think it worries God too much whether people believe in him or not. God isn't proud, and he has the last word, after all. But I do think he grieves that people are denying themselves the freedom, depth and abundance for which he created them. Why live in three dimensions when you could have half a dozen?

But Peter's ebullient opening to his letter is actually meant to put his readers' current experience into a bigger context. They're up against it. They're suffering for their faith. So let's get the big picture straight, he says. So too for us; whatever we're up against, may we never forget the joy of Christ risen. Would you please read that last sentence again?

COLLECT

Almighty God,
who through your only-begotten Son Jesus Christ
have overcome death and opened to us the gate of everlasting life:
grant that, as by your grace going before us
     you put into our minds good desires,
so by your continual help
we may bring them to good effect;
through Jesus Christ our risen Lord,
who is alive and reigns with you,
in the unity of the Holy Spirit,
one God, now and for ever.

Psalms **19**, 147.1-12 *or* **73**
Deuteronomy 17.8-end
1 Peter 1.13-end

Tuesday 5 May

1 Peter 1.13-end

'... as he who called you is holy, be holy yourselves in all your conduct'
(v. 15)

It's a bit daunting, isn't it – to be holy in all our conduct? I feel scuppered before I've started. Couldn't we settle on 40%? The call upwards is undeniable, but the good news is that God doesn't expect us to be flawless and to triumph over our inner and outer chaos by sheer willpower. He asks us to witness to the overwhelming reality of grace in the midst of our chaotic and disordered lives. The point about holiness is that we become transparent to God, not to our own virtue. And Peter is quite clear. It's all about grace. We haven't been ransomed from our failings through society's conventional winning means ('silver or gold' v.18) but with the precious blood of Christ.

I've known a few truly holy people in my life and they've been marked by freedom, enchantment, an at-one-ness with all life. To brush against them was to be invited to be the best that I could be. It was like a bee brushing against pollen in a flower, picking up unintended treasure and taking it elsewhere. But I've known that in most cases these people had come to this place only by having entered the ravages of darkness simply protected by love.

Holiness isn't a goal; it's a by-product of loving. Which means, in all honesty, that it's not as esoteric as we thought. And it doesn't happen next week with different people and in a different context. We can't let ourselves off that easily. Holiness begins where we are, now, and it spins out of that familiar pair of invitations – to love God and to love our neighbour.

Risen Christ,
your wounds declare your love for the world
and the wonder of your risen life:
give us compassion and courage
to risk ourselves for those we serve,
to the glory of God the Father.

COLLECT

141

Wednesday 6 May

Psalms **30**, 147.13-end *or* **77**
Deuteronomy 18.9-end
1 Peter 2.1-10

1 Peter 2.1-10

'... like living stones, let yourselves be built into a spiritual house' (v.5)

Stones that live and houses that are made of spirit seem to belong to the world of cartoons, not of scripture. But Peter is using metaphors and images, piled one on top of the other, to persuade his diverse readers that they are now truly part of God's people, not also-rans outside God's covenant. They are 'a chosen race, a royal priesthood, a holy nation, God's own people' (v.9). He lays it on with a trowel. And they are now part of God's temple because of the cornerstone of the building, Jesus, over whom many are stumbling but over whom they themselves are rejoicing, as they come 'out of darkness into his marvellous light' (v.9). The argument is closely packed but deeply liberating.

As we gather on a Sunday morning with the usual suspects in a luke-warm church for a somewhat predictable service, we may not feel that we are much of a chosen race or a royal priesthood. Something more mundane may come to mind. But beneath the surface something much more important is going on. Christians have been dipped in God and are being re-formed by the Spirit. There's no hurry about this process; God deals in eternities not weekends. So we meet as freshly minted Christians on the royal road to freedom. As we travel, what we need is an ample supply of grace, a pocket full of dreams and a Good Companion.

That motley band of worshippers you meet on Sundays might turn out to be rather special. Why not give them a chance? And why not pray for them today?

COLLECT

Almighty God,
who through your only-begotten Son Jesus Christ
have overcome death and opened to us the gate of everlasting life:
grant that, as by your grace going before us
    you put into our minds good desires,
so by your continual help
we may bring them to good effect;
through Jesus Christ our risen Lord,
who is alive and reigns with you,
in the unity of the Holy Spirit,
one God, now and for ever.

1 Peter 2.11-end

'Conduct yourselves honourably...' (v. 12)

It was the first Sunday after I'd been put in as a new vicar. The evening of the welcome had been wonderful, full of high-sounding words and wonderful aspirations. But now it was a dark, wet, January night, and I found I was expected to fetch the dustbins from behind the church hall and lug them to the main road to be emptied the next day. Was this what I had come for? Actually, why not?

This second section of 1 Peter 2 has that kind of feel about it. It's a bit of a come-down after the glorious affirmations of the first verses of the chapter. It's about accepting the authority of fickle governors, slaves accepting their lot in life, and all of us knuckling down under suffering. Was this what they had become Christians for? Actually, why not?

The Christian life is worked out in details. It's what happens when we're up against it, or just plodding on, that shows how deeply the grace of Jesus Christ has really penetrated. Authority, slavery, suffering? Well, God works through governments and human institutions, and order is far preferable to anarchy. Slavery is a current reality that is completely relativized by the freedom and equality we have in Christ. Suffering is the tragic result of living in God's way in a God-avoiding society. Working out the details of discipleship this very day is where we are most challenged and, perhaps, most energized.

Risen Christ,
your wounds declare your love for the world
and the wonder of your risen life:
give us compassion and courage
to risk ourselves for those we serve,
to the glory of God the Father.

COLLECT

Psalms **138**, 149 *or* **55**
Deuteronomy 21.22 – 22.8
I Peter 3.1-12

1 Peter 3.1-12

'… they too are also heirs of the gracious gift of life' (v.7)

A mere man writing about this passage is more than likely to get it wrong! I could point to the radical reworking of husband–wife relationships to be found in Peter's proposal of mutuality of respect between the two. (Honouring a wife was a very odd idea since honour was usually only given to a husband.) I could point to the subversive intent of a wife accepting her husband's authority so that he might be won over to her faith, rather than the normal practice of a wife accepting her husband's beliefs. I could point to these things, but I expect it would be met with a frosty half-smile.

Peter is working within a set of assumptions that were deeply embedded in the culture. What he knew was that something fundamental had shifted; what he didn't yet know was how far the consequences of that shift would reach. But he knew that this new understanding of faith meant that you had to work from the inside out rather than the outside in. The outer accoutrements of glamour were as nothing compared with 'the lasting beauty of a gentle and quiet spirit' (v.4). What matters is 'love for one another, a tender heart, and a humble mind' (v.8). The gracious gift of new life in Christ flows from the depths; it isn't a superficial cover-up but a top-to-toe make-over. Bubbling up from the deep springs of the Spirit is a revolution on a scale none of us has yet imagined.

We may not understand more than a slice of it, but someone once said: 'Live today as a citizen of the world as you would like it to become.'

COLLECT

Almighty God,
who through your only-begotten Son Jesus Christ
have overcome death and opened to us the gate of everlasting life:
grant that, as by your grace going before us
    you put into our minds good desires,
so by your continual help
we may bring them to good effect;
through Jesus Christ our risen Lord,
who is alive and reigns with you,
in the unity of the Holy Spirit,
one God, now and for ever.

Psalms **146**, 150 *or* **76**, 79
Deuteronomy 24.5-end
1 Peter 3.13-end

1 Peter 3.13-end

'Always be ready to make your defence to anyone who demands
from you an account of the hope that is in you' (v.15)

There's a massive natural disaster and tens of thousands of people are killed. Do you hope no one will ask you why you still believe in God? A dear friend is struck down with an aggressive cancer. Do you trust no one will ask what good praying for that person is supposed to do? A bright A-level student asks how you can reconcile science and faith. Do you wish he'd go away?

Peter says we should always be ready to give an answer for our faith. My fear is that we've neglected the vital teaching of apologetics and we've left the average churchgoer vulnerable if not defenceless. And yet the answers we have are not only intellectual. Just as important is the way we answer ('do it with gentleness and reverence' v.16) and the quality of our lives (our 'good conduct in Christ' v.16). People may not be persuaded by our answers, but they may be moved by our lives, especially when we face suffering. Then, said Peter, we are aligned front and centre with Jesus. No one knows how they will handle suffering until it happens, but the longer we've spent with Jesus, the more resources we'll have if and when the time comes.

When I pick up our cat, I can often tell where she's been – rolling in the catnip or lying on the freshly-washed clothes. Isn't that inevitable? We take on the scent of what – or who – we live close to.

Risen Christ,
your wounds declare your love for the world
and the wonder of your risen life:
give us compassion and courage
to risk ourselves for those we serve,
to the glory of God the Father.

COLLECT

Monday 11 May

Psalms **65**, 67 *or* **80**, 82
Deuteronomy 26
1 Peter 4.1-11

1 Peter 4.1-11

'Whoever speaks must do so as one speaking the very words of God'
(v.11)

Words are dangerous. They can insinuate falsehoods, inflame animosities, undermine truth. They can tempt us to verbal promiscuity as we send them everywhere by email, internet, Facebook, Twitter – even the old-fashioned letter. And yet words keep us sane. When Brian Keenan was kidnapped in Lebanon, he spent many months in solitary confinement and found that the way to survive was to scribble words on every scrap of paper he could find – even on the walls – to prove he existed.

Words sustain us and they damage us. How then can we live with this dichotomy? Peter says we should speak as with the very words of God. In other words, we should only speak words of grace and truth, with love as the benchmark, the filter through which our conversation and comment should pass. 'Maintain constant love for one another, for love covers a multitude of sins' (v.8). The question becomes: does what I'm about to say or write pass the test of love? The world would be a happier place if we all applied that test.

But the words of God, filtered by love, aren't sentimental. When accepting the Nobel Prize for Literature, Polish writer Czesław Miłosz said: 'In a room where people unanimously maintain a conspiracy of silence, one word of truth sounds like a pistol shot.' Love is not love without truth. May we find ways today of speaking with the loving integrity of God.

COLLECT

God our redeemer,
you have delivered us from the power of darkness
and brought us into the kingdom of your Son:
grant, that as by his death he has recalled us to life,
so by his continual presence in us he may raise us to eternal joy;
through Jesus Christ your Son our Lord,
who is alive and reigns with you,
in the unity of the Holy Spirit,
one God, now and for ever.

1 Peter 4.12-end

*'... let those suffering in accordance with God's will entrust
themselves to a faithful Creator, while continuing to do good' (v.19)*

Peter doesn't beat about the bush any longer. He tells his readers not to be surprised that they are suffering but to see it as sharing in the sufferings of Christ. Archbishop Michael Ramsey once bravely wrote to clergy: 'It is doubtful if any of us can do anything at all until we have been very much hurt, and until our hearts have been very much broken.' Suffering goes with the territory of being a Christian. In his book *Christianophobia* Rupert Shortt estimates that roughly 200 million Christians face discrimination or persecution around the world, which makes them the most targeted faith group on earth.

In the face of this, Peter points his readers straight to the beautiful disaster of the cross. He offers advice which from anyone else would sound absurdly romantic or naive: if you suffer as a Christian, 'glorify God because you bear this name' (v.16). But because Peter lived in the thick of persecution his advice has to be heard. These Christians lived so vividly in the expectation of a fast-approaching denoument to the present world order, they could align themselves easily with the cross as a sign of the end.

The task for us is to live with similar faith and urgency but driven by a different fuel. And yet the heart of Peter's message holds true. If things go hard for us, let us entrust ourselves to a faithful Creator, while continuing to do good.

Risen Christ,
by the lakeside you renewed your call to your disciples:
help your Church to obey your command
and draw the nations to the fire of your love,
to the glory of God the Father.

COLLECT

Wednesday 13 May

Psalms **132**, 133 *or* **119.105-128**
Deuteronomy 28.58-end
I Peter 5

1 Peter 5

'Like a roaring lion ... looking for someone to devour' (v.8)

When we experience the discomforts of being people of faith, we in the West will do well not to think we're being persecuted. Persecution is of a quite different order. Nevertheless, it can make us think hard about the origin of evil. Peter likens the devil to a ravenous lion bent on the destruction of anything edible – mostly us. It's a vivid picture, which we tame nicely in the soothing ritual of compline. But Peter is at his clearest. His readers are having a hard time, but the real foe isn't the intermediate persecutors but the lion behind them, the devil. That's why he has insisted throughout the letter that we should treat non-Christians with respect, obey the authorities, behave with humility and patience in all circumstances, and so on. Name the real enemy and 'resist him, steadfast in your faith,' he says (v.9), but remain gracious and Christ-like with everyone.

Modern readers will inevitably ask themselves what they make of talk of the devil. C. S. Lewis was keen to make the point that we should avoid both extremes – the extreme of dismissing the idea of the devil because we can't believe in a ridiculous little chap with horns and red tights, and the other extreme of being fascinated with the idea of a devil and seeing him at work under every stone. For most of us, the personification of the devil doesn't matter so much as the necessity of taking evil seriously, and resisting it, steadfast in our faith. And perhaps even more importantly, instead of asking where this misfortune came from, we could ask the much more telling question: what does this occurrence enable me to do that I couldn't have done before?

COLLECT

God our redeemer,
you have delivered us from the power of darkness
and brought us into the kingdom of your Son:
grant, that as by his death he has recalled us to life,
so by his continual presence in us he may raise us to eternal joy;
through Jesus Christ your Son our Lord,
who is alive and reigns with you,
in the unity of the Holy Spirit,
one God, now and for ever.

Thursday 14 May

Ascension Day

Hebrews 7.[11-25] 26-end

'...a high priest, holy, blameless, undefiled, separated from sinners, and exalted above the heavens' (v.26)

On Ascension Day we celebrate with the Church that our Lord is finally exalted to his proper place at the right hand of the Father. The 'high priest' isn't confined to earth but is 'above the heavens'. But is such a high priest any use? Isn't he so removed from our lives that he's ceased to speak our language or know our terrors? It's all very well, in the ideas-world of Hebrews, to rejoice that there's no more need to offer sacrifices every day as in the old days, but the Jesus of the incarnation was rather more, shall we say, 'in touch'?

One way of approaching the Ascension is to think of it as Christ being put in his right place and we being put in ours. 'God is in heaven, and you upon earth; therefore let your words be few,' (Ecclesiastes 5.2). Now at last we know where Christ is, after the 'now you see him, now you don't' that's been going on ever since the resurrection. And now we know what our task is, left as we are to get on with preparing the ground for the coming of the kingdom. The decks have been cleared; let's get to work. 'The law appoints as high priests those who are subject to weakness' (v.28) (don't I know it!), but now our great high priest can oversee and empower the work of the kingdom, which is the task and privilege of every Christian. In this sense the Ascension is when the starting pistol went off and we started to run the great race. How will today's leg go, I wonder?

COLLECT

Grant, we pray, almighty God,
that as we believe your only-begotten Son
our Lord Jesus Christ
to have ascended into the heavens,
so we in heart and mind may also ascend
and with him continually dwell;
who is alive and reigns with you,
in the unity of the Holy Spirit,
one God, now and for ever.

Friday 15 May

Matthias the Apostle

Acts 2.37-end

'Day by day, as they spent much time together in the temple ...'
(v.46)

This is a classic and greatly loved passage from which we can gain much, but there are two dangers. One is that we take what the first believers did as a kind of blueprint for today. So we think if we preach like this, revival will break out and three thousand people should step forward to make a commitment to Christ. Or we should hold everything in common, sell our possessions, and spend lots of time together in church. But scripture isn't a template whereby we can jump over two millennia of Church and social history. Rather it's an encouragement to do the kind of things in our day that match the kind of things they did in their day. That's true faithfulness to scripture.

The other mistake is to spend too much time on our inner church life when our real task is out there in the helter-skelter, bewildered world of the twenty-first century. If persecution hadn't happened soon (Acts 8.1), maybe those early Christians would have settled down comfortably as a subset of Judaism. It was when they were catapulted out of Jerusalem and encountered the diverse thought-worlds of the wider Middle-East that they had to think furiously about the mission Christ had given them, and come to realize that, in fact, they had a gospel for the whole world.

Do we spend too long in the comfort of church activities and not enough in the discomfort of the secular worlds that surround us? What small step out of that trap could we take today?

COLLECT

Almighty God,
who in the place of the traitor Judas
chose your faithful servant Matthias
to be of the number of the Twelve:
preserve your Church from false apostles
and, by the ministry of faithful pastors and teachers,
keep us steadfast in your truth;
through Jesus Christ your Son our Lord,
who is alive and reigns with you,
in the unity of the Holy Spirit,
one God, now and for ever.

Psalms 21, **47** *or* 96, **97**, 100
Numbers 11.16-17, 24-29
1 Corinthians 2

1 Corinthians 2

'... we have the mind of Christ' (v.16)

In spite of popular perception, Paul had a modest streak. He came to the Corinthians in fear and trembling, he said, not speaking with plausible words of wisdom. Instead, he spoke 'with a demonstration of the Spirit and of power' (v.4). I think I'd settle for that any day! But wisdom is still important.

T. S. Eliot asked what happened to the wisdom we've lost in knowledge and what happened to the knowledge we've lost in information. Good questions. Paul is asking something similar. Ordinary human knowledge doesn't recognize God's wisdom, which is 'secret and hidden' (v.7). Only God's Spirit can access divine wisdom (v.11), but the great thing is 'we have the mind of Christ' (v16).

The trouble with this is that the wrong people often claim to have the mind of Christ! Or if they do have it, God hasn't told the rest of us. It's a problem well known to Church leaders everywhere. That's why what Paul emphasizes elsewhere is important. He says the discernment of what is from God has to be done in community. Wisdom is found when we pray and talk together, rather than when we act alone. The African Church has given us the word *indaba* for this process of corporate discernment. I often think I can see 270 degrees round a problem, but for the last 90 degrees I need the wisdom of the community.

It's not that 'I' have the mind of Christ, but 'we' have the mind of Christ.

Grant, we pray, almighty God,
that as we believe your only-begotten Son our Lord Jesus Christ
to have ascended into the heavens,
so we in heart and mind may also ascend
and with him continually dwell;
who is alive and reigns with you,
in the unity of the Holy Spirit,
one God, now and for ever.

COLLECT

151

Monday 18 May

Psalms **93**, 96, 97 *or* **98**, 99, 101
Numbers 27.15-end
I Corinthians 3

Numbers 27.15-end

'... he laid his hands on him and commissioned him' (v.23)

These days between Ascension Day and Pentecost are traditionally days of prayer for the coming of the Holy Spirit. The readings this week reflect that by pointing to the many and various ways in which God interacts with our human needs and desires through the Holy Spirit. Here, we see Moses asking God for the gift of discernment as he considers who will be his successor as shepherd of Israel. Moses prays for God's guidance and he receives it, but he does not take it for granted – there is a note of humility in his approach to God as he contemplates the end of his extraordinary span as leader of Israel. In many aspects of life, there is an important skill in finding the right person for a particular task. Today's reading suggests that there is also a divine dimension involved. God's will interacts with human choice. Joshua's election is confirmed by ceremony and commitment.

We should think about how we mark the beginnings and endings of the tasks we undertake. As we reflect on the commissioning of Joshua, we could reflect on where the Holy Spirit is calling us to undertake God's work. Are there circumstances in our lives that are nudging us to a new response? And are we actively engaged in prayer for those who will succeed us in the tasks we are today undertaking?

COLLECT

O God the King of glory,
you have exalted your only Son Jesus Christ
with great triumph to your kingdom in heaven:
we beseech you, leave us not comfortless,
but send your Holy Spirit to strengthen us
and exalt us to the place where our Saviour Christ is gone before,
who is alive and reigns with you,
in the unity of the Holy Spirit,
one God, now and for ever.

Psalms **98**, **99**, 100 *or* **106*** (*or* 103)
I Samuel 10.1-10
I Corinthians 12.1-13

Tuesday 19 May

I Samuel 10.1-10

'God is with you' (v.7)

The role of the Holy Spirit in discerning vocation continues today with the story of Samuel's anointing of Saul as the future king of Israel. God has accepted his people's desire for kingship, and Saul is the kind of leader people always want: from a good family, handsome and youthful (1 Samuel 9.1-2). God's choice of Saul requires outer confirmation. The incident of the lost donkeys that sent Saul far from home (1 Samuel 9.3) is part of God's hidden work, leading him to meet with Samuel and the prophets who will confirm him as God's choice. We learn later, of course, that the gifted and good-looking Saul has violent tendencies that arise from dark emotions. He cannot respond to God's choice of him effectively until there has been some dramatic working-through of his inner life. At the end of today's passage, God has – at least temporarily – given Saul 'another heart' (v.9), and he shares the frenzy of the prophets.

This is a fascinating passage because it reveals the work of the Spirit in transforming what today we would probably call the unconscious mind. If we respond to what God is nudging us to become, we will undergo inner change as well as outer change. The Holy Spirit is God's gift to his faithful ones, but we have to be ready to receive the gift, because the Spirit will always reveal the truth.

Risen, ascended Lord,
as we rejoice at your triumph,
fill your Church on earth with power and compassion,
that all who are estranged by sin
may find forgiveness and know your peace,
to the glory of God the Father.

COLLECT

Wednesday 20 May

Matthew 3.13-end

'This is my Son, the Beloved, with whom I am well pleased' (v.17)

The story of Jesus' baptism was embarrassing to the early Church. Why would the sinless one need to be baptized by John for the remission of sins? Matthew is aware of the problem and is careful to try to explain the incident as demonstrating Jesus' willing conformity to fulfilling 'righteousness' (v.15) – that is, to God's plan to save his people from their sins. But the significance of the baptism of Jesus goes beyond this. It is the point at which his sonship is made real to him in his earthly life. He is anointed, not with oil like the kings of Israel, but with the Holy Spirit of which oil is the sign and symbol. Jesus' sonship is of a different order from that of the kings and prophets of Israel. The opening of the heavens signifies his intimate relationship with the Father. He is the beloved of God; he came from God and points the way to God.

Today, as we pray for the coming of the Holy Spirit, remember the gift of the Holy Spirit that all Christians receive in baptism. It is this gift that has made us brothers and sisters of Jesus, this precious gift, which is the pledge of eternal life. We share the sonship that he has with the Father, not by right, as he does, but by love and grace.

COLLECT

O God the King of glory,
you have exalted your only Son Jesus Christ
with great triumph to your kingdom in heaven:
we beseech you, leave us not comfortless,
but send your Holy Spirit to strengthen us
and exalt us to the place where our Saviour Christ is gone before,
who is alive and reigns with you,
in the unity of the Holy Spirit,
one God, now and for ever.

Matthew 9.35 – 10.20

'... it is not you who speak, but the Spirit of your Father' (10.20)

The creed tells us that the Holy Spirit 'proceeds from the Father and the Son'. Here we see the gift of the Holy Spirit proceeding from the Son to the chosen Twelve who will carry the good news of the kingdom to the lost sheep of the house of Israel. Today's reading provides a fundamental insight into the nature of mission. Mission begins in the heart of God, who is the 'Lord of the harvest' (9.38). God's creation exists for his greater glory. He creates to share his goodness. The Son is sent not only to proclaim the kingdom, but also to commission and empower those who follow him. They are sent out with the Spirit's gifts of proclamation, prophecy, healing and exorcism (10.8). They are not to make any charges for the gift they bring, but are to share in the life of the communities they serve. The Holy Spirit is manifested not only when they are successful, but also when they are rejected. They are to witness to Christ through suffering and persecution. That is when they must trust most deeply that the Spirit speaks through them.

It is often assumed in Church life that the Holy Spirit is only present when thing go well; numbers increase, giving goes up. But the presence of the Spirit is not limited to our successes. It is in failure that we are most dependent on the Spirit's strength.

Risen, ascended Lord,
as we rejoice at your triumph,
fill your Church on earth with power and compassion,
that all who are estranged by sin
may find forgiveness and know your peace,
to the glory of God the Father.

COLLECT

Friday 22 May

Matthew 12.22-32

'... whoever does not gather with me scatters' (v.30)

The Holy Spirit manifests the unity of God and draws human beings into community. This is shown in today's reading, where Christ's healing work is challenged by those who claim he is possessed by demonic power. The challenge Jesus throws back is an invitation to true discernment. Demonic power is by its nature divisive. The fact that the crowds question whether Jesus can really be the Messiah ('Can this be the Son of David', v.23) deserves a positive answer. They have all witnessed the cure of the possessed man, who is restored by Jesus so that he can both hear and see; the cured man is now manifesting the fullness of life for which he was created. What evidence could be clearer that this is God's work? But the Pharisees, who should have recognized what was going on, display only cynical disbelief. This shows what they are really about: their concern is with their own status and not with what matters to God. Jesus knows that his ministry is potentially divisive and insists that there is forgiveness for those who attack him verbally and publicly. But to write off God's healing work as demonic is to write oneself out of his promises.

We should ask ourselves whether our words and attitudes are such as to bring unity or division. Are we gathering with God or scattering with Beelzebub?

COLLECT

O God the King of glory,
you have exalted your only Son Jesus Christ
with great triumph to your kingdom in heaven:
we beseech you, leave us not comfortless,
but send your Holy Spirit to strengthen us
and exalt us to the place where our Saviour Christ is gone before,
who is alive and reigns with you,
in the unity of the Holy Spirit,
one God, now and for ever.

Psalms 42, **43** *or* 120, **121**, 122
Micah 3.1-8
Ephesians 6.10-20

Saturday 23 May

Ephesians 6.10-20

'Pray in the Spirit at all times' (v.18)

The Holy Spirit is the comforter, the strengthener of those who seek to follow Christ. This marvellous passage encourages us to realize that, though our spiritual support is invisible to the eyes, it is in reality all-embracing and all-empowering.

Christian life can be likened to warfare, not because we are supposed to be aggressive in our faith, but because the human predicament is full of ambiguities and we need to stay alert. We are all subject to so many influences – from culture, from history, from the media, from economic and social forces. Every day we have to make choices about our own lives. Every choice we make is likely to influence others as well as ourselves. What God provides for us by the Holy Spirit is 'whole armour' (v.13), the moral and spiritual resources to become stable in our faith over time, to grow in the virtues and to resist the vices that destroy lives. The effort that we make is in prayer, not only for ourselves, but also for one another (v.18). Through the Spirit we are part of a community of faith that upholds us, as we uphold others. Irenaeus, one of the early Church Fathers, said that 'the glory of God is a person fully alive'. Being fully alive is what God wills for us; this is the life that the Holy Spirit is forming in us day by day.

Risen, ascended Lord,
as we rejoice at your triumph,
fill your Church on earth with power and compassion,
that all who are estranged by sin
may find forgiveness and know your peace,
to the glory of God the Father.

COLLECT

Ordinary Time

Monday 25 May

Psalms 123, 124, 125, **126**
2 Chronicles 17.1-12
Romans 1.1-17

2 Chronicles 17.1-12

'They went around through all the cities of Judah and taught' (v.9)

The two books of Chronicles are a revision of the earlier sacred histories in the Old Testament. The writer has a clear moral purpose: to show how fidelity to God leads to prosperity, and infidelity to punishment. Unlike earlier writers, he tends to focus on individuals. So here the good king Jehoshaphat is credited with strengthening his kingdom and combating idolatry. He is also concerned that his people are taught the law. As result of his efforts, there is peace, and the surrounding peoples bring tributes to the king.

We live at a time when there is much scepticism about those who govern us. We are fickle in our political loyalties and tend to vote in ways that further our personal interests. Jehoshaphat's emphasis on education in the law encourages us to show concern for the roots of morality in our own society. 'How can young people keep their way pure?' asks the Psalmist (119.9). Today's reading suggests that there is a firm link between the teaching of law, respect and honour, and the health of society. We should support those who teach the importance of faith in schools and in wider society. Neutrality on matters of faith and an emphasis on individual choice in matters of personal morality are not as benign as is sometimes claimed.

COLLECT

O Lord, from whom all good things come:
grant to us your humble servants,
that by your holy inspiration
we may think those things that are good,
and by your merciful guiding may perform the same;
through our Lord Jesus Christ,
who is alive and reigns with you,
in the unity of the Holy Spirit,
one God, now and for ever.

158

Psalms **132**, 133
2 Chronicles 18.1-27
Romans 1.18-end

2 Chronicles 18.1-27

'Inquire first for the word of the Lord' (v.4)

This is a light reworking of 1 Kings 22, which focuses less on Ahab and more on Jehoshaphat. But the central theme is the same. There is a critique here of military adventurism and a brilliant exposition of the role and cost of truthful prophecy. Micaiah, surely, is the heroic figure, resisting the populist call to arms, exposing the fragility of Ahab's conscience towards God and suffering the consequences of his own whistle-blowing. Jehoshaphat, the more virtuous of the two kings, allows himself to be led by Ahab in the whole sorry venture.

It is not difficult to think of parallels in our own time when governments have been led into foolish military interventions at enormous cost. But we should not discount the difficulties of discernment in circumstances of threat. Even Micaiah is well aware that the guidance of God is not always easy to read.

In our personal lives, we may find ourselves having to act prophetically in pointing out the potential destructiveness of what may seem to be an easy or obvious path. Being blamed is part of the burden that truth-tellers bear. It is often a Christian vocation to 'speak truth to power', a clear instance of the gospel challenge that the servant is not greater than the master – we are called to follow Jesus whatever the personal cost.

O Lord, from whom all good things come:
grant to us your humble servants,
that by your holy inspiration
we may think those things that are good,
and by your merciful guiding may perform the same;
through our Lord Jesus Christ,
who is alive and reigns with you,
in the unity of the Holy Spirit,
one God, now and for ever.

COLLECT

Ordinary Time

Wednesday 27 May

Psalm **119.153-end**
2 Chronicles 18.28 – 19.end
Romans 2.1-16

2 Chronicles 18.28 – 19.end

'Nevertheless, some good is found in you' (19.3)

Although Ahab meets a sticky end on the battlefield, Jehoshaphat returns in peace, only to meet prophetic judgement on his own front door. He has made a mistake by supporting Ahab, and yet he is not utterly condemned. His campaign against idolatry is proof that his heart is towards God. Perhaps in penitence, or renewed zeal, he continues with his task of moral and spiritual reform. Significantly, he reminds those who are appointed to be judges that they are not to be swayed by human considerations or loyalties, but to execute judgement for the sake of the Lord, the just judge (19.6-7).

Contrary to much popular belief today, there is a consistent scriptural insistence that God is the source of human justice. Justice is not arbitrary. This is important because we are far too easily seduced by our connections and loyalties, including religious loyalties. A society that does not seek impartial justice can never overcome prejudice and division. In daily life we all have responsibility for ensuring fairness and combating divisive prejudice. As Christians, we need to pray for freedom from making judgements that serve our own interests or protect those dear to us. Sometimes we must speak up for those who differ radically from ourselves in their beliefs and lifestyles. It is not always right to protect those we love from the consequences of their own wrongdoing.

COLLECT

O Lord, from whom all good things come:
grant to us your humble servants,
that by your holy inspiration
we may think those things that are good,
and by your merciful guiding may perform the same;
through our Lord Jesus Christ,
who is alive and reigns with you,
in the unity of the Holy Spirit,
one God, now and for ever.

2 Chronicles 20.1-23

'Believe in the Lord your God and you will be established' (v.20)

Jehoshaphat now faces a real danger: an alliance of armies from across the Jordan is bearing down on Judah with terrifying speed. He has every reason to fear, but fear drives him towards God, and God provides prophetic guidance. This comes in the form of assurance, 'the battle is not yours, but God's' (v.15). It is impossible not to hear an echo of the stories of Joshua (Joshua 1.9) and, before him, Moses (Exodus 13.14). Jehoshaphat and his people will be safe as long as they trust in God. So the congregation 'all Judah' go out to meet the enemy, not in battle order but as though they were going to worship. Jehoshaphat calls the assembly to go ahead of his troops singing praise to God as God intervenes to defeat the aggressors.

Courage is not always easy in the face of threats to our wellbeing and security. There is nothing wrong with being afraid; fearless Christians are sometimes foolish Christians. But the fear of God should drive us to prayer rather than to despair. The habit of praise is also a protection in times of disaster. Remembering the goodness of God, being grateful for his many gifts and immersing ourselves in the promise of his grace is the best way to meet even the most challenging circumstances. Threats are not punishments, but trials.

O Lord, from whom all good things come:
grant to us your humble servants,
that by your holy inspiration
we may think those things that are good,
and by your merciful guiding may perform the same;
through our Lord Jesus Christ,
who is alive and reigns with you,
in the unity of the Holy Spirit,
one God, now and for ever.

COLLECT

2 Chronicles 22.10 – 23.end

'Jehoiada took courage' (23.1)

The Chronicler now tells of another danger to the house of Judah: the wicked Athaliah, granddaughter of the Northern king Omri, who reigned after her son was killed. There is, however, a more promising candidate for the kingship: Ahaziah's son Joash, who is preserved from Athaliah's murderous attempts to secure her throne by killing off the entire royal family. The plot to conceal the boy is probably orchestrated by the priest Jehoiada. The years in which the boy grows up just have to be lived through. When the time is right, Jehoiada announces revolution. As the Chronicler describes it, this coup d'état has massive popular support. Priests, people and military act together to restore a king after the model of David.

We do not live in a society where revolutions on this scale are likely, but plenty of Christians do have the experience of living under oppression and having to discern what God is asking of them in terms of working for a more just order. Today's reading suggests that both patience and courage are needed. Patience to wait for the moment when there is a chance of change; courage to seize the opportunity when it comes.

The same qualities are needed at many points of decision. What balance of patience and courage are you having to exercise at this point in your life? What patience and courage will you need today?

COLLECT

O Lord, from whom all good things come:
grant to us your humble servants,
that by your holy inspiration
we may think those things that are good,
and by your merciful guiding may perform the same;
through our Lord Jesus Christ,
who is alive and reigns with you,
in the unity of the Holy Spirit,
one God, now and for ever.

Psalm **147**
2 Chronicles 24.1-22
Romans 3.21-end

2 Chronicles 24.1-22

'Because you have forsaken the Lord, he has also forsaken you'
(v.20)

Jehoiada's judgement about Joash is proved correct, at least for the first part of his reign while he has Jehoiada to guide him. His major work is one of restoration. He reintroduces an ancient tax to pay for repairs. The Chronicler insists, perhaps implausibly, that this is no burden. The people give gladly to restore the house of the Lord after the desecration of Athaliah's reign.

But Joash is not as stable in his obedience to God as he might have been, and after Jehoiada's death he is easily led astray. However, God does not immediately abandon him, but sends prophets to repeat the message that the prosperity of the land depends on faithfulness to God. When this has no effect, Jehoiada's son Zechariah is moved by the spirit of God to preach the same warning. The response to this is horrific – Zechariah is stoned to death. Joash's refusal to listen seals his own fate and proves the Chronicler's case.

Whenever we are in a position of power over others, we need to be careful who we listen to. The temptation is to listen only to those who have affirming things to say to us. But truth is often found in dissenting and questioning voices. Whose influences hold sway over you? And whose voices do you trust to tell the truth?

O Lord, from whom all good things come:
grant to us your humble servants,
that by your holy inspiration
we may think those things that are good,
and by your merciful guiding may perform the same;
through our Lord Jesus Christ,
who is alive and reigns with you,
in the unity of the Holy Spirit,
one God, now and for ever.

COLLECT

Monday I June

Visit of the Blessed Virgin Mary to Elizabeth

Psalms 85, 150
I Samuel 2.1-10
Mark 3.31-end

1 Samuel 2.1-10

'My strength is exalted in my God' (v.1)

It is a strange time for praise to overflow. A mother has left her child with strangers. She had longed for that son with desperate, uncontrollable tears. Now he is born, now he is weaned, and now he is separated from her. And her praise overflows.

Her hymn is framed by two Hebrew phrases that speak of the 'raising up' of someone's 'horn', an image of triumph and exaltation. NRSV paraphrases on both occasions, somewhat unhelpfully with a different choice of words: 'my strength is exalted in my God' (v.1) and 'exalt the power of his anointed' (v.10). In all that has happened, Hannah sees a pattern: God's action in vindicating the faithful who put their trust in him. This is her testimony, and she weaves it into a prophetic vision of the kingdom of God, which for its fullness requires the one whom God anoints, his messiah. Her hymn declares that in the exaltation of the anointed one, we are also raised up, and in our every witness to God's exaltation, the raising up of the messiah is also proclaimed.

When Mary meets Elizabeth, praise overflows again, moving again from testimony to prophetic vision. Her song, the Magnificat, has become a daily channel for the Church's praise – in the joy of meeting and in the pain of separation, in testimony to what the Lord has done for us today and in witness to the kingdom that extends to 'the ends of the earth', and into eternity.

COLLECT

Mighty God,
by whose grace Elizabeth rejoiced with Mary
and greeted her as the mother of the Lord:
look with favour on your lowly servants
that, with Mary, we may magnify your holy name
and rejoice to acclaim her Son our Saviour,
who is alive and reigns with you,
in the unity of the Holy Spirit,
one God, now and for ever.

2 Chronicles 28

'... carrying all the feeble among them' (v.15)

Victory and defeat easily distort our perceptions. This chapter describes what appears to be a decisive defeat. Since the division of the kingdom, there has been constant tension between Judah, Samaria and Aram, with alliances, skirmishes and sometimes all-out war. Suddenly, it appears to be all over: Judah is defeated, and the way lies open for it to be wiped from the map. Yet this local drama is about to be eclipsed by wider developments. The armies of Assyria are stirring.

The Chronicler focuses attention on two responses to all this. One is the desperation of King Ahaz, who gives up on the God of his ancestors and makes pathetic attempts to curry favour instead with those human and divine powers that appear to be on the winning side of history. The other is the mercy of the Israelites, who eventually recognize in the captives they have taken in war their own 'kindred' (v.11). These bodies are not raw material to be turned into money and power, but persons to whom they have obligations in the sight of the Lord, who is God of both victors and vanquished. And so these Samaritans clothe them, give them food and drink, anoint the wounded and take them home (v.15).

This is the victory of God, and this is the true heart of human history: mercy, love of neighbour, even enemy. We need to be very careful that apparent conquests and perceived successes do not blind our eyes to that truth.

Almighty and everlasting God,
you have given us your servants grace,
by the confession of a true faith,
to acknowledge the glory of the eternal Trinity
and in the power of the divine majesty to worship the Unity:
keep us steadfast in this faith,
that we may evermore be defended from all adversities;
through Jesus Christ your Son our Lord,
who is alive and reigns with you,
in the unity of the Holy Spirit,
one God, now and for ever.

COLLECT

Wednesday 3 June

Psalm 119.1-32
2 Chronicles 29.1-19
Romans 5.1-11

2 Chronicles 29.1-19

'... the Lord has chosen you to stand in his presence' (v.11)

According to the Chronicler, God chose a people, a king and a line of succession, and God chose for them a land, a city and a temple. And he chooses the Levites to maintain the temple's life.

Perhaps we feel uncomfortable with such statements. Is it not true that God is the God of all, and cares for all – so how can it be true that God chooses some rather than others? And is it not too often the case that those who talk confidently about being called and chosen – not least the clergy – can fall into a kind of offensive superiority, as if they are the ones around whom the Church or indeed the world revolves?

Here, as elsewhere in the Scriptures, God chooses some for the sake of many, and in Christ, God chooses one for the sake of all. It is a great thing to grasp that we are chosen to follow a particular vocation, but it is not primarily for our sake that this happens, but for the good of others and for the glory of God, in which, of course, our own good finally lies. In the Scriptures, to be chosen is to be set aside for some work, which may well be hard and difficult, wearying and even boring – like cleansing the temple from top to bottom along with everything in it for a solid fortnight. It is no reason to feel superior to anyone else.

COLLECT

Almighty and everlasting God,
you have given us your servants grace,
by the confession of a true faith,
to acknowledge the glory of the eternal Trinity
and in the power of the divine majesty to worship the Unity:
keep us steadfast in this faith,
that we may evermore be defended from all adversities;
through Jesus Christ your Son our Lord,
who is alive and reigns with you,
in the unity of the Holy Spirit,
one God, now and for ever.

Psalm 147
Deuteronomy 8.2-16
I Corinthians 10.1-17

Thursday 4 June

Day of Thanksgiving for the Institution of the Holy Communion (Corpus Christi)

Deuteronomy 8.2-16

'... to test you, and in the end to do you good' (v.16)

The gifts of God do not come to us here on earth without testing. This in no way qualifies divine generosity. Receiving God's gifts will test us and humble us, shape us and form us, for we cannot receive them and stay just as we are. And therefore the place of grace is also the place of trial. We cannot bypass the wilderness in the life of faith.

At the root of this is the unbreakable bond between the things God gives and the word God sends: 'One does not live by bread alone, but by every word that comes from the mouth of God' (Matthew 4.4). What kept the children of Israel alive in the desert? Yes, it was the manna, but the manna could only be received by trusting in the word that accompanied it, by following God's guidance. To try to take what God gives without receiving God's word makes the gift turn sour and vanish in our hand. For the word reveals the precious mystery in every holy gift, the gift of God's own self to us in loving, patient freedom.

Anglicans do not, by and large, follow medieval traditions in observing Corpus Christi. Yet it might still remind us of the need for seriousness about holy things. We cannot take what God gives without putting our very life in God's hands. We cannot receive Christ's body and blood without opening our heart to his word. It will test us, and incalculable good will flow from it.

COLLECT

Lord Jesus Christ,
we thank you that in this wonderful sacrament
you have given us the memorial of your passion:
grant us so to reverence the sacred mysteries
of your body and blood
that we may know within ourselves
and show forth in our lives
the fruits of your redemption;
for you are alive and reign with the Father
in the unity of the Holy Spirit,
one God, now and for ever.

Friday 5 June

2 Chronicles 30

'But Hezekiah prayed for them' (v.18)

Reconciliation is never easy. Hezekiah wants to bring people together for the feast of Passover as set out in the law of Moses – but although he has done everything properly in Jerusalem, the people from across the country who have responded to his invitation are a rather mixed bunch, and many are not in a fit state to participate (vv.17-18). So what is to be done? That which brings them together is a ritual event defined by rules: to say the rules do not matter is to erode its character, its very power to unite people. Yet to send some away, or make them second-class participants, would be to miss the opportunity that is here for those 'who set their hearts to seek God' (v.19) to be united in God's presence.

The things that divide us from others tend to be bound up inseparably with what really matters to us, what gives us our deepest identity, what provides the central point for our meeting together as one. Reconciliation cannot mean saying that this does not matter, or that our identity can be rewritten, or that we can meet around something more diffuse and more vague. It must mean welcoming the other into our place – the place that matters most to us, the place that speaks most deeply of who we are, the place where we find the strongest roots of community. And it must mean bearing, with continual prayer, the disruption that is threatened by such welcome.

COLLECT

Almighty and everlasting God,
you have given us your servants grace,
by the confession of a true faith,
to acknowledge the glory of the eternal Trinity
and in the power of the divine majesty to worship the Unity:
keep us steadfast in this faith,
that we may evermore be defended from all adversities;
through Jesus Christ your Son our Lord,
who is alive and reigns with you,
in the unity of the Holy Spirit,
one God, now and for ever.

Psalms 20, 21, **23**
2 Chronicles 32.1-22
Romans 6.15-end

Saturday 6 June

2 Chronicles 32.1-22

'... as if he were like the gods of the peoples of the earth' (v.19)

Much of the Chronicler's presentation of Hezekiah is relatively independent of the material we know from 2 Kings, but here he rejoins it for the story of the confrontation with Sennacherib. The confrontation is a military one, but it is also theological: Sennacherib offers a sustained critique of Israel's faith, which he intends to prove by force of arms. For him, Israel's God is just a god like any other god of a nation, and nations rise and fall. Right now, the Assyrians are rising, and all other nations, all other gods, must give way before them.

Jerusalem stands firm (just), refuting the Assyrians' theology. Still, questions remain once their army has retreated. If God rules over the nations, and Hezekiah was his faithful servant, why did God let the Assyrians invade in the first place (v.1)? Behind that, however, lies a deeper issue. Why is Israel's God not 'like the gods of the peoples of the earth' (v.19)? Is he superior to them but essentially on the same level, doing what they do only more effectively than them: better at winning battles, better at making crops grow, better at guaranteeing his own people's survival? Or is this God truly and radically unique, beyond any comparison, because he is the creator of all things and therefore essentially unlike all things, yet also somehow attached to them all, present in them all, loving them all as their maker and sustainer – even Assyrians, even Sennacherib?

Holy God,
faithful and unchanging:
enlarge our minds with the knowledge of your truth,
and draw us more deeply into the mystery of your love,
that we may truly worship you,
Father, Son and Holy Spirit,
one God, now and for ever.

COLLECT

Monday 8 June

Psalms 27, **30**
2 Chronicles 33.1-13
Romans 7.1-6

2 Chronicles 33.1-13

'Then Manasseh knew that the Lord indeed was God' (v.13)

Sometimes we have to go abroad before we realize where home is. Manasseh, the son of faithful Hezekiah, becomes one of the worst of Judah's kings, drawing God's people more deeply into sin than ever before (v.9). But in a distant country, he comes to his senses, humbles himself before 'the God of his ancestors', and is freed to set out on the journey home. Once back, he will remove the idol he had once 'set' in the place where God had 'put' his name forever (v. 7 – the two words in Hebrew come from the same verb) and return to the one who in all his wanderings never ceased to be his God.

God's judgement never comes without mercy: its painful surgery can also bring healing and restoration. Manasseh was surrounded by so many gifts from God, so many signs of God's faithfulness and love – and yet in the midst of it all, he could not see who God was and what God was asking from him. So he is taken away from the place of God's choosing, the site of God's name. And then he feels the loss, the lack, and entreats the favour – literally, 'the face' – of the Lord his God (v.12). He returns, repents, is converted. So exile, the place of judgement, becomes a space where grace can do its work. Distance from the things of God becomes the condition for him to draw near, all alone, to the one who welcomes him home.

COLLECT

O God,
the strength of all those who put their trust in you,
mercifully accept our prayers
and, because through the weakness of our mortal nature
we can do no good thing without you,
grant us the help of your grace,
that in the keeping of your commandments
we may please you both in will and deed;
through Jesus Christ your Son our Lord,
who is alive and reigns with you,
in the unity of the Holy Spirit,
one God, now and for ever.

Psalms 32, **36**
2 Chronicles 34.1-18
Romans 7.7-end

2 Chronicles 34.1-18

'... he began to seek the God of his ancestor David' (v.3)

The life of faith may steadily unfold in accordance with the stages of life, and it may also be suddenly transfixed by the word that is always new and always now. Perhaps it is normal that it embraces both – the former creating space for the latter, the latter giving direction to the former.

Something stirs in the spirit of the adolescent Josiah. For a while nothing changes, but four years later, fully in charge of the kingdom, he acts with the energy and the violence of youth, embarking on a systematic national programme of iconoclasm. It takes six years, after which he returns to Jerusalem and begins 'to repair the house of the Lord his God' (v.8): not tearing down but building up; not travelling around but staying in one place; not facing down evil so much as becoming a project manager. But in the midst of this project, an old book is found, and God's word is heard anew.

Is it possible that we can become so intent on our own projects for God, our hard-won progress in ministry, that we might lose our readiness to receive the word that cuts across it all and speaks of overwhelming judgement and overwhelming blessing right here, right now? And is it also possible that we can be searching so hard for some new and exciting word that we neglect the ordinary and ancient wisdom that should be shaping us day by day for knowing God?

God of truth,
help us to keep your law of love
and to walk in ways of wisdom,
that we may find true life
in Jesus Christ your Son.

COLLECT

Wednesday 10 June

2 Chronicles 34.19-end

'So Hilkiah ... went to the prophet Huldah' (v.22)

There are not many women who are named in 2 Chronicles: occasionally as mothers of kings, and Athaliah as queen in her own right – though that ends very badly (2 Chronicles 23.12-15). Otherwise, they tend to appear as bystanders, sharing anonymously in both joy and suffering. Yet at this pivotal moment in the reign of the great Josiah, the men who run the country pay a visit to a woman.

The reason they visit Huldah is that she is a prophet. 'The law and the prophets' appears as a kind of shorthand for Israel's Scriptures in the New Testament, a conjunction reflected also in the dual presence of Moses and Elijah at the Transfiguration. The prophets proclaim what it means to be faithful to the law of God here and now, the shape of its promises for us and the shadow of its judgements. The law God gave needs interpretation that is God-breathed; the letters on the page seek a living voice so that they might come alive in our midst. Law and prophets go together. Hence the unexpected discovery of the book of God's law sends its finders off in search of God's prophet.

How was Huldah known to be a prophet? We are not told. Evidently her gender did not prevent her gift from being recognized. To understand the Scriptures in all their urgency and power, we may need to listen to some surprising voices and make detours to visit people whom the world usually passes by.

COLLECT

O God,
the strength of all those who put their trust in you,
mercifully accept our prayers
and, because through the weakness of our mortal nature
we can do no good thing without you,
grant us the help of your grace,
that in the keeping of your commandments
we may please you both in will and deed;
through Jesus Christ your Son our Lord,
who is alive and reigns with you,
in the unity of the Holy Spirit,
one God, now and for ever.

Psalms 100, 101, 117
Jeremiah 9.23-24
Acts 4.32-end

Barnabas the Apostle

Acts 4.32-end

'Barnabas (which means "son of encouragement")' (v.36)

The next time we encounter Barnabas in Acts, he is the one Christian in Jerusalem prepared to believe Saul's story of conversion. The time after that he has been sent on a fact-finding mission to the Church in Antioch. 'When he came and saw the grace of God, he rejoiced, and he exhorted them all to remain faithful to the Lord with steadfast devotion; for he was a good man, full of the Holy Spirit and of faith' (Acts 11.23-24a).

The verb translated as 'exhorted' there comes from the root *parakaleo*, which also gives us the noun *paraklesis* in today's passage: 'encouragement'. It is a word with a broad range of meaning, but these verses perhaps help us to see how Barnabas got his nickname, 'son of encouragement'. He spoke words that brought encouragement, but not just in the generic sense of keeping one's chin up. Barnabas encouraged disciples 'to remain faithful to the Lord', and was able to do this because he was 'full of the Holy Spirit and of faith'.

Jesus tells the disciples he will send them 'another Advocate': another *parakletos*, one who gives encouragement (John 14.16). How will the Spirit do this? '[He] will teach you everything, and remind you of all that I have said to you' (John 14.26). Let us pray to the Son to be filled anew with the Spirit who comes from the Father, so that we too may speak true encouragement to the Church of Christ, and to the world that seeks him.

Bountiful God, giver of all gifts,
who poured your Spirit upon your servant Barnabas
and gave him grace to encourage others:
help us, by his example,
to be generous in our judgements
and unselfish in our service;
through Jesus Christ your Son our Lord,
who is alive and reigns with you,
in the unity of the Holy Spirit,
one God, now and for ever.

COLLECT

Friday 12 June

2 Chronicles 35.20 – 36.10

'All Judah and Jerusalem mourned for Josiah' (35.24)

The Chronicler can appear to hold to a simple, indeed naive, theology, in which faithlessness to God is always punished and faithfulness always rewarded. Josiah, according to the Chronicler, 'did not turn aside to the right or to the left' (2 Chronicles 34.2) and was devoted to the temple of which God said to Solomon, 'my eyes will be open and my ears attentive to the prayer that is made in this place' (2 Chronicles 7.15). So how can it be that he dies after defeat in battle by the King of Egypt, from which Israel was once rescued by God to be brought into the land of promise – a defeat precipitating a sequence of disasters that will end with a new exile, a new slavery?

It is, however, also naive, indeed patronizing, to presume that such tensions would not have occurred to an ancient author, or to ancient readers. The Chronicler's account of Josiah's exchange with King Neco is absent from the parallel passage at 2 Kings 23, and may represent an attempt at explanation – but it might be better to say exploration, for it yields no simple answer. Did Josiah, at the last, 'turn aside' and refuse to heed God's guidance, unable to believe it might come from the successor of the Pharaohs? Or is it the case that faithfulness to God and love of God's name do not make us immune from errors of judgement, nor act as a magic charm to protect us from their sometimes tragic consequences?

COLLECT

O God,
the strength of all those who put their trust in you,
mercifully accept our prayers
and, because through the weakness of our mortal nature
we can do no good thing without you,
grant us the help of your grace,
that in the keeping of your commandments
we may please you both in will and deed;
through Jesus Christ your Son our Lord,
who is alive and reigns with you,
in the unity of the Holy Spirit,
one God, now and for ever.

Psalms 41, **42**, 43
2 Chronicles 36.11-end
Romans 8.31-end

2 Chronicles 36.11-end

'Let him go up' (v.23)

It has looked like the end of the road, the end of the story, at various points in 2 Chronicles, but here it finally comes. God 'chose' this people, this land, this place for God's name – and now all is shattered and scattered.

Yet even as it ends, the story is also beginning, beginning again. Kingdoms rise and kingdoms fall, and a new kingdom creates a new space, a new opportunity. God spoke to David and Solomon about building a house, and now God speaks to the King of Persia. God led Israel out of bondage in Egypt, and now God opens a way for Israel's return from exile in Babylon. It is a new story, but it is also the same story: it shares the same rhythm, the same pattern, and what God did once is not lost and forgotten but taken up in what God is doing now. It is the story of resurrection. 'Let him go up.'

Sooner or later, we face loss, tragedy and failure so comprehensive that we want to say, if it is not said to us by others: 'This is the end; this is finished.' But because of one who said as he died, 'It is finished,' there is no end to the beginning of new life, and no end to the story that unfolds from the gospel and gathers up all the threads of God's promise, all the fragments of God's purpose, from the foundation of the world.

God of truth,
help us to keep your law of love
and to walk in ways of wisdom,
that we may find true life
in Jesus Christ your Son.

COLLECT

Monday 15 June

Psalm **44**
Ezra 1
Romans 9.1-18

Ezra 1

'... in order that the word of the Lord ... might be accomplished'
(v. 1)

It is 50 years since Jerusalem was destroyed. Fifty years of living in exile, far from home. Those who knew Jerusalem best have died. With every year that passes, its memory is more distant, return an ever more impossible dream. But the stories are told, the songs are sung, and the dream lives on. Babylon is a good place to live, but Jerusalem is still home.

Then international politics once more intervene in the fate of God's people. There is a new regime in power, one that rules by taxation rather than by force. Emperor Cyrus needs stability in his provinces. Suddenly everyone captured and moved by the Assyrians is encouraged to go home, taking their treasures with them.

But that is not how our author tells the story. For him, Cyrus' decree has nothing to do with the practical demands of empire building, and everything to do with the major player in this story, the Lord 'the God of heaven' (v.2). Going home is not about a return to familiar comfort, but about rebuilding the house of the Lord. The vision is not political but theological. It is not a nation that is being rescued but a faith, the faith that we will come to call Judaism, emerging out of the ashes of destruction to make Jerusalem its centre once more. God's plan for the salvation of the world has been resurrected.

COLLECT

Lord, you have taught us
that all our doings without love are nothing worth:
send your Holy Spirit
and pour into our hearts that most excellent gift of love,
the true bond of peace and of all virtues,
without which whoever lives is counted dead before you.
Grant this for your only Son Jesus Christ's sake,
who is alive and reigns with you,
in the unity of the Holy Spirit,
one God, now and for ever.

Ezra 3

'But many ... wept with a loud voice' (v.12)

It wasn't like the good old days. The old folks watched sadly, and agreed that things would never be the same as before. The temple in Jerusalem had been a thing of great beauty, of fine cedar wood and gold, a fit dwelling place on earth for the God of Israel. Seeing it in ruins had been bad enough, but it was even worse to see it now, the small foundations that told of a small building to come. Even the grant from the emperor, even all their trading activities, would never bring in enough money to build anything approaching the great edifice of King Solomon. And even if the money could be found from somewhere, there was still the distraction of trouble brewing on the borders, taking resources from the building work.

But the young people sang. Against all the odds they had come home and begun. There was a foundation and an altar, and the ancient festivals could be kept. The priests had their vestments, and the musicians their instruments. It was the start of something new.

To grieve over the past, or to rejoice in the present? This is a choice faced by many faith communities. Looking back at the days when churches were packed can lead us to despair. But seeing the innovative work done by churches today in their communities may encourage us to shout with delight.

Faithful Creator,
whose mercy never fails:
deepen our faithfulness to you
and to your living Word,
Jesus Christ our Lord.

COLLECT

Wednesday 17 June

Psalm **119.57-80**
Ezra 4.1-5
Romans 10.1-10

Ezra 4.1-5

'... we alone will build to the Lord' (v.3)

It is common for neighbours to fall out over building work. A new window overlooking someone's garden, a wind farm changing the long-cherished view – these can cause bitter enmity. In this case, though, it is not a case of not wanting a temple in my back yard. It is what the temple stands for.

The former exiles and their descendants are back from Babylon and taking charge. But the land has not been empty during their absence. Many ordinary people, left behind, have been living in the land for the past 50 years. And then there are the people very nearby across the border in what was the northern kingdom of Israel, people redistributed many years earlier by the Assyrians and, according to them at least, worshipping the God of Israel all that time.

How inclusive is the new community to be? On the one hand, the help and support of neighbours would be valuable. On the other, the little community and its worship may be too fragile to withstand an influx of people with their own ways of doing things and their differing slants on faith in the Lord. The leaders of the community choose to send them away.

Where should people of faith make a stand? How far should they widen their borders to include everyone, and how far should they keep pure the belief system and practice of their faith? This is not only an ancient question.

COLLECT

Lord, you have taught us
that all our doings without love are nothing worth:
send your Holy Spirit
and pour into our hearts that most excellent gift of love,
the true bond of peace and of all virtues,
without which whoever lives is counted dead before you.
Grant this for your only Son Jesus Christ's sake,
who is alive and reigns with you,
in the unity of the Holy Spirit,
one God, now and for ever.

Thursday 18 June

Ezra 4.7-end

'... issue an order that ... this city be not rebuilt' (v.21)

No good ever comes of upsetting the neighbours. Refuse to discuss your building work with them and they are liable to complain to the planning office – in this case the emperor. It is a clever objection to the work, one that appeals to the emperor's nervousness about the stability of this province of his empire.

Enemies and emperor misunderstand what is happening, but the storyteller spells out for us its deep significance. There is no resurgence of national identity here. The real aim of Ezra and his followers is to renew the worship of the Lord the God of Israel in the place where he has been most clearly known in the past. That, not the construction of a building, is what is being prevented here.

How important are religious buildings? On one hand, not important at all. We can worship God anywhere. But when a small country church with no congregation is about to close, we see what these buildings can stand for – a heart in the community, a hallowed place, representing something permanent and good, a place where heaven and earth meet.

The Jews know that God can be worshipped without a building. But this particular building is a place where God has always met with a particular historic people, chosen to fulfil his purposes. Its rebuilding must not be prevented. And it will not be prevented, because God, not the emperor, will have the last word.

Faithful Creator,
whose mercy never fails:
deepen our faithfulness to you
and to your living Word,
Jesus Christ our Lord.

COLLECT

Friday 19 June

Ezra 5

'Who gave you a decree to build this house?' (v.3)

Two can play the game of using records of the past to make a case in the present. There is a new emperor now, and the Jews take the risk of restarting their building project. This time, when they are challenged, they have their answer ready, an answer that results in a fresh search of the archives.

The Persian empire is not the enemy here; opposition comes from elsewhere. Contrary to what the enemies suggest, the Jews do not want to rule themselves. They are content to be a small corner of a province of the empire, to pay their taxes and rely on the benign protection of the emperor. Of course, when the Persians are succeeded by the Greeks and then the Romans, it all becomes more problematic. But here we have an example of a positive relationship between faith and secular power. The empire can function as a protection for the worship of God in Jerusalem, which is all that really matters.

Every faith community needs the wisdom to decide how far to work with the rules imposed by the secular authority, and how far to resist them. Here what looks at first like resistance is backed up by an appeal to the system, in the confidence that the God who once gave Cyrus his power over the Jews will work his influence once more on his successor.

COLLECT

Lord, you have taught us
that all our doings without love are nothing worth:
send your Holy Spirit
and pour into our hearts that most excellent gift of love,
the true bond of peace and of all virtues,
without which whoever lives is counted dead before you.
Grant this for your only Son Jesus Christ's sake,
who is alive and reigns with you,
in the unity of the Holy Spirit,
one God, now and for ever.

Psalm **68**
Ezra 6
Romans 11.13-24

Ezra 6

'... they set the priests in their divisions and the Levites in their courses for the service of God in Jerusalem' (v.18)

Thank goodness for Persian efficiency. Apparently the Persian civil service is a model of effective filing and archiving, even at its far flung bases. Even more fortunately, King Darius is not minded to overturn the decree of his predecessor. So the building work is back on, though apparently not without its problems. If you look up the words of the prophet Haggai, mentioned here, you will find him berating the people for putting the building of their own homes ahead of the building of the temple. However, eventually the work gets done, and there is a magnificent rededication festival.

But where are the leaders of this new community? There are no more kings, and the prophets are mentioned only in passing. Instead we have the religious officials, priests and Levites, whose names have been listed in chapter 2. The restored community is no longer in the business of war and conquest, of wealth creation through trade. This community is in the business of worship. It is led not by warriors or kings, but by worship leaders.

And where is the Lord the God of Israel? Not at the head of armies doing battle for Israel, not fighting pharaohs or parting seas. God is encountered in the temple. The Passover is no longer eaten on the move. Sometimes we see God in dramatic events, but more often we are like the Jerusalem Jews, meeting God quietly as we gather for worship.

Faithful Creator,
whose mercy never fails:
deepen our faithfulness to you
and to your living Word,
Jesus Christ our Lord.

COLLECT

Monday 22 June

Ezra 7

'Blessed be the Lord ... who put such a thing as this into the heart of the king' (v.27)

Some years have passed. The Jews are now well established in Jerusalem. Worship is happening in the rebuilt temple. It is a good beginning. But as we know, all worshipping communities need to grow in faith and understanding, and today we meet the man who is going to help them, the hero of our story who gives his name to this book.

Ezra has an impeccable pedigree reaching all the way back to Aaron, the priest of the exodus. He has grown up in Babylon, a place of culture and learning, steeped in the traditions of his people and in the law of the God of Israel. Also, importantly, he has earned the respect of the king, who sends him on his way to Jerusalem with a guarantee of all the resources he can possibly need to develop worship in the Jerusalem temple.

But there is more. Ezra is given authority to appoint legal officials to ensure that the law of the Lord becomes the law of the land in the area around Jerusalem. Does this represent the first step towards the legalism condemned by Jesus in the Jewish leaders of his day? We may be able to form a judgement as we read on. For the moment, Ezra himself takes up the story, and he is in no doubt about recent developments. God's hand is upon him, he tells us, and all his authority flows from God's grace.

COLLECT

Almighty God,
you have broken the tyranny of sin
and have sent the Spirit of your Son into our hearts
    whereby we call you Father:
give us grace to dedicate our freedom to your service,
that we and all creation may be brought
    to the glorious liberty of the children of God;
through Jesus Christ your Son our Lord,
who is alive and reigns with you,
in the unity of the Holy Spirit,
one God, now and for ever.

Ezra 8.15-end

'... the gracious hand of our God was upon us' (v.18)

Into the Jerusalem temple sweep Ezra and his entourage. They bear with them vessels of gold, silver and polished bronze. Among them are priests from the tribe of Levi, descendants of the priests of old, whose ancestors served the Lord in the great temple of Solomon. They have the authority of the emperor and the blessing of the Lord. They have prepared for the journey with rituals of purification. They have triumphed over the dangers of the wilderness with no more protection than their commission from their God. Once arrived, they set about organizing a great ceremony, with sacrifices to rival those at the temple's dedication.

Do we perhaps feel a little uncomfortable? Such unshakeable belief in the rightness of your commission, such certainty that God is on your side, such confidence in future success – it all sounds rather like a crusade, and woe betide anyone who gets in its way. For all people of faith, there is a fine line between confidence in God's calling and pride in our own efforts. It is easy for faith in God's blessing to become a certainty of our own rightness that prevents us from hearing opposing views. The Church's history is full of the damage done by confident crusaders.

At least Ezra has the humility to know whose doing it all is; 'the gracious hand of our God was upon us' is his repeated refrain.

God our saviour,
look on this wounded world
in pity and in power;
hold us fast to your promises of peace
won for us by your Son,
our Saviour Jesus Christ.

COLLECT

Wednesday 24 June

Birth of John the Baptist

Psalms 50, 149
Ecclesiasticus 48.1-10
or Malachi 3.1-6
Matthew 11.2-19

Matthew 11.2-19

'A prophet? Yes, I tell you, and more than a prophet' (v.9)

Not Ezra today, but John the Baptist, whose birth we celebrate. Another of the Bible's uncompromising, uncomfortable characters; another fanatic in God's cause; another man with a clear vision of the future of the people of God, prepared to go out on a limb to help that future along; another with a priestly ancestry. But while Ezra is a leader, and knows it, John is the advance guard for a leader beyond Ezra's wildest imagining.

Both Ezra and John are hinges between past and future. Ezra sits at the transition from Israel to Judaism, from nation to faith. John bridges BC and AD. He is the last prophet of ancient Israel, and the first of the Christian era. When we meet him in Matthew 11, his mission is over. He has preached and baptized; he has cursed the wicked and complacent, and stirred the souls of those who waited. He is in the prison from which he will never emerge.

But in prison he receives the message that makes it all worthwhile. John is a good enough prophet to recognize the signs of the messianic age when he hears about them. He can die knowing that he has been right; that although they may not know it yet, the one to whom he pointed truly is the fulfilment of all the hopes and dreams of his people, Ezra included.

COLLECT

Almighty God,
by whose providence your servant John the Baptist
    was wonderfully born,
and sent to prepare the way of your Son our Saviour
by the preaching of repentance:
lead us to repent according to his preaching
and, after his example,
constantly to speak the truth, boldly to rebuke vice,
and patiently to suffer for the truth's sake;
through Jesus Christ your Son our Lord,
who is alive and reigns with you,
in the unity of the Holy Spirit,
one God, now and for ever.

Psalm **78.1-39***
Ezra 10.1-17
Romans 13.1-7

Thursday 25 June

Ezra 10.1-17

'... separate yourselves from the peoples of the land' (v.11)

This chapter is something of a horror story.

The purity of the community is at stake, and a dreadful deed needs to be done. Even the sky seems to be weeping at the terrible choice that the men have to make – to send their foreign wives and children away or leave the community for ever.

Centuries before there had been another entry into the land and another temple. But it had all gone horribly wrong, partly, the biblical writers tell us, because the people had been drawn away from their God by the attractions of the gods of the people of the land. Now, in the time of the new exodus, the new temple, the mistakes must not be repeated. This time there must be no little shrines to Baal, no house goddesses, no compromising of the absolute loyalty owed to their God. To survive this time, the community must be clearly defined by God's law, God's worship, alone. There must be nothing, and no one, to lead them astray.

Purity or openness? Faithfulness to God or human loyalty? It is easy to condemn what happens here, but if it were us, small, alone, surrounded by enemies, what would we do?

Even so, at the end of the chapter, behind the long list of the names of the men who send their families away lies an even longer list of unnamed women and children, silent in the rain.

Almighty God,
you have broken the tyranny of sin
and have sent the Spirit of your Son into our hearts
whereby we call you Father:
give us grace to dedicate our freedom to your service,
that we and all creation may be brought
to the glorious liberty of the children of God;
through Jesus Christ your Son our Lord,
who is alive and reigns with you,
in the unity of the Holy Spirit,
one God, now and for ever.

COLLECT

Friday 26 June

Nehemiah 1

'O Lord, let your ear be attentive' (v.11)

Ezra has dealt with the restoration of the temple. Now Nehemiah turns his attention to the state of the city in which it is set. Jerusalem is defenceless. It walls and gates, destroyed many years ago by the invading Babylonians, have never been rebuilt.

What plan would we make when faced with this task? Perhaps work out how to get funds from the Persian Heritage Fund? Get in touch with Jerusalem and see what materials and workforce were available locally? Nehemiah starts in a different place. Before the practical planning comes the prayer. Before a new start can be made, the sins of the past must be confessed once more.

The Jews have learned the hard way that sin and disaster go together. Their story is shot through with the reflections of prophets and theologians who explain that the disasters that have befallen them are the result of their unfaithfulness rather than of God's neglect. Of course they, and we, know that life is more complicated than that, that God's purposes are more complex than a simple transaction of sin = punishment.

Nevertheless, Nehemiah's prayer is a good model for the start to a new venture. Sin is confessed; God's promises are recalled, and God's forgiveness and blessing are sought. The past is dealt with and the present acknowledged so that God's grace may prosper the future. Then Nehemiah is ready for action.

COLLECT

Almighty God,
you have broken the tyranny of sin
and have sent the Spirit of your Son into our hearts
    whereby we call you Father:
give us grace to dedicate our freedom to your service,
that we and all creation may be brought
    to the glorious liberty of the children of God;
through Jesus Christ your Son our Lord,
who is alive and reigns with you,
in the unity of the Holy Spirit,
one God, now and for ever.

Psalms **76**, 79
Nehemiah 2
Romans 14.1-12

Nehemiah 2

'Let us start building!' (v.18)

Jesus' parable of the houses built on sand and on rock comes to mind today. Nehemiah has all his foundations in place before he begins to build. If yesterday we formed a picture of a pious man of prayer, today we meet the sharp man of action. Before any work on the walls begins, Nehemiah has secured planning approval, scoped out the job, energized his workforce, and, temporarily at least, seen off the project's opponents. Prayer is all very well, but if the project is to have any chance of success, Nehemiah needs to get his hands dirty.

Any church or cathedral that has embarked on a building project knows that, although prayer may be the starting point, it is by no means the only thing needed. Planning expertise, fundraising skill, business acuity and effective marketing must follow, before the first spade hits the ground. And there will be times when it is hard to remember what it is all about.

People of faith need to be engaged with the world and its ways. It is hard to maintain a balance between worldly wisdom and spiritual vision, but it is essential for whatever we embark on in God's name.

Nehemiah holds on to the vision. 'The God of heaven is the one who will give us success' is his reply to opposition (v.20). Willingness to play the political and strategic game is combined with an unshakeable faith in God's future.

God our saviour,
look on this wounded world
in pity and in power;
hold us fast to your promises of peace
won for us by your Son,
our Saviour Jesus Christ.

COLLECT

Monday 29 June

Peter the Apostle

Psalms 71, 113
Isaiah 49.1-6
Acts 11.1-18

Acts 11.1-18

'... God gave them the same gift that he gave us when we believed'
(11.17)

This account has significant meaning for Christian mission today. It tells us that God's loving gift of the Holy Spirit is available to everyone. The 'first fruits' of Jesus' promise – that repentance and forgiveness of sins would be proclaimed to all nations (Luke 24.47) – are visible.

Often, our outreach programmes are hindered by our unwillingness to engage with others who look, dress or speak differently from us. The early Jewish-Christians followed the Mosaic Law, its festivals and dietary restrictions. They did not foresee 'unclean' gentiles being added to their congregations. However, Peter's vision signalled God's saving grace at work *outside* their community, and they received the news with joyous celebration. Do we celebrate all who accept God's gracious invitation? Does our worship include all ages, as well as those of different ethnicities, cultural backgrounds or socio-economic status?

Peter's humble question – 'who was I that I could hinder God?' (v.17) – is a reminder that, ultimately, the Church belongs to God, and the Holy Spirit draws and gathers at will all those included in his kingdom. When we are obedient to the instructions of the Holy Spirit to go and 'not to make a distinction between them and us' (v.12), we too can anticipate an outpouring of his grace on others.

COLLECT

Almighty God,
who inspired your apostle Saint Peter
to confess Jesus as Christ and Son of the living God:
build up your Church upon this rock,
that in unity and peace it may proclaim one truth
and follow one Lord, your Son our Saviour Christ,
who is alive and reigns with you,
in the unity of the Holy Spirit,
one God, now and for ever.

Psalms 87, **89.1-18**
Nehemiah 5
Romans 15.1-13

Nehemiah 5

'Restore to them, this very day ... [all] that you have been exacting from them.' (v.11)

The rebuilding programme in Jerusalem is fraught with problems, and Nehemiah faces an ethical dilemma. Should he halt the financial oppression of others? Or, should he appease his wealthy contributors? His decision could have a disastrous impact on the building project.

It's often difficult to stand up against those that wield power, wealth and influence in our congregations and civic communities. However, positions of leadership, governance and patronage, by their very nature, come with the burdensome responsibility of ethical administration – good stewardship.

As God's people, we are called to be good stewards, but also to hold others accountable for their actions. Today, many of our communities are affected by a sluggish economy, work redundancies, food shortages, unaffordable mortgages and dependency on high-interest payday loans. Food banks and work clubs are a necessity to assist displaced families and those most vulnerable – children and elderly.

Ethical responsibility should not be taken lightly or compromised, even for the most noble or worthy initiatives. Rather, benevolence to the poor and needy strengthens and builds our communities, and is the ultimate service that honours God. Building or restoration programmes placed on hold temporarily, may find that Church growth sparked by compassion has made the original plans obsolete.

O God, the protector of all who trust in you,
without whom nothing is strong, nothing is holy:
increase and multiply upon us your mercy;
that with you as our ruler and guide
we may so pass through things temporal
that we lose not our hold on things eternal;
grant this, heavenly Father,
for our Lord Jesus Christ's sake,
who is alive and reigns with you,
in the unity of the Holy Spirit,
one God, now and for ever.

COLLECT

189

Wednesday 1 July

Psalm **119.105-128**
Nehemiah 6.1 – 7.4
Romans 15.14-21

Nehemiah 6.1 – 7.4

'For they all wanted to frighten us, thinking, "Their hands will drop from the work" ...' (6.9)

Those opposing the renovation project in Jerusalem – Sanballat, Tobiah and Geshem – are obstructionists. How often do we encounter others opposed to change? Sometimes, individuals may move beyond being 'nay-sayers,' instead resorting to deception or subterfuge to halt progress. What should we do?

New initiatives represent change. When sanctioned by God, they become symbols of hope in our faith communities, signalling the Holy Spirit at work in our midst. Spirit-led projects renew Christian identity, often uniting congregations and communities in a common purpose. This is why Nehemiah remained focused on the task at hand, even when accused of sedition and threatened with assassination. Like Nehemiah's struggle, our Christian work should be underpinned in prayer that echoes Nehemiah's '... O God, strengthen my hands' (6.9).

When we find that the very activities that unite, re-energize and restore hope in our lives and Christian fellowships are being afflicted by 'little foxes' (Song of Solomon 2.15), we need to respond to seeds of opposition with prayer, rather than allow them to distract us or cause doubt. In prayer, God gives us the courage and strength to persevere against everything that would hinder divine fruitfulness and restoration of our communities.

COLLECT

O God, the protector of all who trust in you,
without whom nothing is strong, nothing is holy:
increase and multiply upon us your mercy;
that with you as our ruler and guide
we may so pass through things temporal
that we lose not our hold on things eternal;
grant this, heavenly Father,
for our Lord Jesus Christ's sake,
who is alive and reigns with you,
in the unity of the Holy Spirit,
one God, now and for ever.

Psalms 90, **92**
Nehemiah 7.73*b* – 8.end
Romans 15.22-end

Nehemiah 7.73*b* – 8.end

'This day is holy to the Lord your God; do not mourn or weep' (8.9)

Have you noticed how God often uses new Christians to infuse renewed hope and zeal into our fellowships and worship services? 'Baby' Christians often radiate a wellspring of joy that appears unquenchable, reminding us that 'for God all things are possible' (Matthew 19.26). Often their enthusiasm challenges our joyfulness (or lack thereof) and encourages us to rededicate ourselves to God in humble adoration.

Today's reading makes a powerful and faithful proclamation in acknowledging the ability of God's word to break yokes, while evoking tears of repentance *and* joy. Often those who are new in Christ help us recognize just how complacent our relationship with him has become, or how we may have drifted away from God's divine plan for us. Ezra's encouraging words, 'do not mourn' affirm God's forgiveness.

Perhaps this is why the gospel holds such importance in worship and evangelism. God's word gently reminds us of *his* love and *our* sinful frailties. It pierces our hearts, brings repentance, gives ongoing reassurance and allows us to move closer to God. And, as we learn to accept God's will for our lives, those tears of repentance vanish. They are swept away by joyous celebration as we come to recognize how God's protective arm has faithfully been at work in our lives, ever present, guiding and drawing us toward reconciliation.

Gracious Father,
by the obedience of Jesus
you brought salvation to our wayward world:
draw us into harmony with your will,
that we may find all things restored in him,
our Saviour Jesus Christ.

COLLECT

Friday 3 July

Thomas the Apostle

Psalms 92, 146
2 Samuel 15.17-21
or Ecclesiasticus 2
John 11.1-16

John 11.1-16

'Let us also go, that we may die with him' (v.16)

Thomas is often remembered as the apostle who doubted Jesus' resurrection. However, in today's reading, Thomas shows great courage and faithful commitment to Jesus. How often do we begin our Christian walk in the same way? We boldly express our willingness to follow Jesus whatever the cost and often encourage others to do likewise. However, as life's journey continues, and we endure the many challenges that emerge, we find that those confident expressions of faithful trust in God become less frequent.

Jesus' decision to go on to Bethany – at the risk of further angering those threatening to stone him – reveal his unshakeable trust in God's divine protection. He also lets his disciples know this journey is for *their* benefit. So, regardless of the peril – Jesus *must* go, and Thomas acknowledges his determination to be present.

What changed? How did this courageous, faithful disciple, who saw Jesus restore Lazarus' life, later doubt Jesus' resurrection? At times during our Christian journey, our confidence and commitment appears unshakeable; Jesus speaks to our hearts, and we eagerly anticipate God's miraculous power in our lives as well as in others'. At other times – during periods of extreme difficulty – we doubt. Today, our reading challenges us to remember our commitment to die with Christ and trust God during periods of unbelief so 'that we will also live with him' (Romans 6.8).

COLLECT

Almighty and eternal God,
who, for the firmer foundation of our faith,
allowed your holy apostle Thomas
    to doubt the resurrection of your Son
till word and sight convinced him:
grant to us, who have not seen, that we also may believe
and so confess Christ as our Lord and our God;
who is alive and reigns with you,
in the unity of the Holy Spirit,
one God, now and for ever.

Psalms 96, **97**, 100
Nehemiah 9.24-end
Romans 16.17-end

Saturday 4 July

Nehemiah 9.24-end

'… yet when they turned and cried to you, you heard from heaven'
(9.28)

Each day is an opportunity to renew afresh our relationship with God. In our daily prayers, we reflect on our words, thoughts and deeds – crying out to a loving God who forgives and liberates us according to his great mercies. We pray for our nation, world leaders and the suffering of others. Because, like Nehemiah we believe in a God who 'saves', 'rescues' and never forsakes his people. This is *our* God!

Special celebrations such as Social Justice Sunday or the World Day of Prayer or Reconciliation Sunday are designed for us to focus *collectively* on national repentance while personally recommitting ourselves to follow God's will. Unity in prayer reminds us that without God's help we often fall short of his plans, but through him all things are possible.

We may never be able to comprehend fully God's love for us; however, when we reflect on all that is good in our nation and lives, we can see God's mercy and faithfulness constantly at work. It's the 'little things' habitually taken for granted – food, water, shelter, clothing, physical health and personal freedom – that Nehemiah associates with God's generous provision. Today, we remember that while the outcome of heartfelt confession is renewal and restoration, the process includes prayer, recommitment, reflection and thankful worship of a merciful God who saves.

O God, the protector of all who trust in you,
without whom nothing is strong, nothing is holy:
increase and multiply upon us your mercy;
that with you as our ruler and guide
we may so pass through things temporal
that we lose not our hold on things eternal;
grant this, heavenly Father,
for our Lord Jesus Christ's sake,
who is alive and reigns with you,
in the unity of the Holy Spirit,
one God, now and for ever.

COLLECT

193

Monday 6 July

2 Corinthians 1.1-14

'For just as the sufferings of Christ are abundant for us, so also our consolation is abundant through Christ' (v.5)

Paul doesn't avoid writing about his sufferings, as he recognizes affliction and persecution as crucial elements of his Christian journey. However, total dependence on Christ – to console every pain, sorrow and affliction – can be challenging for us today, mainly because modern medicine readily offers remedies to counteract physical or emotional pain. Sometimes we may even find ourselves 'desensitized' to the daily sufferings of our Christian brothers and sisters around the world. If we're not careful, they become mere images on mission leaflets or media appeals for money. Alternatively, our concern for the suffering of others in distant places can consume us, making us 'insensitive' to those suffering in our local churches or communities.

Paul's sees his relationship with Christ as his primary curative and relief. As Christians, we share in this sacred connectedness. Even as all are united through a common faith in Jesus, all look to him during periods of rejection, affliction and suffering. And, he empowers *us* to comfort one another (v.4).

When we extend God's divine consolation to others during seasons of great suffering, these encounters produce faith-building testimonies – personal stories – that, when shared, bring consolation to others during times of their greatest need. In our prayers today, we ask the Holy Spirit to make us into anointed vessels of comfort, bringing healing and restoration to others.

COLLECT

Almighty and everlasting God,
by whose Spirit the whole body of the Church
    is governed and sanctified:
hear our prayer which we offer for all your faithful people,
that in their vocation and ministry
they may serve you in holiness and truth
to the glory of your name;
through our Lord and Saviour Jesus Christ,
who is alive and reigns with you,
in the unity of the Holy Spirit,
one God, now and for ever.

Psalms **106*** (*or* 103)
Nehemiah 13.1-14
2 Corinthians 1.15 – 2.4

2 Corinthians 1.15 – 2.4

'For in him every one of God's promises is a "Yes."' (1.20)

We've all experienced disappointment, when we (or someone else) have been unable to keep a promise. Of course, this doesn't mean that the promise was made capriciously, as hindrances often impede our plans daily. So, how do we handle disappointment?

Today, human relationships are fragile – marriages fail, children and the elderly are abandoned, and local neighbourhood friendships are quickly being replaced by 'cyber friendships' existing in remote 'chat rooms'. There are correlations between disappointment, internet usage, social escapism and physical human interaction. How we accept disappointment directly impacts on our rapport with others.

Our reading reminds us that Christian relationships are formed and nurtured *through* Christ *in* the Spirit. These relationships are expected to be loving and trusting, for '...love is not envious or boastful or arrogant or rude' (1 Corinthians 13.4-5). Are we eager to blame others? Do we grumble? Or, do we bear all things, believe all things, hope all things and endure all things? Loving Christian relationships allow room for human failings, while readily extending God's grace to others.

Broken promises need not destroy a relationship. Rather, we avoid making promises we have no intention of keeping, and avoid complaining or thinking less of others when commitments are broken. Spiritual maturity in Christ challenges us to accept, forgive and love one another even during times of great disappointment.

> Almighty God,
> send down upon your Church
> the riches of your Spirit,
> and kindle in all who minister the gospel
> your countless gifts of grace;
> through Jesus Christ our Lord.

COLLECT

Ordinary Time

Wednesday 8 July

Psalms 110, **111**, 112
Nehemiah 13.15-end
2 Corinthians 2.5-end

2 Corinthians 2.5-end

'So I urge you to reaffirm your love ...' (v.8)

How do we resolve relationships breached by conflict? Try as we may, we cannot avoid the tension or difficulties that arise when opinions differ from our own. As we find in many of Paul's letters to the early Church, bringing individuals together from different ethnic, cultural and social backgrounds – and, in some instances, varying religious practices – discord is inevitable!

When conflict occurs, prayerful discernment may reveal that the Holy Spirit is challenging us to 'build bridges', compromise and learn to work eagerly together in identifying viable solutions. We would find our Christian communities quite banal if *everyone* agreed about *everything* all the time. Healthy conflict reveals that we are growing and being 'stretched' outside our comfort zones. In fact, it often means that God is giving us 'fresh wineskins' (Matthew 9.17).

Alternatively, ongoing conflict among Christian brothers and sisters obstructs God's plans for our communities. So, for the sake of Christ and proclamation of the gospel, forgiveness is needed and broken relationships need to be restored. This is not always easy; nevertheless, a genuine effort must be made for reconciliation. Jesus' life-giving sacrifice on the cross reveals the significance of resolution and restoration. His death satisfied the penalty for our sin, and his resurrection restored us to loving relationship with God. Reconciliation requires loving forgiveness, and Jesus has revealed the way for us through his example.

COLLECT

Almighty and everlasting God,
by whose Spirit the whole body of the Church
is governed and sanctified:
hear our prayer which we offer for all your faithful people,
that in their vocation and ministry
they may serve you in holiness and truth
to the glory of your name;
through our Lord and Saviour Jesus Christ,
who is alive and reigns with you,
in the unity of the Holy Spirit,
one God, now and for ever.

2 Corinthians 3

'...how much more will the ministry of the Spirit come in glory?' (v.8)

At some point, we've all listened to the introduction of a speaker with a distinguished list of credentials and then expectantly awaited to be impressed. Why? Are we hoping to receive their message better because of their celebrity or credentials? Like the Corinthian Church, do we (unintentionally) place individuals in a position to recommend themselves or somehow to *prove* their ministerial worthiness to us?

When Paul is placed in the position of recommending himself, he asks, 'Surely we do not need ... letters of recommendation to you or from you, do we?' (v.1). His question may appear strange to us, familiar with the mass-media technological network. We are bombarded daily with messages from '*tele*-evangelists', unsolicited email and 'tweets' recommending worthy initiatives, life-changing ministries, prominent charities and remarkable individuals. However, Paul emphasizes that it is the loving relationships *within* the Church that commend us to each other.

He reminds us that our qualifications in proclaiming the 'good news' come directly from God, and we are free to share the gospel in ways that are most comfortable for us. There is no set format or structure; we simply allow the Holy Spirit to guide us. As we faithfully share our personal stories of our transformation by the gospel story, others will come to see us as mirror reflections of the 'glory of Christ'.

COLLECT

Almighty God,
send down upon your Church
the riches of your Spirit,
and kindle in all who minister the gospel
your countless gifts of grace;
through Jesus Christ our Lord.

Friday 10 July

Psalm **139**
Esther 2
2 Corinthians 4

2 Corinthians 4

*'…since it is by God's mercy that we are engaged in this ministry,
we do not lose heart' (v.1)*

It's hard to understand how our service to others produces treasure in
both us and them. Each day we learn of some new scandal that exposes
human selfishness and our insatiable desire for wealth, prominence and
power. Our generosity when sharing with others provides an alternative
message that speaks to our relationship with Christ – we too have died
to the material lure this world offers.

The *death* Paul writes of in today's reading is analogous to the *life* of a
slave – a lifetime of selfless service to others. A slave begins work early
each morning and concludes late every night. Their life is one where, in
every waking moment, the personal needs and expectations of another
takes precedence over their own. For many of us, it's difficult to imagine
living our lives this way; we might even consider it a *living death*.

The 'extraordinary power' that allows us to serve others selflessly comes
from God (v.7)! It is the same divine power that resurrected Jesus. God
empowers and encourages us, and gives us the resolve to continue to
serve even when we have nothing to gain personally. Rather, our service
to others is an authentic expression of our faith. As we extend God's
grace to others – their praise and thanksgiving mingles with our own,
thereby increasing the glory given to God.

COLLECT

Almighty and everlasting God,
by whose Spirit the whole body of the Church
    is governed and sanctified:
hear our prayer which we offer for all your faithful people,
that in their vocation and ministry
they may serve you in holiness and truth
to the glory of your name;
through our Lord and Saviour Jesus Christ,
who is alive and reigns with you,
in the unity of the Holy Spirit,
one God, now and for ever.

2 Corinthians 5

'For the love of Christ urges us on' (v.14)

What motivates us to serve? Sometimes it is friendship – we enjoy being with friends and those who share our common interests. We enjoy knitting so we form a knitting club and make garments for infant baptisms or donate them to disaster victims.

However, somehow extending loving acceptance is different – it's more personal – or, is it? Christ died to restore *all* humanity to right relationship with God. Understanding this should prompt us to form relationships with those who wouldn't otherwise enter our circle of friends.

We all know at least one person who is quick to point out the personal, shameful actions of another – often revealing their former sins or misdeeds. Little do we know that fear of rejection, ridicule for past deeds, or shame associated with former sin often prevents those who don't know Christ from entering our churches. We all share a common grace – a past buried in the death of Jesus and new life birthed in the love of Christ. Our relationship with him is the common thread that binds us together. Today's reading challenges us to extend the grace we have received to others by becoming more inclusive in our relationships. When we reject those whom God brings through our doors, we also reject the diverse gifts he has given them needed to bless our communities.

Almighty God,
send down upon your Church
the riches of your Spirit,
and kindle in all who minister the gospel
your countless gifts of grace;
through Jesus Christ our Lord.

COLLECT

Monday 13 July

2 Corinthians 6.1 – 7.1

'... having nothing, and yet possessing everything' (6.10)

I've got a new thermos flask. I use it to keep the hot things hot and the cold things cold. In it I've got a cup of coffee. And a choc ice!

Please excuse the lame joke. The moral is that some things don't mix. Paul's straightforward advice for a holy life is to recognize that there are some activities that so deeply compromise our desire to follow Jesus that the only way to deal with them is to reject them altogether. How can you hold together the values of Beliar (a mythical demon whose name meant 'good-for-nothing') and Jesus Christ the Saviour? Well, you can't. They are coffee and choc ice.

There is a paradox in this chapter. God intends us to be part of our society, engaging with and enjoying the company of all. But at the same time he wants us to be set apart, recognisably distinct from people without faith.

Should I befriend someone who uses pornography? Of course, because that is how he or she will observe what difference a relationship with God can make to a life, and that is urgent because 'now is the day of salvation' (v.2). Should I go into a business partnership with someone for whom pornography is a money-spinner? Absolutely not, because that means being yoked together in a way that will inevitably drag Christian standards down.

If only all the distinctions were as blatant as that.

COLLECT

Merciful God,
you have prepared for those who love you
such good things as pass our understanding:
pour into our hearts such love toward you
that we, loving you in all things and above all things,
may obtain your promises,
which exceed all that we can desire;
through Jesus Christ your Son our Lord,
who is alive and reigns with you,
in the unity of the Holy Spirit,
one God, now and for ever.

2 Corinthians 7.2-end

'God, who consoles the downcast' (v.6)

A familiar scene? An email contains news you do not want to hear, so you dash off a furious reply, copying in others. Moments after clicking 'Send', you regret most of what you wrote and hurriedly pick up the phone in the hope of limiting the damage before it escalates.

Twenty centuries ago, with different technology, Paul did precisely that. A letter to the Christians in Corinth, now lost to us, had taken sides in a dispute and been intemperately critical. He regretted it and sent Titus in pursuit to make amends. Titus returned with good news. The Christians had responded with grace. They had been hurt, but instead of reacting with fury, they had paused, tried to understand what had made Paul write, put right what was wrong, and found it in their hearts to appreciate Paul for his integrity and honesty. The result was a healed relationship, a godly change of behaviour, and a burst of encouragement and joy.

There are lessons to learn about trying to work out what was in someone's mind when they slighted us. People rarely do things with no reason. A thought-out reply is almost always better than an immediate one. A spoken reply is usually better than an impersonal one. And as the wise men of Judah knew, a thousand years before Paul wrote to the Corinthians, 'A soft answer turns away wrath' (Proverbs 15.1).

Creator God,
you made us all in your image:
may we discern you in all that we see,
and serve you in all that we do;
through Jesus Christ our Lord.

COLLECT

Wednesday 15 July

2 Corinthians 8.1-15

'Your present abundance and their need' (v.14)

The decades after the resurrection of Jesus, during which the Christian Church expanded, coincided with a devastating famine in which the people of Jerusalem suffered particularly badly. Churches found themselves dealing for the first time with this question: As Christians are we responsible for people in need whom we don't know in places we will never visit?

The answer was an unambiguous 'yes'. Church leaders launched a scheme whereby Christians in flourishing towns could give money that was transported in a trustworthy manner to towns where there was poverty. It is so much part of Christian practice today that we forget there was a first time. But these events were taking place as the first books of the New Testament were being written. Paul's letters were, in part, fundraising appeals.

The Christians in Macedonia got it right. They themselves were relatively poor. But when they heard what was happening in Jerusalem, they knew they had to help. In fact, they gave more than the relatively wealthy Christians in Corinth, which is why Paul wrote the reprimand disguised as an exhortation that we read today. The Church in Macedonia became a model for every succeeding generation of Christians because they wanted to be like their Lord – wholeheartedly generous to a needy world (v.9).

Why should Christians in 2015 give money to allow suffering people to rise out of poverty? Because it makes them like Jesus.

COLLECT

Merciful God,
you have prepared for those who love you
such good things as pass our understanding:
pour into our hearts such love toward you
that we, loving you in all things and above all things,
may obtain your promises,
which exceed all that we can desire;
through Jesus Christ your Son our Lord,
who is alive and reigns with you,
in the unity of the Holy Spirit,
one God, now and for ever.

2 Corinthians 8.16 – 9.5

'... we intend to do what is right' (8.21)

At first sight these verses seem to be someone's private travel arrangements. Paul warned the Christians in Corinth to expect a visit from two men – Titus and a stranger. Paul had chosen them for this journey because they were known for their integrity with money. The Church had organized a financial collection on behalf of famine-stricken Christians in Jerusalem. Titus and his companion were to be the couriers.

However, important principles were being established in this letter. Paul knew that if he was asking Christians to be generous on behalf of the poor, they needed to be confident that every penny would end up in the hands of those for whom it was intended. There is nothing new about worrying that money given for those in need will end up in the pockets of corrupt officials. These were the principles of accountability that Paul established:

– It was not enough to say, 'God knows we are honest people,' but there was to be manifest transparency.
– There were to be two couriers for the money to reduce the risk of one of them absconding.
– They were formally appointed by a committee who knew they had a track record of honourable behaviour.
– They had references provided so that those giving the money could make an informed decision.

Every church treasurer will recognize these principles. They deserve our thanks for maintaining them.

Creator God,
you made us all in your image:
may we discern you in all that we see,
and serve you in all that we do;
through Jesus Christ our Lord.

COLLECT

Friday 17 July

Psalms 142, **144**
Esther 8
2 Corinthians 9.6-end

2 Corinthians 9.6-end

'Thanks be to God for his indescribable gift!' (v.15)

If you give liberally and gladly to work that builds the kingdom of God, you will be blessed by God in return. There is nothing suspicious about that. It is the straightforward truth.

Of course, that truth can be abused. When a preacher tells you that if you give money to his fund, you will get even more in return, you have every reason to distrust him. Giving to God's work is not a lottery in which an outlay now will win you a jackpot later.

So in what sense does this blessing come about? People who have extravagant hearts for God find themselves giving extravagantly. They love doing it. God loves them doing it. The needy people who benefit from the money love it too. Everyone, absolutely everyone, is blessed by generosity.

It is the indescribably lavish giving of God, leaving the wealth of heaven in order to be born among us with nothing, that inspires cheerfully generous giving by those who love him.

Paul originally wrote this letter in Greek, and the word he used for 'cheerful' is *hilarion*. It's not difficult to guess which English word derives from that. The literal translation of verse 7 is: 'God loves a hilarious giver.' It offers a vision of a congregation doubled up with joyful laughter as the collection plate passes along the pews.

Well, Sunday's coming. Why not!

COLLECT

Merciful God,
you have prepared for those who love you
such good things as pass our understanding:
pour into our hearts such love toward you
that we, loving you in all things and above all things,
may obtain your promises,
which exceed all that we can desire;
through Jesus Christ your Son our Lord,
who is alive and reigns with you,
in the unity of the Holy Spirit,
one God, now and for ever.

2 Corinthians 10

'... those whom the Lord commends' (v.18)

At the same time that Paul wrote to the Christians in Corinth, other missionaries were travelling through the region telling the story of what Jesus did. They had a different vision from Paul for what the life of a first-century follower of Jesus should be like. Suppose it had been their version of the faith that endured, what would Christianity be like? It would flee from hard work and mess into a spiritually elevated enclave. It might expect Christians to take part in rituals associated with Judaism. And it would almost certainly be a long-lost sect that only academics have heard of.

Instead, we have the faith that mostly we love and occasionally we are frustrated by. It's the faith that shows its best qualities when it is weak, because when the meekness and gentleness of Jesus are emulated, they are a powerful influence for good (v.1). It's also the faith in which people sometimes shout assertively because they see things happening that will ultimately damage everyone's joy in being human (v.2).

Christian leaders do their best to get the balance right between the two. Sometimes they succeed – hence the love. Sometimes they don't – hence the frustration. How do we tell which is which? One indication is that anyone who is bigging themselves up in the process will never help us discern the mind of God (v.18).

Creator God,
you made us all in your image:
may we discern you in all that we see,
and serve you in all that we do;
through Jesus Christ our Lord.

COLLECT

205

Monday 20 July

2 Corinthians 11.1-15

'... I proclaimed God's good news to you' (v.7)

In the twenty-first century, there are many people trying to attract our attention with answers to the big questions about human existence. There are shops dedicated to spirituality where it's possible to buy a personalized tarot reading or horoscope. There are knocks on the door from personable Mormons or Jehovah's Witnesses. There are psychics claiming special powers who present theatrical evenings of messages from beyond the grave. Are these worth your attention?

There is nothing new about the need to work out whose message to trust and whose to disdain. The Christians to whom Paul wrote were having to make the same judgements. Here are four ways to investigate whether the message you are being given will lead you towards the Way, the Truth and the Life:

- If someone tells you that recent revelations have uncovered more about Jesus than the four Gospels that have sustained the Christian Church for two thousand years, politely take your leave (v.4).

- Examine the content of what people are saying, rather than being captivated by the exhilaration of the presentation (v.6).

- If you are asked to purchase an experience that will give you enlightenment, it's likely that you are being sold a fake. Salvation is God's free gift (v.7).

- Do some investigation and find out who is funding an event so that you are not deceived by something that uses the language of mainstream Christianity but is actually an unhelpful variant (v.9).

COLLECT

Lord of all power and might,
the author and giver of all good things:
graft in our hearts the love of your name,
increase in us true religion,
nourish us with all goodness,
and of your great mercy keep us in the same;
through Jesus Christ your Son our Lord,
who is alive and reigns with you,
in the unity of the Holy Spirit,
one God, now and for ever.

2 Corinthians 11.16-end

'I am under daily pressure.' (v.28)

In Greek mythology, Hercules slew giants, captured beasts and fathered enough children to fill a primary school. If you lived in Corinth in the first century, you were brought up with that as your role model for heroism. So it was obvious what a Christian leader should do to earn your respect. He should order you around, swagger like a grandee and slap you if you stepped out of line. There were Christians in Corinth asserting their leadership by doing just that (v.20).

At the same time there was a puny little guy who kept getting arrested, flogged, starved, betrayed, and when he had a chance to stand up and fight preferred to escape by hiding in a vegetable basket (vv.24-33). Pah!

However, something unexpected happened after Paul wrote these words. The leadership style that he espoused became the one that allowed the Christian faith to prosper.

Occasionally during the history of the faith, Christian leaders have made attempts to establish their authority using the Hercules method. Without exception they have been catastrophic. Think of the Crusades, the Spanish Inquisition or any number of warmongers.

In contrast, unchurched people come to faith when what Paul jokingly called 'weak' Christians share their lives and stories with their friends. Why? Because people the world over respond to integrity. Staying faithful to Jesus through hardship speaks powerfully of the blessing of going through life in the company of a good and loving God.

Generous God,
you give us gifts and make them grow:
though our faith is small as mustard seed,
make it grow to your glory
and the flourishing of your kingdom;
through Jesus Christ our Lord.

COLLECT

Wednesday 22 July

Mary Magdalene

Psalms 30, 32, 150
I Samuel 16.14-end
Luke 8.1-3

Luke 8.1-3

'... bringing the good news' (v.1)

It is possible to romanticize the circumstances in which Jesus' travelling ministry took place. We tend to picture him and his twelve disciples as if they were Robin Hood and his merry men, living hand-to-mouth under the open skies, sustained by sympathetic locals who rustled together a few leeks and onions to make a pot roast.

The truth was far from that. Jesus' project was disciplined, organized and paid for. The Bible tells us who sustained it. There was a group of women who, with great generosity, did the practical things that were necessary to allow Jesus and his entourage to focus on preaching and healing.

We know the names of some of them. Joanna was the prosperous one. Her husband was the manager of King Herod's household. There is a great irony that money earned by Chuza for maintaining that place of cruelty was leaving the palace through a back entrance and being recycled into good news for the poor.

It is hard to imagine, though, that Mary Magdalene was wealthy. Having lost her way through life, she had been calmed from a mental illness by Jesus. But it is clear that she was not just receiving Jesus' help. She was contributing financially to his work.

And what of Susanna? All that is known of her is this solitary reference to giving. Was she rich or poor? She could be you!

COLLECT

Almighty God,
whose Son restored Mary Magdalene to health of mind and body
and called her to be a witness to his resurrection:
forgive our sins and heal us by your grace,
that we may serve you in the power of his risen life;
who is alive and reigns with you,
in the unity of the Holy Spirit,
one God, now and for ever.

Psalms 14, **15**, 16
Jeremiah 30.1-11
2 Corinthians 13

2 Corinthians 13

'Do you not realize that Jesus Christ is in you?' (v.5)

There was a verb in Greek whose literal meaning was 'to act like you're in Corinth'. It meant to get up to no good on a Friday night, if you catch my drift. It shows the kind of reputation the city of Corinth had. It was like living in ... well, most cities on a Friday night in 2015.

The followers of Jesus, then as now, were called to have distinctive lifestyles. In the letters Paul wrote to the recently converted Christians of Corinth, he repeatedly had to tell them that, although they had a new faith, it wasn't being matched by a new set of standards. In particular, they were still acting as though Jesus' teaching made no difference to their sexual relationships, their arguments, and the way rich and poor regarded each other.

But what was Paul to do about it? As we have been reading, other leaders had addressed the issue by lording it over the believers. Paul was considering visiting in person with an uncompromising approach, but he was genuinely reluctant to do so (v.10). Better far would be for the Christians to reflect on their lives, consider what Jesus had done for them, and make the changes needed out of sheer gratitude to their Saviour (v.5). Paul's message reverberates down the centuries because having a lifestyle that is not merely self-pleasing can stand out in a city (or just in a family) and offer a rich and fulfilling alternative.

Lord of all power and might,
the author and giver of all good things:
graft in our hearts the love of your name,
increase in us true religion,
nourish us with all goodness,
and of your great mercy keep us in the same;
through Jesus Christ your Son our Lord,
who is alive and reigns with you,
in the unity of the Holy Spirit,
one God, now and for ever.

COLLECT

209

Friday 24 July

Psalms 17, **19**
Jeremiah 30.12-22
James 1.1-11

James 1.1-11

'... the testing of your faith produces endurance' (v.3)

Tradition has it that this letter was written by the James who was a relative of Jesus and leader of the Church in Jerusalem. Scholarship questions that. But if it's true, it was written in a setting of urgent poverty. Jerusalem was the famine-afflicted city for which Paul organized the appeal about which we read last week. If someone from that context writes that there are reasons to be joyful in the face of immense difficulty, we can be sure that he speaks from experience, not from easy piety.

It would be understandable if someone beleaguered with poverty recommended praying for money. But instead the writer urges people to pray that they will become wise (v.5). To be wise is a spiritual matter and it allows us to know the ways of God. But wisdom is also a practical matter and it shapes the day-to-day business of living as a follower of Jesus. Wealth cannot help us do either of those.

So if God is generous in making those who worship him wise, why do Christians keep making asses of themselves? Because we so often fail to be single-minded about wanting everything we do to be permeated by God's wisdom (v.6). If half our mind is set on God's values, but the other half cannot let go of the world's values, we will be as restless as a storm on the sea.

COLLECT

Lord of all power and might,
the author and giver of all good things:
graft in our hearts the love of your name,
increase in us true religion,
nourish us with all goodness,
and of your great mercy keep us in the same;
through Jesus Christ your Son our Lord,
who is alive and reigns with you,
in the unity of the Holy Spirit,
one God, now and for ever.

Psalms 7, 29, 117
2 Kings 1.9-15
Luke 9.46-56

Luke 9.46-56

'... he turned and rebuked them' (v.55)

This was not the first time there had been a tense stand-off on the hill outside this Samaritan village. Seven centuries earlier King Ahaziah had broken his hip. He sent troops to the shrine of the god Baal to have his fortune told. On the way they encountered Elijah, who was enraged that they planned to worship a meaningless god. When they tried to arrest him he called down fire from the sky, which incinerated them. You can read the story in 2 Kings 1.

Now the villagers were insulting Jesus in the same way that Elijah had been abused all those years before. James and John must have been told the story in their childhood. They were outraged on behalf of their friend, dismissing the Samaritans as a half-caste tribe who had no idea of the significance of the man at their gates. Surely it was time for another inferno.

Jesus too was furious. However he wasn't angry with the villagers, but with his own disciples. Revenge had no place in his plan for humankind, and has no place in the lives of his followers today. Instead, Jesus turned his face toward another hill. There he would submit to brutality on behalf of an entire needy world.

Where does greatness lie? Not in the bravado of violent men, but in the kindness of those who take a stand on behalf of the needy, the despised or the young (v.48).

Merciful God,
whose holy apostle Saint James,
leaving his father and all that he had,
was obedient to the calling of your Son Jesus Christ
and followed him even to death:
help us, forsaking the false attractions of the world,
to be ready at all times to answer your call without delay;
through Jesus Christ your Son our Lord,
who is alive and reigns with you,
in the unity of the Holy Spirit,
one God, now and for ever.

COLLECT

Monday 27 July

Psalms 27, **30**
Jeremiah 31.23-25, 27-37
James 2.1-13

James 2.1-13

'You do well if you really fulfil the royal law ...' (v.8)

The French Revolution's cry of 'Liberty, Equality, Fraternity' seems unexpectedly to find a precursor here in the Letter of James. God in Christ, according to James, has called Christians to 'the law of *liberty*'. And what is this law of liberty? It is to show no favouritism; to avoid making distinctions on the grounds of wealth or social status; to put such distinctions away forever. *Equality* is its watchword: equality of regard. And what is to be the fruit of this equality of regard? Love and mercy. These create the special bond of Christian fellowship whose French Revolutionary equivalent was *fraternity*.

Where the French Revolutionary would surely baulk, however, is in the claim that this 'law of liberty' is also a 'royal' law. What has royalty to do with such ideals? Why talk of kingship in the same breath as saying we must make no social distinctions?

Yet here is the secret: this is the true royalty that puts a revolutionary end to all the most unjust or self-serving pretensions of earthly rule. It is not the royalty that the Judges in ancient Israel knew was a dangerous burden for the people to take upon themselves: a royalty so easily corrupted. It is the royalty that alone guarantees the mercy, the love, the freedom from favouritism that allows humans to flourish together, while even the most high-minded revolutionaries fall back into being victims of their own 'evil thoughts'. It is the royalty of the crucified.

COLLECT

Almighty Lord and everlasting God,
we beseech you to direct, sanctify and govern
    both our hearts and bodies
in the ways of your laws
    and the works of your commandments;
that through your most mighty protection, both here and ever,
we may be preserved in body and soul;
through our Lord and Saviour Jesus Christ,
who is alive and reigns with you,
in the unity of the Holy Spirit,
one God, now and for ever.

James 2.14-end

'… just as the body without the spirit is dead, so faith without works is also dead' (v.26)

You cannot have the Spirit without the Son. This is what Christians have believed for centuries, on the basis that it is the Son, in John's Gospel, who promises to send the Holy Spirit, as a guide and comforter after he is gone. In theological terms, it is often said that the sanctification (the making holy) that the Spirit works in the lives of believers is only possible because of the justification (the reclaiming of sinners for God) that the Son accomplishes on the Cross. No grass, no milk, as the dairy farmer might put it. No justification, no sanctification.

What James wants us to know is that it runs the other way too. You cannot have the Son without the Spirit. The Son might give grounds for a proclamation of justification that is no more than a proclamation: uneaten grass. The truth of the good news is only fully known – only fully *real* – when the grass is eaten and the milk follows. The Son, though the incarnate one, becomes (ironically) the subject of a disembodied and abstract message until the Spirit – who has no body – begins to flesh out that message in the deeds of Christ's followers.

Lord God,
your Son left the riches of heaven
and became poor for our sake:
when we prosper save us from pride,
when we are needy save us from despair,
that we may trust in you alone;
through Jesus Christ our Lord.

COLLECT

James 3

'... the tongue is a small member, yet it boasts of great exploits' (v.5)

If asked to name people who occupy positions of power, we might first describe decision-makers: politicians, heads of corporations, bank managers. Every tax bill and every traffic light is a reminder that someone with the power to do so has made a decision about our lives. But there are other kinds of power, and a key one – a kind of power that even decision-makers depend on – is the power of description. Without a good description, a good decision is hard to make. And objective descriptions are hard to come by: every description has an angle.

The tongue is a small part of our bodies, but as the Letter of James reminds us, it has immense influence, and this is partly because of its power to tell the truth or to distort it. The lying tongue is such a dangerous force in our world because it describes falsely. One fake call to the emergency services in the middle of the night can mean that someone else loses a loved one.

We use our tongues to tell others 'how things are', and this is a wonderful but grave responsibility, one that has special claims on parents, on preachers, on teachers, on journalists, on scholars.

If we manage to fool ourselves that no one is influencing us, we no longer pay attention to who is telling us what we think are facts. But we are also influencing others whenever we offer our own descriptions of things. So we should mind our tongues.

COLLECT

Almighty Lord and everlasting God,
we beseech you to direct, sanctify and govern
    both our hearts and bodies
in the ways of your laws
    and the works of your commandments;
that through your most mighty protection, both here and ever,
we may be preserved in body and soul;
through our Lord and Saviour Jesus Christ,
who is alive and reigns with you,
in the unity of the Holy Spirit,
one God, now and for ever.

Psalm **37***
Jeremiah 33.14-end
James 4.1-12

James 4.1-12

'Draw near to God, and he will draw near to you.' (v.8)

'You do not have, because you do not ask', says the Letter of James (v.2). Could asking be somehow a way of life? A disposition of the soul? In his poem *Frost at Midnight*, Coleridge addresses his sleeping infant son, and anticipates hopefully that God will make him an asker:

*'Great universal Teacher! he shall mould
Thy spirit, and by giving make it ask.'*

It's a peculiar construction, because it makes 'ask' into an intransitive verb. There is no specific object of the asking. Coleridge's assumption is simply that it is good for a human being to be open to receiving, and open to what comes. This is a receptivity to grace, but not a pre-emption of it. It is the agency of availability.

What would this mean in our own lives: to exist 'askingly'? The paradox of Christian living is that action is unavoidable, but that we attribute even our acting to God's action in us. Our language struggles to accommodate this paradox, though there are moments (especially in worship) when we come close. 'Ascribe to the Lord the glory due his name ...' (Psalm 96.8). Ascribing is an act that subverts its own agency by giving all to another – a drawing near to God so that God may draw near to us.

Indeed, in all worship, we learn to be 'prone' to God, and this is perfectly captured in those most familiar words 'Let us pray ...'.

Lord God,
your Son left the riches of heaven
and became poor for our sake:
when we prosper save us from pride,
when we are needy save us from despair,
that we may trust in you alone;
through Jesus Christ our Lord.

COLLECT

Friday 31 July

James 4.13 – 5.6

'... the cries of the harvesters have reached the ears of the Lord of hosts' (5.4)

Here, in chapter 5, verse 4, the rich are called to 'Listen!'. To what are they meant to listen? At one level – as always when the Lord speaks – it is a call to listen to the voice of God. But in this passage, as in so much of the law given to Moses, there is an extra twist. The rich are called to listen to what God listens to. Indeed, listening to what God listens to is – in this situation – the form that listening to God actually takes.

What God listens to is the cry of the oppressed. The rich are thus called to listen to the voice of those who are their own victims, and to do this as a mode of listening to God.

God hears the cry of the oppressed as a parent hears the cry of his or her own child. Even in a busy place full of noise, or even when they are asleep, the cry of a child has an extraordinary power to penetrate the consciousness of its parents. God hears the oppressed in that sort of way.

What the rich must do is attune their ears accordingly – filtering out all the reassuring background noise that shields them from the effects of their own actions. They must learn to hear as God hears – to learn to *relate* to those who labour on their behalf.

COLLECT

Almighty Lord and everlasting God,
we beseech you to direct, sanctify and govern
    both our hearts and bodies
in the ways of your laws
    and the works of your commandments;
that through your most mighty protection, both here and ever,
we may be preserved in body and soul;
through our Lord and Saviour Jesus Christ,
who is alive and reigns with you,
in the unity of the Holy Spirit,
one God, now and for ever.

James 5.7-end

'The farmer waits for the precious crop from the earth' (v.7)

This passage presents us with a conundrum. It suggests that prayer is answered (especially, in this case, prayer for the sick) in real and healing ways. 'The prayer of the righteous is powerful and effective' (v.16). But it makes the prelude to this claim a series of injunctions to learn from those who are especially patient – those who are models of how to wait. Be like a farmer, the passage says; be like a prophet; be like Job.

This is to capture two aspects of the experience of prayer, both of which are well and widely attested to in the Christian Church. There are very many Christians who will testify with joy to the fact that they have known their prayers to be answered and felt the effectiveness of God's grace powerfully in their lives. But there are others who have dwelt in a dark night of the soul, questioning where God is and what God's will might be.

I am not sure that the Letter of James wants to resolve the apparent tension between these two aspects of prayer; equally, it does not want to deny either type of experience. Christians are to pray with a patience that sets no ultimatums. And yet … they are to pray in the real expectation of an answer. The waiting that strains forward needs accompaniment by a straining forward that knows how to wait.

Lord God,
your Son left the riches of heaven
and became poor for our sake:
when we prosper save us from pride,
when we are needy save us from despair,
that we may trust in you alone;
through Jesus Christ our Lord.

COLLECT

Monday 3 August

Mark 1.1-13

'... and he was with the wild beasts; and the angels waited on him'
(v. 13)

This passage begins with John the Baptist in the wilderness and ends with Jesus in the wilderness.

These two kinsmen had a lot in common in terms of their message – even though the Baptist cuts a more rough-and-ready figure. They wanted to give people a sense of the primordial goods of life, and a suspicion of some of the constructions of human society that make life more complicated than it should be. Locusts and wild honey were probably not some sort of penitential diet for John – they were quite rich and nourishing fare. The real point was that they weren't farmed or sold at market; they were part of God's bounty in nature. Jesus would later celebrate that same bounty when he invited his followers not to be over-anxious about how they would clothe or feed themselves, and asked them to consider the example of lilies and birds (Matthew 6.26,28).

Even the wilderness immediately around the Jordan where John preached and baptized wasn't (and isn't) arid and desert-like either; it is quite lush and verdant.

So perhaps John and Jesus offer us reminders of Eden – the fundamental goodness of creation – in which humans, wild beasts and angels all coexist well with one another. We can live well on what God provides, if we do not live with too much fear or with too much greed.

COLLECT

Almighty God,
who sent your Holy Spirit
to be the life and light of your Church:
open our hearts to the riches of your grace,
that we may bring forth the fruit of the Spirit
in love and joy and peace;
through Jesus Christ your Son our Lord,
who is alive and reigns with you,
in the unity of the Holy Spirit,
one God, now and for ever.

Psalms **48**, 52
Jeremiah 37
Mark 1.14-20

Tuesday 4 August

Mark 1.14-20

'... and his brother John' (v.19)

Right from the start of his ministry, Jesus begins to subvert and play with our assumptions about those to whom we are related; those to whom we have obligations; those to whom we belong. The poor and the socially repugnant are celebrated as *near* to God. Jews are asked to accept that Samaritans are their neighbours. Gentiles, tax-collectors and women are shown special treatment by Jesus. Perhaps most dramatically of all, the natural family is redefined. All who love God and do his will are Jesus' mother and brothers and sisters.

Traditional Jewish interpretation of Scripture (and a long Christian tradition too) makes the distinction between plain-sense readings and deep-sense readings of the text. Perhaps Jesus wants us to think about 'deep-sense family' (spiritual family) and not suppose that the only meaning of family is the 'plain-sense' (natural) one.

However, Jewish interpreters will also insist that deep-sense readings do not undo or replace plain-sense ones; they extend and deepen them, and are based on them. It is very striking that the Jesus who preached a radical reconsideration of what the meaning of 'family' might be also called two pairs of ('natural') brothers as some of his first disciples: Simon and Andrew, James and John. Even this moment of radical decision, dramatic in its reconfigurations of relationship, is not in every way a break. Family bonds are both sundered and preserved – our kith and kin given back in a new light.

Gracious Father,
revive your Church in our day,
and make her holy, strong and faithful,
for your glory's sake
in Jesus Christ our Lord.

COLLECT

Wednesday 5 August

Mark 1.21-28

'What have you to do with us?' (v.24)

People are waking up to Jesus' 'authority'. It is more than that he says knowledgeable and interesting things; he has power to change people and situations by his interventions. Here, even the unclean spirit whom Jesus confronts acknowledges his authority, calling him the Holy One of God. But what – in this situation – does Jesus do with his authority?

He turns an incoherence at the heart of the possessed man into a coherence. Like Tolkien's Gollum, this unclean spirit calls himself 'us', and when the possessed man is addressed by Jesus, it is this 'us' who responds. After the exorcism, the man is restored to being an 'I'.

Could part of the authority that Jesus exercises be the power to turn our possession by many voices into a settled attachment in which we truly become ourselves? Does he deliver us from being multiply torn, divided people, into the state of being true persons, whose hearts, in a much-loved phrase from the Anglican Collect for the Third Sunday before Lent, are 'surely fixed where lasting joys are to be found'?

Straight after this incident, the elaborations and distortions of many chattering tongues kick in once again, and the authority of Jesus becomes gossiped abroad as 'fame'. Perhaps the rumour-mongers and wonder-seekers who begin to spread this 'fame' of Jesus around the region have their own 'possession' to overcome before they can find the still centre in which the healed demoniac now has his peace.

COLLECT

Almighty God,
who sent your Holy Spirit
to be the life and light of your Church:
open our hearts to the riches of your grace,
that we may bring forth the fruit of the Spirit
in love and joy and peace;
through Jesus Christ your Son our Lord,
who is alive and reigns with you,
in the unity of the Holy Spirit,
one God, now and for ever.

Psalms 27, 150
Ecclesiasticus 48.1-10
or I Kings 19.1-16
I John 3.1-3

1 John 3.1-3

'... what we will be has not yet been revealed' (v.2)

The very first chapter of this epistle – the First Letter of John – begins by celebrating what has been revealed in Christ. 'We declare to you what was from the beginning, what we have heard, what we have seen with our eyes, what we have looked at and touched with our hands, concerning the word of life – this life was revealed, and we have seen it.' It is all in the past tense. It is all about the 'givens' of revelation that help us to orientate ourselves in the present moment. They are vital points by which we steer.

But two chapters later, the emphasis has shifted to the future, to 'what has not yet been revealed'. This is a crucial reminder that the Christian life is not all about the 'given'; it must be radically open to what is yet to be 'found'.

There can be something off-puttingly complacent about a Christianity that thinks it has the answer to everything already, so that in any new situation all it has to do is to root around in its bundle of 'givens' in order to produce just the right answer for just the right occasion, all ready-made. But the God who has stocked our backpacks for the journey also places things up ahead of us on the road – and both the givens and the founds are equally 'of God'.

Father in heaven,
whose Son Jesus Christ was wonderfully transfigured
before chosen witnesses upon the holy mountain,
and spoke of the exodus he would accomplish at Jerusalem:
give us strength so to hear his voice and bear our cross
that in the world to come we may see him as he is;
who is alive and reigns with you,
in the unity of the Holy Spirit,
one God, now and for ever.

COLLECT

221

Mark 2.1-12

*'… some people came, bringing to him a paralysed man,
carried by four of them' (v.3)*

It's often said by Christianity's despisers that Christianity, like all religion, is a 'crutch'. Religious people, it's said, cannot stand on their own two feet. They cannot cope with life's demands like mature people who have learnt to take responsibility for themselves: to think and act by their own lights.

So what model of being a human well do these crutch-haters have in mind? It is a model that owes a great deal to the Enlightenment, and to give it a little more thought is to begin to realize that it has disturbing undertones. It presupposes that the normal state of the human being is to be healthy, self-sufficient and independent of others. Children, the elderly, the sick, the disabled are all departures from this norm, and patterns of life can ensue that make few concessions to them.

Actually, none of us can be this norm consistently, at every point in our lives – and the Christian model of being a human well makes this a cause for celebration. It is not as those who deny their need of others that Christians find blessing, but as members of the Church where all, at different times, carry one another, and in which this interdependence is the norm. The bringing of the paralysed man to Jesus by his friends is a scene of exceptional tenderness and tenacity that shows something profound about the best that humans can be.

COLLECT

Almighty God,
who sent your Holy Spirit
to be the life and light of your Church:
open our hearts to the riches of your grace,
that we may bring forth the fruit of the Spirit
in love and joy and peace;
through Jesus Christ your Son our Lord,
who is alive and reigns with you,
in the unity of the Holy Spirit,
one God, now and for ever.

Psalm **68**
Jeremiah 40
Mark 2.13-22

Mark 2.13-22

'Those who are well have no need of a physician,
but those who are sick' (v.17)

There are many models of what salvation is in the Christian tradition:
being liberated by a victory over death and the devil; being ransomed
from slavery; having one's sins expiated by sacrificial offering; being let
off in a court of law; and many more. They all have scriptural licence.

Although it is tucked away in what is almost a passing remark, Jesus
here offers us one of the most important of all, though it is sometimes
neglected. Salvation is healing. This is a precious safeguard against a
moralizing gospel in which it is secretly implied that we ought to pull
ourselves together and try harder. Sin is a condition of woundedness
or sickness.

St Augustine of Hippo (354–430) knew this well, as he showed when
he described the condition of being a sinner by analogy with the figure
of the man left beaten and half-dead by the side of the road in the
story of the Good Samaritan. The man had no power to help himself.
He needed radical care from beyond his own resources.

If we read this passage from Mark chapter 2 alongside the story of
the Good Samaritan, we see that our need of Christ to heal us is as
absolute as our need of God to create us in the first place – which is
why Levi's calling is like a sort of new creation, in which he even
receives a new name.

Gracious Father,
revive your Church in our day,
and make her holy, strong and faithful,
for your glory's sake
in Jesus Christ our Lord.

COLLECT

Monday 10 August

Mark 2.23 – 3.6

*'The sabbath was made for humankind,
and not humankind for the sabbath' (v.27)*

A friend of mine, and a biblical scholar, says that if you want to understand Jesus, you have to appreciate that he was a bit of a rebel when it comes to Judaism. My friend blames Joseph and Mary for this. It was the way they raised him.

We know that by working in Joseph's trade – carpentry and building – Jesus had, by living in Nazareth, been exposed to the nearby Roman settlement of Sepphoris. This was a Hellenized community of almost 30,000, compared to the population of Nazareth, which boasted a mere 300. So Nazareth was a dormitory village supplying labour to a much larger cosmopolitan community nearby. It would have been full of gentiles of every kind. So, from an early age, Jesus would have been exposed to a world beyond his native parochial Judaism.

The theatre at Sepphoris seated 5,000. It is almost certain that Joseph took Jesus there. For in his adult life, Jesus uses the Greek word 'hypocrite' quite a few times, which simply means 'actor' – one who is masked and playing a part. Jesus has got no time in his adult life for a religion that is merely being acted out and gets in the way of commonsense compassion. The sabbath is for humanity, not humanity for the sabbath.

This is not orthodox Judaism. Indeed, some would say that Jesus was a bad Jew. But he embodies good religion. That's why Jesus often praised gentiles for their faith, and often scolded the apparently 'orthodox' belief of his kith and kin for its insularity and purity. Jesus saw that God was for everyone; he lived, practised and preached this.

COLLECT

Let your merciful ears, O Lord,
be open to the prayers of your humble servants;
and that they may obtain their petitions
make them to ask such things as shall please you;
through Jesus Christ your Son our Lord,
who is alive and reigns with you,
in the unity of the Holy Spirit,
one God, now and for ever.

Psalm **73**
Jeremiah 42
Mark 3.7-19*a*

Mark 3.7-19*a*

'Jesus departed with his disciples to the lake' (v.7)

Jesus had reasons for spending time at the Sea of Galilee. It's the politics and geography that give the clue. The western shore was predominantly Jewish; the eastern shore was mainly gentile, with borders on Gaulanitis and Decapolis. Perea and the Jordan valley are also within striking distance, as was the eastern part of Samaria. Why might this matter?

Simply because we see that Jesus' ministry starts by reaching not only into Judaism, but also reaching out to regions and tribes beyond Judaism. You can see this in the healing miracles of Jesus – a Canaanite girl, a Samaritan woman or a Roman centurion's servant. It is there in parables, too, with Jesus constantly teaching us about the edges and those beyond them; all those on the other side of the shore.

The kingdom of God, initiated and embodied in Jesus, begins both by and in international waters; for that is what the Sea of Galilee was. The kingdom Jesus proclaims will be open to the peoples and lands outside Judea. The gospel is radically inclusive: Jew, Greek, gentile, slave, free – all shall be welcome in the kingdom of God.

The ministry of Jesus, simply by making a start at the Sea of Galilee, carries a strong but often hidden message. And it is this: God brings us all together. He's all done with working through a single tribe or race. The Church that begins at Pentecost has been dress-rehearsed in Jesus' ministry: it will be multilingual, multicultural and multiracial. It will be multiple. Yet we, though being many, are one body.

> Lord of heaven and earth,
> as Jesus taught his disciples to be persistent in prayer,
> give us patience and courage never to lose hope,
> but always to bring our prayers before you;
> through Jesus Christ our Lord.

COLLECT

Wednesday 12 August

Mark 3.19*b*-end

'... he has gone out of his mind' (v.21).

We should not be surprised that the disruption Jesus' ministry caused – to the prevailing culture, society and faith of his day – prompts onlookers and commentators to surmise that this is the work of Satan. Jesus' critics are searching for an explanation of what is going on. The key to understanding their concerns lies in the telling comment that he (Jesus) 'has gone out of his mind' (v.21). And that is why the family of Jesus effectively try to serve a detention order on him: 'they went out to restrain him' (v.21).

But Jesus' ministry is not madness. Or evil. This is the arrival of the kingdom of God. And this entails letting out, freeing and liberating lots of issues, infirmities and people that have, hitherto, been locked up. But it is hugely traumatic and disruptive for wider society. People living with tormenting afflictions are suddenly, beautifully, wildly and wonderfully free. For the onlookers, this is unsettling, to say the least. Even today, when the mad start to say they are completely cured, we tend to proceed with caution. It was no different in Jesus' day. When the patients revert to being people again, society has suddenly to readjust. Sometimes it is easier to keep the delineations clear between sick and well, sane and insane. But Jesus, by healing so many afflicted people, radically reorders society. Some would prefer to restrain Jesus at this point, or say that he has gone out of his mind and has an unclean spirit. Jesus' response is simple: whoever does the will of God is my kindred (v.35).

COLLECT

Let your merciful ears, O Lord,
be open to the prayers of your humble servants;
and that they may obtain their petitions
make them to ask such things as shall please you;
through Jesus Christ your Son our Lord,
who is alive and reigns with you,
in the unity of the Holy Spirit,
one God, now and for ever.

Psalm **78.1-39***
Jeremiah 44.1-14
Mark 4.1-20

Mark 4.1-20

'Other seed fell into good soil' (v.8)

Like many parables, this one – the 'Parable of the Sower' – has been misnamed in the subheading. This parable is not about the sower or seed. It is about soil. The question it poses for your life, or perhaps your ministry, is simple: what kind of ground have you got to work with? Not everyone has fertile soil that produces a rich and abundant crop. Some have stony ground. Others have soil choked with fast-growing weeds or plagued by predatory birds that take the seeds. Some get lovely soil; everything grows. Some have it hard-going; others, a mixture.

What does the parable invite us to do here? Three things, I think. First, be honest about what your and your neighbours' soil is like. Not all soils are the same; some are receptive to seed, and some are not. Second, be generous to those who have less than you. If you are part of a wonderful, growing church, rejoice. But do remember those who toil in ground that is less receptive and much tougher – and don't assume that your growth and harvest are linked to your faithfulness, talent or success. Others are working just as hard and faithfully, but are toiling in much harsher conditions. Third, remember that the soil can be changed. No one wants to spend their life picking up rocks and stones. But sometimes, this very slow, patient work creates the conditions for better soil. Can you help your neighbour here?

So, don't be jealous of the growth of others, or despise those with less than you. This parable is saying that God intends to plant everywhere. And the onus is on the fruitful places to share what they have with those toiling in the less easy soil.

> Lord of heaven and earth,
> as Jesus taught his disciples to be persistent in prayer,
> give us patience and courage never to lose hope,
> but always to bring our prayers before you;
> through Jesus Christ our Lord.

COLLECT

Friday 14 August

Psalm **55**
Jeremiah 44.15-end
Mark 4.21-34

Mark 4.21-34

'... nor is anything secret, except to come to light' (v.22)

George Fox, one of the early leaders of Quakerism, instructed his followers to 'turn within to meet the light, and then wait in that which is pure'. This might seem like strange advice, but there is a link between the lighting and the waiting – or, as Jesus suggests, between the lampstand and growth. Illumination and patience are related. The secret of a deepening discipleship is, as Fox knew, to allow the cultivation of inward journeying, growth and transformation. To move on with God, and to go deeper, requires a listening and a certain kind of openness.

There is no formula for this, strictly speaking. It is not something to be 'done', 'achieved', 'realized' or 'made to happen'. It is, rather, something about being in the waiting. Understanding, perhaps, that as we wait, God will slowly shine a light on what is hidden and what needs attention or even correction. So as our hearts become prepared – letting God work through the purity, silence and quality of illumination that comes through listening and patient attention – so we find growth.

Consider then, how God might teach you. Sometimes God speaks to us through the smallest things, in order to remind us that the weak and foolish things of the world can often be his lively oracles. So if God can speak through Balaam's ass (Numbers 22), he might be able to say something to you through an acquaintance whose opinion you might not normally seek – or even a colleague that you wouldn't normally consider your equal. Listening, then, to the voice of God, requires humility and openness on our part. We do not know from whom or where he will say something. Sometimes light and growth begin with the smallest seed.

COLLECT

Let your merciful ears, O Lord,
be open to the prayers of your humble servants;
and that they may obtain their petitions
make them to ask such things as shall please you;
through Jesus Christ your Son our Lord,
who is alive and reigns with you,
in the unity of the Holy Spirit,
one God, now and for ever.

Psalms 98, 138, 147.1-12
Isaiah 7.10-15
Luke 11.27-28

Saturday 15 August

The Blessed Virgin Mary

Luke 11.27-28

'Blessed is the womb that bore you and the breasts that nursed you!'
(v.27)

This is the day when large numbers of Christians the world over celebrate the Assumption of the Blessed Virgin Mary. Like Elijah, she does not die in the usual sense, but is simply taken up into heaven. Because they are so holy and so pure, they are simply lifted from our sight at the end of their lives, rather than buried in the ground. Whatever you think of the doctrine, the reading turns on a single word: 'blessed'.

It is for this reason that the curious aphorism of Jesus – 'it is more blessed to give than to receive' – is so interesting. It is one of those unusual texts that does not appear in the Gospels. This saying comes at the end of a long speech from Paul (Acts 20.35), in which he declares that he has given everything he has to give.

We should not be surprised that holiness and piety are linked to gifts and giving, rather than abstinence and withdrawal. In the Christian faith, true religion is judged not by its seeds but by its fruits. Christianity is known by what is reaped, not what is sown; holiness is found in the bounty of harvest. It is not judged by its origins, but by its ends. So Christians only have one thing to invest: their lives. The only possession we have – ourselves – is asked to be surrendered. And we cannot truly give until we give up ourselves.

'God rules creation by blessing' claimed the rabbis of Jesus' day. Truly, it *is* more blessed to give than to receive. And that is what we remember today, with Mary. As she surrenders and gives her all, she is able to say 'my soul proclaims the greatness of the Lord'.

Almighty God,
who looked upon the lowliness of the Blessed Virgin Mary
and chose her to be the mother of your only Son:
grant that we who are redeemed by his blood
may share with her in the glory of your eternal kingdom;
through Jesus Christ your Son our Lord,
who is alive and reigns with you,
in the unity of the Holy Spirit,
one God, now and for ever.

COLLECT

229

Monday 17 August

Psalms **80**, 82
Micah 1.1-9
Mark 5.1-20

Mark 5.1-20

'Go home to your friends ...' (v.19)

The healing of the Gerasene demoniac is one of the more dramatic Gospel accounts. As is often the case, the best details of the story are implied rather than explicit. It takes place on the eastern shore of the Sea of Galilee – an overwhelmingly gentile area, which helps explain the pigs that would not be found in Jewish territory. So here is Jesus, again, reaching out to the gentiles.

But it is perhaps the unnamed demoniac who is most interesting. He has been chained up in a graveyard by the villagers. In their attempts to keep him confined and imprisoned among the tombs, we are given a real insight into social exclusion. This man has been banished from his community, and has almost no contact with people. So Jesus seeks out not only a demoniac in gentile territory – but, by implication, visits someone that even an excluded community has marginalized.

What happens next is astounding. The healed man – sensibly and reasonably – begs Jesus to take him with him. After all, why would you, as an ex-demoniac, want to return to the village that had excluded you and chained you up in the tombs? But Jesus refuses and insists on the demoniac returning to the community that expelled him from their midst.

Unsurprisingly, the villagers beg Jesus to leave. They have had quite enough disruption for one day. I imagine they went home, double-locked their doors and windows, and drew the curtains. I imagine the demoniac returning to his home village later, hoping for a meal and a bed from some kind soul. He sees the lights are on in all the houses and knocks on each door. But no one is home.

COLLECT

O God, you declare your almighty power
most chiefly in showing mercy and pity:
mercifully grant to us such a measure of your grace,
that we, running the way of your commandments,
may receive your gracious promises,
and be made partakers of your heavenly treasure;
through Jesus Christ your Son our Lord,
who is alive and reigns with you,
in the unity of the Holy Spirit,
one God, now and for ever.

Psalms 87, **89.1-18**
Micah 2
Mark 5.21-34

Mark 5.21-34

'Daughter, your faith has made you well' (v.34)

The accounts of the haemorrhaging woman are always paired with the raising of Jairus' daughter. Jesus goes out of his way to affirm the faith of the older woman in this story. Yet apart from healing her, he also seems to challenge the social and religious forces that have rendered this woman 'contagious'; he calls her 'daughter' in all three Gospels, all of which stress the woman's faith.

Although modern readers of the text may find this aspect of the narrative difficult, the significance of Jesus' action should not be under-estimated, since her continuous menstruation renders her permanently unclean. Her poverty – she 'had spent all that she had' (v.26) – is a direct result of her affliction.

There is a double issue of impurity here: touching a corpse, and a continually menstruating woman. The girl is twelve, and her untimely death clearly prevents her from entering womanhood. Jesus declares her 'not dead, but sleeping', and his touch, resulting again in his defilement, raises her.

Mark gives prominence to the narrative by the sharing of the number twelve: the girl is twelve, the woman has been ill for twelve years. This coincidence suggests that there is a narrative relation of some kind between the woman and the girl. An older woman is cured of a menstrual disorder of twelve years' standing and is sent back into society; a girl who has not yet reached puberty is about to be reborn and take her place in society. Jesus, by absorbing and absolving their taint through the simple power of healing touch, enables this.

God of glory,
the end of our searching,
help us to lay aside
all that prevents us from seeking your kingdom,
and to give all that we have
to gain the pearl beyond all price,
through our Saviour Jesus Christ.

COLLECT

Wednesday 19 August

Mark 5.35-end

'... twelve years' (vv.25,42)

What is radical about Jairus' daughter and the bleeding women is this: they are not the deviant ones – Jesus is. It is he who crosses the boundaries of acceptable behaviour and reverses the notion of taboo. No one would argue that the women were 'unclean'; the shock of the stories is that Jesus brings them both back to life through his touch.

But is there another relationship between Jairus and the bleeding woman? Remember, Jairus is one of the leaders of the synagogue (5.22), and would therefore have an instrumental role in policing its precincts, keeping the impure and undesirable out. So now we have a story about immediacy and patience. The woman has waited for twelve years – and probably been excluded from worship for all that time. The girl is twelve too. Neither can truly live until Jesus acts.

One of the subtle yet blunt exercises of power is to make people wait. If you are in power, people wait to see you. Only the powerless wait. Jairus has kept this woman waiting for years, but he wants Jesus for his daughter here and *now*. What does Jesus do? He gets distracted by an apparently pointless brush with a member of the crowd and he keeps Jairus waiting as a result. And this must have seemed too long, as Jairus' daughter dies. I wonder if, when his twelve-year-old daughter was raised, the penny ever dropped? This is a miracle with a moral.

COLLECT

O God, you declare your almighty power
most chiefly in showing mercy and pity:
mercifully grant to us such a measure of your grace,
that we, running the way of your commandments,
may receive your gracious promises,
and be made partakers of your heavenly treasure;
through Jesus Christ your Son our Lord,
who is alive and reigns with you,
in the unity of the Holy Spirit,
one God, now and for ever.

Thursday 20 August

Mark 6.1-13

'Prophets are not without honour, except in their home town' (v.4)

It is hard not to feel some sympathy for the complainants in today's Gospel reading. Jesus is someone they know. They have eaten with him, played ball with him, and watched him grow up. Now, almost suddenly, so it seems, he's different. He's preaching, healing, drawing large crowds, and everyone is interested in his background. What were his parents like? Tell us about his schooling? Has he always been special? How did he become a celebrity healer-preacher?

The friends and family of Jesus are a bit piqued, to say the least. But this causes Jesus not to acknowledge his humble origins, and affirm his nearest and dearest. Rather, he steps up a gear in proclaiming the kingdom of God project. He calls the Twelve, and clearly states that they are to come on this new mission without too many ties. The next few years will require utter dedication and few distractions.

Yet these exchanges in Mark 6 also serve to remind us of the deep importance of the Nazareth years. Simply put, Jesus has been with us. He has lived and eaten among us. He has slept in beds and on boats. He has, truly, richly and deeply, been Emmanuel – God with us. God knows what it is like to be human. In Jesus, we have heaven in ordinary, so that we too might, in the end, be ordinary in heaven. He became like us so we might become like him.

> God of glory,
> the end of our searching,
> help us to lay aside
> all that prevents us from seeking your kingdom,
> and to give all that we have
> to gain the pearl beyond all price,
> through our Saviour Jesus Christ.

COLLECT

233

Friday 21 August

Mark 6.14-29

*'...when Herod heard of it, he said,
"John, whom I beheaded, has been raised"' (v.16)*

Mark, the first and briefest of evangelists, places John the Baptist at the start of his Gospel. The road is wide open, and the prophecies of Isaiah all seem to be coming true. And yet, it is already the case that 'unless a grain of wheat falls into the earth and dies, it remains just a single grain; but if it dies, it bears much fruit' (John 12.24). We already know how John's story will end, I think.

The connection here is one of paradox. Unless we step aside – die to ourselves – we cannot bear fruit. This is no easy lesson, to be sure. But it is the only one we have to ponder on as we learn from the example of John the Baptist. For in the end, John the Baptist's example embodies a kind of prayer, one that I think we all wish for every Christian – namely, to have a good death. Not necessarily one of peace, surrounded by friends; that is not always granted to us. By a good death, I mean one that brings life-bearing possibilities to others. That in letting go, finally, we make way for life.

Like Elijah, John the Baptist cared enough about society, and his enemies, to protest about abuses of power. He loved individuals and society enough to summon the words that spoke against the forces of evil. Like Elijah with Ahab, John the Baptist loved his enemies – and probably prayed for those who persecuted him. Like other prophets before him, and since, his passion and love meant he paid with his life. His ministry could not have been more costly.

COLLECT

O God, you declare your almighty power
most chiefly in showing mercy and pity:
mercifully grant to us such a measure of your grace,
that we, running the way of your commandments,
may receive your gracious promises,
and be made partakers of your heavenly treasure;
through Jesus Christ your Son our Lord,
who is alive and reigns with you,
in the unity of the Holy Spirit,
one God, now and for ever.

Psalms 96, **97**, 100
Micah 6
Mark 6.30-44

Saturday 22 August

Mark 6.30-44

'Those who had eaten the loaves numbered five thousand ...' (v.44)

The ministry of Jesus is startling in its inclusivity. Consider, for example, the feedings of both the 5,000 and the 4,000 – the latter occurs in Mark 8.1-10. It is customary, in a kind of lazy-liberal and rather reductive way, to suppose that the Gospel writers simply got their maths muddled and were a bit confused about a single event. But in actual fact, there may be good reasons to regard the two miracles as quite separate.

The feeding of the 5,000 takes place on the western banks of the Sea of Galilee. The region was almost entirely Jewish, and the twelve baskets of leftovers symbolize the twelve tribes of Israel. What then, of the feeding of the 4,000, and the seven baskets of leftovers? The event occurs on the eastern shores of the Sea of Galilee, and the region was almost entirely gentile in composition. The seven baskets of leftovers correspond to the seven gentile regions of the time (i.e. Phoenicia, Samaria, Perea, Decapolis, Gaulanitis, Idumea and Philistia). Moreover, the baskets in the feeding of the 5,000 (*kophinos*) are smaller than those mentioned in the feeding of the 4,000 (*spuridi* – a basket big enough for a person, as with Paul in Acts 9.25).

The point here is that the new manna from heaven will be distributed evenly, across all lands. There is plenty for all. This new gospel is fundamentally broad and all-embracing: Jew, Greek, gentile, slave, free, male, female, adult and child – all are now welcome in the kingdom of God. Come, feast.

God of glory,
the end of our searching,
help us to lay aside
all that prevents us from seeking your kingdom,
and to give all that we have
to gain the pearl beyond all price,
through our Saviour Jesus Christ.

COLLECT

Monday 24 August

Bartholomew the Apostle

Psalms 86, 117
Genesis 28.10-17
John 1.43-end

Genesis 28.10-17

'... he dreamed that there was a ladder ... and the angels of God were ascending and descending on it' (v.12)

The link between this passage and St Bartholomew is not immediately obvious, but is found in John 1.51, when Jesus quotes these words in conversation with Nathanael. Nathanael is identified by many scholars with the Bartholomew who is listed with Philip in Mark 3.18. Nathanael and Philip appear together in John's Gospel, where Bartholomew is never mentioned. This is an argument from silence, so the link cannot be certain.

In Genesis 28, the fugitive Jacob lies down in the open and has a dream in which the angels of God are ascending and descending on a ladder between earth and heaven. In the accompanying message, God assures him that it is through his offspring that all the families of the earth shall be blessed (v.14). Headstrong Jacob may have seen this as a sign of his importance to God; and again and again in the Old Testament God has to remind his people Israel that they have been chosen not because of merit, but for the sake of the world.

It is Nathanael, an Israelite in whom there is no deceit, who nearly 2,000 years later is allowed to see the ultimate fulfilment of this vision in Jesus, who by his death and resurrection would open the door of heaven. In John 1, Jesus describes heaven being opened and the angels ascending and descending not on a ladder but 'upon the Son of Man'.

COLLECT

Almighty and everlasting God,
who gave to your apostle Bartholomew grace
    truly to believe and to preach your word:
grant that your Church
may love that word which he believed
and may faithfully preach and receive the same;
through Jesus Christ your Son our Lord,
who is alive and reigns with you,
in the unity of the Holy Spirit,
one God, now and for ever.

Psalms **106*** (*or* 103)
Micah 7.8-end
Mark 7.1-13

Mark 7.1-13

'Whatever support you might have had from me is Corban ...' (v.11)

This incident, coming so soon after the feeding of the 5,000 (Mark 6.30-44), shows the Pharisees in a rather unflattering light – instead of rejoicing in the abundant provision of food for the hungry, they are hung up on Jesus' failure to keep the tradition of the elders, which required the ceremonial washing of hands before eating (v.5). Jesus replies with a counter-attack, pointing out that the Pharisees keep their oral tradition to the letter, even when it prevents them honouring the very commandment that it was meant to protect.

'Corban' is an Aramaic word that translates the Hebrew for 'an offering to God'. According to the tradition of the Pharisees, something could be declared to be Corban (set apart for God) even while still in private hands, meaning that it could not then be given to those (like dependent relatives) whom one would otherwise be obliged to help. A religious tradition could thus be misused as a convenient way to duck one's proper duty.

Few individuals or organizations last very long without any traditions – witness the many new churches and Christian communities that began with a rejection of all tradition, only to produce their own in time. Traditions can be healthy, when they help us remember to do things that are good. The important thing is to keep our traditions in proper perspective – are they helping or hindering us as a family, or as a Church, in following Jesus?

Almighty and everlasting God,
you are always more ready to hear than we to pray
and to give more than either we desire or deserve:
pour down upon us the abundance of your mercy,
forgiving us those things of which our conscience is afraid
and giving us those good things
which we are not worthy to ask
but through the merits and mediation
of Jesus Christ your Son our Lord,
who is alive and reigns with you,
in the unity of the Holy Spirit,
one God, now and for ever.

COLLECT

Wednesday 26 August

Psalms 110, 111, 112
Habakkuk 1.1-11
Mark 7.14-23

Mark 7.14-23

'It is what comes out of a person that defiles' (v.20)

We live in a world where food safety is a big issue, to the point where organizations sometimes worry about accepting home baking on grounds of 'health and safety'. However, we are much less fussy about the things we fill our minds with, from television, the internet and social media. Research suggests that by age 18 an American child will have seen 16,000 simulated murders and 200,000 acts of violence.

I recently sat in court with a parishioner whose daughter had been brutally murdered by a young man heavily influenced by images of sexual violence he had collected on his computer. This experience has made me much more aware of, and disturbed by, the graphic images that find their way into the dark storylines of many prime-time television dramas.

Old Testament dietary laws were focused not so much on hygiene (though various of them make good sense), but on ritual purity – that is, being clean in the eyes of God. Jesus points out that what we eat cannot make us clean in God's sight, for the things that defile us come from within, not without.

If we want to be clean in God's eyes, are there things which we should choose no longer to watch for entertainment? For it is what we fill our minds with that will, sooner or later, influence how we think and behave. Jesus said, 'Out of the abundance of the heart the mouth speaks' (Matthew 12.34).

COLLECT

Almighty and everlasting God,
you are always more ready to hear than we to pray
and to give more than either we desire or deserve:
pour down upon us the abundance of your mercy,
forgiving us those things of which our conscience is afraid
and giving us those good things
    which we are not worthy to ask
but through the merits and mediation
of Jesus Christ your Son our Lord,
who is alive and reigns with you,
in the unity of the Holy Spirit,
one God, now and for ever.

Psalms 113, **115**
Habakkuk 1.12 – 2.5
Mark 7.24-30

Mark 7.24-30

'... it is not fair to take the children's food and throw it to the dogs'
(v.27)

How do we react when events take us by surprise? Jesus has gone away from Jewish territory and apparently without his disciples, because it seems he wants to be alone (v.24). Reflecting perhaps on his recent ministry, opposed by his own religious leaders, doubted by his loved ones, followed often for the wrong reasons by the crowd, suddenly Jesus finds in this gentile woman a response of expectant faith that has not been forthcoming at home.

Jesus' initial response seems dismissive, but the word 'first' in verse 27 is significant, indicating that the Gospel will in time reach and nourish the gentiles, just not yet. The word Jesus uses for 'dogs' is a diminutive, 'puppies', which was used of household pets rather than the scavenging dogs of the street.

In this story Jesus shows that he has set clear limits for his earthly ministry (which will enable him later to cry from the cross 'It is accomplished'), but is also flexible enough to change his mind, when confronted by human need and persistent faith.

Lord, help me to take time out to reflect on what I am doing, so that I may have the wisdom to set realistic limits, and to know when to make gracious exceptions.

God of constant mercy,
who sent your Son to save us:
remind us of your goodness,
increase your grace within us,
that our thankfulness may grow,
through Jesus Christ our Lord.

COLLECT

Friday 28 August

Psalm **139**
Habakkuk 2.6-end
Mark 7.31-end

Mark 7.31-end

'He has done everything well' (v.37)

How I envy Jesus this testimony from the crowd! As working lives get more and more hectic, often we find ourselves having to move on to the next task, or the next deadline, hoping that we have done things if not well, at least 'well enough'. That Jesus gained a reputation for 'doing all things well' may be linked with his willingness to set clear boundaries, as we saw yesterday. It is also for the writer Mark a clue to his Messiah-ship. The word for the man's speech impediment is found only in one other place in the whole of the Greek Bible, in Isaiah 35.6, which describes the coming of the messiah. That verse finds its echo in the astonished verdict of the crowd in verse 37.

However verse 34 makes clear that, even for Jesus, the work of setting a man free is not without real struggle – the word translated 'he sighed' is the same word translated 'groaning' in Romans 8.22-27 and 2 Corinthians 5.2,4, describing the Christian's inner struggle, as we await the redemption of our bodies. This man's healing is part of the wider struggle against pain and evil to which Jesus and his followers are called as we seek the in-breaking of God's kingdom. If it was hard work for Jesus, it will be for us too. Readiness to persevere and struggle is also part of 'doing all things well'.

COLLECT

Almighty and everlasting God,
you are always more ready to hear than we to pray
and to give more than either we desire or deserve:
pour down upon us the abundance of your mercy,
forgiving us those things of which our conscience is afraid
and giving us those good things
    which we are not worthy to ask
but through the merits and mediation
of Jesus Christ your Son our Lord,
who is alive and reigns with you,
in the unity of the Holy Spirit,
one God, now and for ever.

Saturday 29 August

Mark 8.1-10

'... and after giving thanks he broke them and gave them to his disciples' (v.6)

The word for giving thanks here is *eucharisto*, also used at the Last Supper, from where comes our word Eucharist. In the next verse the Greek word for blessing represents the Hebrew *berek*, 'to say the blessing'; this usually refers to blessing God for the food, rather than the food itself. The ancient Hebrew *berekah*, or blessing for bread, is: 'Blessed art Thou, O Lord our God, King of the world, who bringest forth bread from the earth.'

The giving of thanks before meals has somewhat fallen out of favour in many Western countries today, even in the families of church members. Perhaps we are over-anxious not to offend those who don't share our faith – though I am challenged by the example of Christian friends in Malaysia who will always say grace before meals, even in restaurants and public places.

Or perhaps we take our daily bread for granted. When staying at a busy dispensary in a poor, remote part of Kenya, I was struck by the example of Ruth, the Kenyan nurse in charge. She said an extempore and heartfelt prayer of thanks not only before meals, but even when we sat down for mid-morning coffee. In comparison with her English visitors, Ruth had so little, and yet she took nothing for granted and always thanked God for his many blessings. When we got back to England, saying grace before meals suddenly felt very different.

God of constant mercy,
who sent your Son to save us:
remind us of your goodness,
increase your grace within us,
that our thankfulness may grow,
through Jesus Christ our Lord.

COLLECT

Monday 31 August

Psalms 123, 124, 125, **126**
Haggai 1.1-11
Mark 8.11-21

Mark 8.11-21

'he sighed deeply in his spirit and said, "Why does this generation ask for a sign?"' (v.12)

Another groan from Jesus – see Mark 7.34. This time it is provoked by the Pharisees' demand that he perform a miracle to prove his identity. Jesus consistently resisted the temptation to perform spectacular acts to prove who he was – as he had in the testing in the wilderness (Luke 4.9-12). Jesus had only just fed 4,000 people, as we saw in the previous passage, but he acted out of love and compassion for the crowd (8.2), not in an attempt to convince the cynics. There is a sense in which miracles become signs, and in John's Gospel, Jesus' miracles are called 'signs' (see for example, John 2.11), but they are signs for those who believe, not for those who don't.

We live in a world that wants the Church to demonstrate its relevance and usefulness, by doing good. In these circumstances it is tempting to draw attention to our good works, or to pray for miracles, in order to try to win over the sceptics. However, we need to take care, like Jesus, that our ministry is conducted out of love and compassion for those in need, not a desire to authenticate or justify ourselves.

Over the years I have witnessed some remarkable signs from God, some of which have awakened or deepened faith in Christ, but they have always happened when the Church has been seeking to bless, not to impress.

COLLECT

Almighty God,
who called your Church to bear witness
that you were in Christ reconciling the world to yourself:
help us to proclaim the good news of your love,
that all who hear it may be drawn to you;
through him who was lifted up on the cross,
and reigns with you in the unity of the Holy Spirit,
one God, now and for ever.

Psalms **132**, 133
Haggai 1.12 – 2.9
Mark 8.22-26

Mark 8.22-26

'I can see people, but they look like trees, walking' (v.24)

This man had clearly not been blind from birth, since he knew what trees and people should look like. This incident shares with other Gospel stories Jesus' concern for privacy – both in taking the man away from the village to heal him and in his command not to return to the village. The use of saliva and of the laying-on of hands also occur in other healing miracles.

What is distinctive about this narrative is that the healing does not take place immediately, but in stages. This strikes a chord with many of us involved in the healing ministry, who find that God often works through continued prayer for an individual, often with the laying-on of hands being repeated regularly over time. If healing was not always instantaneous even for Jesus, that is a real encouragement to persist in prayer, rather than to assume too easily that physical healing may not be the Lord's will in a particular case.

Yet on the other hand, I have also been at the bedside of those with terminal illness who have felt burdened by the prayers of well-meaning Christian friends, expecting that they will be healed, even in the last stages of cancer. The challenge of course is to discern God's will in a particular situation, whether it is for a significant physical healing, or for the person to receive inner peace and spiritual strength to face what lies ahead.

Almighty God,
you search us and know us:
may we rely on you in strength
and rest on you in weakness,
now and in all our days;
through Jesus Christ our Lord.

COLLECT

243

Wednesday 2 September

Psalm **119.153-end**
Haggai 2.10-end
Mark 8.27 – 9.1

Mark 8.27 – 9.1

'Peter took him aside and began to rebuke him' (v.32)

Don't you just love Peter? Even though he has just grasped that Jesus is God's anointed, he can't help himself taking Jesus on one side and presuming to correct his theology! And what does this story tell us about Jesus, that he created the kind of dynamic within his disciples that enabled them to be completely honest with him, even when they thought he was wrong?

These days, more and more people find themselves having to work as part of a team, and many of us will have worked in effective teams where the boss would not have been able to cope with such honest and open criticism. In his bestselling book, *The Five Dysfunctions of a Team*, business guru Patrick Lencioni identifies the first dysfunction as the absence of trust – unwillingness to be vulnerable within the group. And when Peter says something that is clearly off-message, Jesus is not afraid to confront him, for the sake of the team (v.33). Too often the effectiveness of teams is hampered when a leader shies away from confronting behaviour which they know is harmful – as Lencioni also notes.

And what does it say about Jesus that he created the type of team where the members were willing to be open about their mistakes so that others could learn from them? One of Mark's primary sources for his Gospel was probably the personal reminiscences of Peter, which makes me love Peter all the more.

COLLECT

Almighty God,
who called your Church to bear witness
that you were in Christ reconciling the world to yourself:
help us to proclaim the good news of your love,
that all who hear it may be drawn to you;
through him who was lifted up on the cross,
and reigns with you in the unity of the Holy Spirit,
one God, now and for ever.

Mark 9.2-13

'Elijah has come, and they did to him whatever they pleased …' (v.13)

Peter, James and John seem more interested in having seen Elijah than Moses, perhaps because of the expectation that Elijah would return before the Messiah; this was based on the prophecy in Malachi 4.5-6, the closing verses of the Old Testament. Their question enables Jesus to point out that Elijah has come, in the person of John the Baptist (a link made explicit in Matthew's account: Matthew 17.13), but was not recognized. However, even the Baptist himself seems unconscious of this role when, in John's Gospel, he is specifically asked and denies it (John 1.21).

Jesus warns his disciples that just as John the Baptist was treated with contempt and killed, so it will be for the Son of Man. The experience of the transfiguration seems to have been significant for Jesus himself; his intimate relationship with the Father was reaffirmed, with words recalling his baptism (v.7) coming from a cloud, an expression so often in the Old Testament of the glory and presence of God. The conversation with Moses and Elijah (about the 'exodus' he would accomplish at Jerusalem, Luke 9.31), affirmed that his coming suffering was part of God's purpose, fulfilling the Hebrew Scriptures.

For the inner core of disciples also it must have been a significant learning experience, as they were trusted by the leader with a secret they could not share until after an event they could not comprehend. No wonder they questioned among themselves what the Son of Man rising from the dead could mean.

> Almighty God,
> you search us and know us:
> may we rely on you in strength
> and rest on you in weakness,
> now and in all our days;
> through Jesus Christ our Lord.

COLLECT

Friday 4 September

Psalms 142, **144**
Zechariah 1.18 – 2.end
Mark 9.14-29

Mark 9.14-29

'This kind can come out only through prayer' (v.29)

In St Peter's Basilica in Rome, there is a stunning painting by Raphael depicting this incident. In the top half of the painting is a patch of light, in which Jesus is transfigured, his closest disciples hiding their faces from the brightness; below, at the foot of the mountain, there is a patch of darkness, where Christ is not, around which are gathered the possessed boy, the other disciples and an angry crowd.

This painting expresses for me the twin calling of the Church – to stand apart to be with Christ, and to engage, to enter into the pain and suffering of the world. Our local church has just chosen as its vision statement, 'Called to be closer to Christ, sent to be closer to others'. Both aspects are as vital to the health of the body of Christ as breathing in and breathing out are to the human body, and both are reflected in Jesus' own example of alternating times of engagement and withdrawal.

Coming down the mountain, Jesus and the disciples find a boy who appears to the modern reader to have the classic symptoms of epilepsy, but whose father identifies him as having a spirit (v.17). Jesus accepts the diagnosis, commands the spirit to leave, and the boy is healed. Jesus' enigmatic explanation to the puzzled disciples in verse 29 underlines the fact that prayer and action go together. As disciples, we have no power of ourselves, but must prayerfully depend on God in every situation.

COLLECT

Almighty God,
who called your Church to bear witness
that you were in Christ reconciling the world to yourself:
help us to proclaim the good news of your love,
that all who hear it may be drawn to you;
through him who was lifted up on the cross,
and reigns with you in the unity of the Holy Spirit,
one God, now and for ever.

Psalm **147**
Zechariah 3
Mark 9.30-37

Mark 9.30-37

*'Whoever welcomes one such child in my name …
welcomes the one who sent me' (v.37)*

The other day, a church member asked me what I was going to do about the behaviour of two young children who had recently started coming to church. This incident put me in mind of this verse, where Jesus, having declared that true greatness is a matter of humble service, goes on to give as an example of humble service the way in which we welcome young children. Children had little by way of rights or status in the Greco-Roman world, and so Jesus says that how we welcome young children is actually a measure of how we welcome God the Father.

The status of children in society may have risen hugely since Jesus' day, but are we any better at welcoming children in our churches? When I was a diocesan missioner, I was invited to speak to many different PCCs about how to help their churches grow. I used to ask them, 'What do you really, really want?' Time and again their replies boiled down to this: 'What we really, really want is to see more children and young people coming to the kind of services that we (the PCC members) like.' How realistic is that?

And yet Jesus said the welcome we give to a child is the welcome we give to God the Father.

Almighty God,
you search us and know us:
may we rely on you in strength
and rest on you in weakness,
now and in all our days;
through Jesus Christ our Lord.

COLLECT

Monday 7 September

Mark 9.38-end

'Whoever is not against us is for us' (v.40)

You can hear Jesus gearing up for what is to come. It's no good shilly-shallying around anymore. The disciples are missing the point; they just don't get it. And unless they do, they are worse than useless – 'a stumbling block' to others – and no fate is bad enough for them. They need to know that their discipleship is for real. It's not about who belongs to the in-group, and who doesn't; it's much bigger than that. Jesus exaggerates for effect, to stress just how crucial it is that these disciples of his are there, for him, as he faces life and death. His call burns like fire; it purifies like salt.

Think of the times when a commitment is required, a decision has to be made. The run-up is hard: your mind goes back and forwards, weighing over different options, arguments with others rehearsed in your mind, unsure what to do for the best. Then, suddenly, sometimes out of the blue, the way forward becomes clear. You know where you are going. The doubts and uncertainties fall away.

Jesus uses the image of an ordinary cup of water, given to you to drink (v.41). You are thirsty, and the water is fresh and cold. You feel the shock as it reaches your stomach and begins to revive you. That's what the clarity is like, when an ordinary decision is made, commitment taken. How much greater the clarity when we respond and say 'yes' to the name of Jesus Christ!

COLLECT

Almighty God,
whose only Son has opened for us
a new and living way into your presence:
give us pure hearts and steadfast wills
to worship you in spirit and in truth;
through Jesus Christ your Son our Lord,
who is alive and reigns with you,
in the unity of the Holy Spirit,
one God, now and for ever.

Psalms **5**, 6 (8)
Zechariah 6.9-end
Mark 10.1-16

Tuesday 8 September

Mark 10.1-16

'Therefore what God has joined together, let no one separate' (v.9)

In the sacrament of marriage, Jesus teaches that this is what happens: God joins together two people for life, through good or ill, sickness or health, until death parts them. All should respect that bond as a divine gift of grace, including the couple themselves. Divorce is for the hard-hearted.

But there's another sense in which individuals are joined together by marriage. Jesus goes on, immediately, to teach about the love and respect due to children. When children are born or adopted by that married couple, they too deserve not to be separated from that primary bond between parent and child. That is what divorce does. The pain of divorce can be extreme for the adults who go through it, but how much more damaging it is for the children. They have no control over the course of events, as they watch their parents bicker and fight, tearing apart themselves and the family created by their union. Hearts are attacked and broken.

There is good reason why these two passages are held together. Jesus' teaching on divorce is unequivocal: one flesh should not be divided, once it has been made one. That gift of marriage is like receiving the kingdom of God. Children, likewise, are a gift – one that needs the nurture and protection of marriage in which to grow and flourish, and to receive blessing.

Merciful God,
your Son came to save us
and bore our sins on the cross:
may we trust in your mercy
and know your love,
rejoicing in the righteousness
that is ours through Jesus Christ our Lord.

COLLECT

Wednesday 9 September

Psalm 119.1-32
Zechariah 7
Mark 10.17-31

Mark 10.17-31

'Jesus, looking at him, loved him ...' (v.21)

You can't help feeling rather sorry for this rich young man. And it seems that Jesus did too. Again, from Mark's Gospel we receive a clear and unequivocal message about what it takes, and what it means, to follow Jesus. Jesus has been teaching about eternal life, the age to come, when God will bring in his kingdom. Who enters that kingdom was the big question for those who lived around Jesus, as they began to realize that he held the key. So, it is not enough to fulfil the commandments – the rich young man had done so since he was young. Entry into the kingdom means total response, so that nothing is more important. That's treasure in heaven.

The conversation evidently left Peter uncomfortable. 'How much is enough?' He wants to know. Jesus' response has a sting in the tail that challenges even further. Yes, Peter, you have left everything – and in due course you'll receive everything back a hundredfold. But don't forget the persecutions thrown in for good measure: Peter, who will hang upside down on a cross to die. It's hardly an attractive option, the way Mark presents discipleship. This good news is strange indeed.

I wonder what happened to the rich young man. Did life just continue as before? Or did that gaze of love enter his soul? Perhaps, in an age to come, he was St Francis.

COLLECT

Almighty God,
whose only Son has opened for us
a new and living way into your presence:
give us pure hearts and steadfast wills
to worship you in spirit and in truth;
through Jesus Christ your Son our Lord,
who is alive and reigns with you,
in the unity of the Holy Spirit,
one God, now and for ever.

Mark 10.32-34

'... the Son of Man will be handed over' (v.33)

The story that Mark tells pivots around the beginning of chapter 11, where we begin to hear the unfolding events of the last week of Jesus' life. Everything beforehand, in this fast-moving tale, is an extended prologue to the real drama of the passion. Three times, before they reach Jerusalem, Jesus tells his disciples what is to happen – at chapter 8.31, and then at 9.31, and now here. Each time the disciples can't, or won't, hear what Jesus is saying.

He couldn't be clearer, this third time; here is the Passion narrative in just 61 words. A short, succinct account of what Jesus believed was to happen as his life came to its climax. Those following were amazed and afraid, still not sure how to respond to the challenge to follow Jesus wholeheartedly, this all-or-nothing discipleship. How could they know where this story was going? How it would all end?

How hard it must have been for them without the evidence of the resurrection. No wonder they didn't understand. No wonder Jesus was so frustrated at times.

We are given, in the Gospel of St Mark, a story that shapes all stories. Those disciples couldn't know where it would end. We know – or do we? Not for nothing does the Gospel itself end in such deliberate confusion, for that's when we need to let the story unfold and shape the meaning of our lives.

Merciful God,
your Son came to save us
and bore our sins on the cross:
may we trust in your mercy
and know your love,
rejoicing in the righteousness
that is ours through Jesus Christ our Lord.

COLLECT

251

Friday 11 September

Psalms 17, **19**
Zechariah 8.9-end
Mark 10.35-45

Mark 10.35-45

'Are you able to drink the cup that I drink?' (v.38)

In today's reading we see just how much in the dark the disciples are about what's going on. They want something back for the trouble of following this man. He has asked for total commitment; now James and John want him to reciprocate, to make it all worthwhile. Jesus takes the opportunity for more teaching about what it will all mean, which is not what they were hoping for, but merely more enigmatic stuff that leaves them even deeper in the dark.

They hear of a cup, of a baptism, and then of the tyranny of powerful rulers. With the benefit of hindsight, we can see how the cup takes us back to Jeremiah, to the cup of God's wrath that becomes the cup of salvation, the chalice of the Blood of Christ. We can see how Christ's baptism becomes ours, membership of the Body of Christ, where our sins are forgiven and we are washed clean. We know how the cross is also the beginning of a new order in society, where violence and power are destroyed by love and truth. With hindsight, we can read this, and more, into the words that Christ uses. But we see all this from a post-cross perspective.

James and John ask for glory and honour, only to be told that they must be slaves of all. You wonder why they stuck it at all..

COLLECT

Almighty God,
whose only Son has opened for us
a new and living way into your presence:
give us pure hearts and steadfast wills
to worship you in spirit and in truth;
through Jesus Christ your Son our Lord,
who is alive and reigns with you,
in the unity of the Holy Spirit,
one God, now and for ever.

Saturday 12 September

Mark 10.46-end

'Jesus, Son of David, have mercy on me!' (v.47)

Walking on the road to Jerusalem, accompanied by the disciples and other stragglers, Jesus has struggled to explain what it's all about. His disciples are confused, anxious, frightened. Jesus keeps asking the world of them, but they don't know what's in it for them, beyond an uneasy sense that it's not going to be good. They are in the dark.

So Mark illustrates that their blindness will not be for ever. Just as the blind beggar, Bartimaeus, gains his sight, so they will too. All they need to do is ask the Son of David, the Son of Man, for mercy, and to show faith in Him.

Instead of words and more words, Jesus uses action: he heals to illustrate what he is about, to show what it means to follow him. The contrast between being blind and having sight could not be more marked as a way of trying to open the eyes of his disciples to understand what Jesus offers. But they've got to want it with as much keenness as this blind man, who springs up at the call of Jesus and is very clear about what he wants when asked. 'Let me see again' (v.51).

It's not always easy to know what we're not seeing. We can be very blind to our own blindness.

Merciful God,
your Son came to save us
and bore our sins on the cross:
may we trust in your mercy
and know your love,
rejoicing in the righteousness
that is ours through Jesus Christ our Lord.

COLLECT

Monday 14 September

Holy Cross Day

Psalms 2, 8, 146
Genesis 3.1-15
John 12.27-36a

John 12.27-36a

'And I, when I am lifted up from the earth, will draw all people to myself' (v.32)

Today is Holy Cross Day, a day on which we contemplate the Christ, lifted up from the earth, drawing all people to himself. But it is a strange kind of pedestal, this cross – a prominent positioning that is nothing of the sort, but rather a brutal killing of an innocent man who shows forth the light of love as he dies. Visiting a local church recently where there was a choir, I was delighted to see the young boys and girls crossing themselves – at the proclamation of forgiveness of sins, at the blessing. For many, I suspect, it was something to do because everyone else did it, but perhaps they will come to reflect that in making this simple gesture, they are writing the cross onto their bodies, making it their own. For the holy cross is the mark of the Christian; it recalls us to that central reality of self-sacrificial love that is at the heart of the gospel.

'All people' is a tall order. The cross stirs hatred and anger among many people. For them it is a symbol of violence and blame for the times when Christians have exhibited not self-sacrificial love, but evil greed, arrogance, unconcern. For such people the cross is anything but holy. It's hard to see how the enemies of Christianity today might be drawn to Jesus, the Christ, except by the way of forgiveness and blessing – forgiveness, which is the only way through cycles of revenge and anger, however difficult it is to ask for, to give and to receive, and blessing, that impulse of love and good will that is God's generous initiative. I continue to cross myself, in hope.

COLLECT

Almighty God,
who in the passion of your blessed Son
made an instrument of painful death
to be for us the means of life and peace:
grant us so to glory in the cross of Christ
that we may gladly suffer for his sake;
who is alive and reigns with you,
in the unity of the Holy Spirit,
one God, now and for ever.

Psalms 32, **36**
Zechariah 11.4-end
Mark 11.12-26

Tuesday 15 September

Mark 11.12-26

'Have faith in God' (v.22)

The good news of Jesus is something altogether new. It overturns old practices and tired ways – even lucrative ones such as money-changing and dove-selling. The temple has harboured 'a den of robbers' (v.17), hardly the fruits of righteousness and holiness. Jesus is hungry for something different: the fruits of faith and prayer; he is angry that he does not find such things in the temple, where such things should be found.

The fig tree is out of season and not in fruit; the temple is never in season nor fruitful. The tree has leaves, but from a distance they deceive. Jesus curses that which leads people astray, empty promises of material gain and false hopes carried back and forth through the temple. All in the temple is sterile, cursed like the fig tree and withered away to its roots.

'My house shall be called a house of prayer for all the nations', says Jesus, quoting Isaiah (56.7). This is a tree that provides fruit for all comers, at all times of the year. How do we discern, today, the health or otherwise of our religious institutions? Especially at a time when for many what the Church provides is the bitter, withered fruit of sex scandal and hypocrisy? The only recourse is prayer – the most powerful nutrient of all – and particularly the prayer of forgiveness of others and the prayer of faith that our trespasses may be forgiven.

God, who in generous mercy sent the Holy Spirit
upon your Church in the burning fire of your love:
grant that your people may be fervent
in the fellowship of the gospel
that, always abiding in you,
they may be found steadfast in faith and active in service;
through Jesus Christ your Son our Lord,
who is alive and reigns with you,
in the unity of the Holy Spirit,
one God, now and for ever.

COLLECT

Wednesday 16 September

Mark 11.27-end

'By what authority are you doing these things?' (v.28)

Oh, for Jesus' quick mastery of a situation and clever words, his fearless wit. He has the chief priests, the scribes and the elders totally on the back foot with a few, well-chosen words that establish his authority in this, the first of a number of arguments with the authorities. Jesus claims divine legitimacy by pointing to his forerunner, John, and they don't dispute the connection between the two religious leaders. John, like Jesus, had command of the crowd. So partly Jesus' authority comes from the crowd itself, but he is more concerned to establish its heavenly source. He leaves it unspoken, but clear.

How someone uses words, and silence, is an interesting indication of their authority. Often the point is carried most effectively when it is argued less forcefully, when silence is left for the principle or point to sink in where it needs to. But first one needs to be clear about why the authority is being exercised at all: it isn't genuine if it's simply an empty assertion of personality or power. Real authority takes us back to the Author, the begetter of words, the Word that was in the beginning with God.

Rowan Williams, in *Dostoevsky*, argues that Christ is never the final word; there is always more to come. Christ's authority never comes to an end. Perhaps we should be more cautious when we attempt to have the last word.

God, who in generous mercy sent the Holy Spirit
   upon your Church in the burning fire of your love:
grant that your people may be fervent
in the fellowship of the gospel
that, always abiding in you,
they may be found steadfast in faith and active in service;
through Jesus Christ your Son our Lord,
who is alive and reigns with you,
in the unity of the Holy Spirit,
one God, now and for ever.

COLLECT

Psalm **37***
Zechariah 13
Mark 12.1-12

Mark 12.1-12

'What then will the owner of the vineyard do?' (v.9)

The cultural reference to the vineyard would not have been lost on those listening to Jesus; all would have heard his meaning– that the vineyard, Israel, is kept by those who are betraying God's purposes. The priests, scribes and Pharisees are unscrupulous in taking what belongs to God, and will even go as far as to kill the beloved son. Mark's Gospel, by this point, is focused on one thing: calling Israel to account. It's a yes/no response that is required as the narrative gathers pace and intensity.

The betrayal of the landlord and the consequent promise of the destruction that will follow is a message that can be difficult to square with a loving, ever-patient God. Perhaps we should ask more often about the consequences of humanity's betrayal of the gifts that we are entrusted with. Think of the stewardship of God's creation: should we not be liable for the poor job we have made of the rich resources of nature that are put at our disposal? As the oceans warm and the climate changes, we live with adverse weather that threatens our livelihood and wellbeing. Previous generations would have seen God's anger in the destruction of coast lines and rain forests, his grief at the extinction of species. The vineyard has not been cultivated properly and as well as it deserves. Are we, too, guilty of killing the Son, the firstborn of the new creation?

Lord God,
defend your Church from all false teaching
and give to your people knowledge of your truth,
that we may enjoy eternal life
in Jesus Christ our Lord.

COLLECT

Friday 18 September

Psalm **31**
Zechariah 14.1-11
Mark 12.13-17

Mark 12.13-17

*'Give to the emperor the things that are the emperor's,
and to God the things that are God's' (v.17)*

Another neat sidestep out of a trap. Jesus does it by deliberately confusing the question of ownership, for surely the coin belongs to the person who has earned it, and not to the emperor at all. And if that is so, then he is going right to the heart of the payment of tribute money, which was a real cause of grievance to the Jews, a constant reminder of their subjection to Roman rule. If he says 'Pay the tax!', then the crowd will be angry; if he says 'Don't!', the Pharisees and Herodians can report him. Jesus refuses to play that game.

Instead he draws attention to the image of the emperor Tiberius, whose head was there, on the coin – distasteful enough to a devout Jew who did not believe in images of human beings, let alone one of an emperor who claimed to be divine, the son of the divine Augustus. Let this 'shame go where it doth deserve', as the poet George Herbert puts it, and let us concentrate on what's really important. What belongs to God?

Time? Money? Prayer? Love? It's a question to take with us through today – and every day. What belongs to God in what I do? How much do I give? Bearing in mind, of course, that all things come from God, 'for all things come from you, and of your own have we given you' (1 Chronicles 29.14).

Jesus gave the ultimate gift of himself, proving that images on coins are nothing compared to the human being made in God's image, a gift for all eternity.

COLLECT

God, who in generous mercy sent the Holy Spirit
    upon your Church in the burning fire of your love:
grant that your people may be fervent
in the fellowship of the gospel
that, always abiding in you,
they may be found steadfast in faith and active in service;
through Jesus Christ your Son our Lord,
who is alive and reigns with you,
in the unity of the Holy Spirit,
one God, now and for ever.

Psalms 41, **42**, 43
Zechariah 14.12-end
Mark 12.18-27

Saturday 19 September

Mark 12.18-27

'He is God not of the dead, but of the living' (v.27)

'Get a life!' Jesus might have said, as the Sadducees stand up to have a go. They didn't believe in the resurrection, and so present him with this challenge, a legalistic quibble we can imagine took them hours and hours of endless argument, and now they want to draw Jesus in. Short shrift, again, is his response. If God is the God of Abraham, Isaac and Jacob, then they obviously endure in some existence beyond death, waiting for the resurrection that is to come.

Such questions don't go away. We all wonder what awaits us, if anything, after death. For Jesus, it seems he held the belief that we are resurrected into a new order, a new kingdom, in which aspects of human life – like marriage – simply pale into insignificance, as all enjoy the glory of God.

How we answer that question of what awaits us makes a real difference to how we live life now. Life is precious, and all too short, galloping away with us as the years pass by.

If Jesus were to say to us 'Get a life!', what would we do to change things?

Lord God,
defend your Church from all false teaching
and give to your people knowledge of your truth,
that we may enjoy eternal life
in Jesus Christ our Lord.

COLLECT

Monday 21 September

Matthew, Apostle and Evangelist

Psalms 49, 117
1 Kings 19.15-end
2 Timothy 3.14-end

2 Timothy 3.14-end

'... the sacred writings that are able to instruct you' (v.15)

The four gospels – Matthew, Mark, Luke and John – form a familiar list that, for those who spend any time in church regularly, trips off the tongue. But it is a commonplace in our contemporary society that biblical literacy – familiarity with and knowledge of the stories, characters and themes of Scripture – is low. Matthew, the disciple we celebrate today, by tradition a Jewish official who co-operated with the occupying forces as a collector of taxes, writes the gospel placed first in the New Testament, although it's by no means the first to be written. What's more, to imagine that a single person called Matthew scribed every sentence is no longer credible after a scholarly enterprise that has long since accepted the gospels were oral for many years before they were written.

The gospels, including Matthew's, were written in community and are designed to be read in community, argued over, discussed, and, as theologian Carlos Mesters puts it, they must be read not only with our head and heart, but with our feet, as a companion on a journey (*God's Project* 1987).

Several translations of this passage of Paul render verse 16 as 'God-breathed'. This, together with the encouragement to read with our feet, gives me a clue as to how intimate my relationship with the living Scriptures brought to me by Matthew and others could be. Grand gestures and big moments are sometimes part of a faith journey, but it is the everyday inspiration and adjustments of direction that make the Scriptures the travelling companion they should be.

O Almighty God,
whose blessed Son called Matthew the tax collector
to be an apostle and evangelist:
give us grace to forsake the selfish pursuit of gain
    and the possessive love of riches
that we may follow in the way of your Son Jesus Christ,
who is alive and reigns with you,
in the unity of the Holy Spirit,
one God, now and for ever.

Psalms **48**, 52
Ecclesiasticus 1.11-end
or Ezekiel 1.15 – 2.2
Mark 12.35-end

Tuesday 22 September

Mark 12.35-end

'... all she had to live on' (v.44)

Over the next few days' readings, as Mark's Gospel progresses, it becomes obvious that Jesus of Nazareth is in increasingly serious conflict with the organized religion of his day. He is in the temple promoting what the religious leaders ultimately come to believe is seditious teaching. The fact that he is challenging some religious practices from within the temple itself is highly provocative.

The Jesus we meet in these chapters of Mark is a singular, energetic, challenging individual. The comment he makes about the widow and the fact that she gives away to the temple authorities all that she has is a curious one. It is often preached about as an encouragement to the rest of us; that Jesus is commending her for her commitment, even though it leaves her destitute. In the context of everything else that is happening in these chapters, however, I can't interpret it like this myself. It seems to me that Jesus is furious that she has been taught that this is necessary. He is in the middle of excoriating criticism of the leaders of the temple, he sees this incident played out in front of him, and he calls his disciples together in defence of this woman who has given two copper coins, 'all she had to live on'. Jesus' words that she gave more than the others are not so much commending her as criticizing the leaders who have taught that this destitution is demanded by religion. It has the sense of 'that can't be right'. Jesus' anger is energizing not paralysing and his social comment is based on close observation of the abuses around him infused by a deep spiritual connection with the God of justice and compassion.

O Lord, we beseech you mercifully to hear the prayers
of your people who call upon you;
and grant that they may both perceive and know
what things they ought to do,
and also may have grace and power faithfully to fulfil them;
through Jesus Christ your Son our Lord,
who is alive and reigns with you,
in the unity of the Holy Spirit,
one God, now and for ever.

COLLECT

Wednesday 23 September

Psalm **119.57-80**
Ecclesiasticus 2
or Ezekiel 2.3 – 3.11
Mark 13.1-13

Mark 13.1-13

'... all will be thrown down' (v.2)

Jesus, still teaching around the temple, the huge and dominating presence within the city of Jerusalem, turns his attention to the building itself. If you visit Jerusalem today and go up to the Temple Mount or, in Arabic, Haram al Sharif, it becomes obvious how impressive and dominant the building and all its outer courtyards would have been. It dwarfed the people who visited, reminding them of the transcendent and unimaginable power of God. By interpreting the walls and the stones, the jewelled adornments and the craftsmanship in the way that he does, Jesus is not only making a comment about a historic building, but is also making the point that, however impressive the achievement of human endeavours, even in service of God and to indicate the glory of God, this is as nothing compared with the transcendent power of God, who cannot be seen or touched.

It's a beautiful teaching and one that up-ends the way we live. What is real is not what we can touch or prove; what is real is what lies beyond this. It's as if all the buildings, all the roads with which we are surrounded are not ends in themselves but are signs of a greater reality – a spiritual reality. They point, signify, indicate something beyond. This doesn't make life as a Christian in the modern world less real or practical, but more so. We see beyond that which looks permanent but is truly temporary, and in reflecting on this, we discern what deeper truths endure.

COLLECT

O Lord, we beseech you mercifully to hear the prayers
    of your people who call upon you;
and grant that they may both perceive and know
    what things they ought to do,
and also may have grace and power faithfully to fulfil them;
through Jesus Christ your Son our Lord,
who is alive and reigns with you,
in the unity of the Holy Spirit,
one God, now and for ever.

Psalms 56, **57** (63*)
Ecclesiasticus 3.17-29
or Ezekiel 3.12-end
Mark 13.14-23

Thursday 24 September

Mark 13.14-23

'... let the reader understand' (v.14)

It was the writer Mark Twain who said that it wasn't the parts of the Bible he didn't understand that troubled him; it was the parts that he did understand. The words from Jesus in today's passage, when taken literally, have caused people over the centuries to act in cruel ways, believing often that they are saving others from the fate described here at the end of days. Some scholars have wanted to cast Jesus of Nazareth as a failed preacher predicting the end of the world, and nothing more. It is passages like this that have added fuel to that debate.

At 2000 years' distance, we should take seriously Jesus' contemporary context, in which the desert around Jerusalem was febrile with prophets, soothsayers, people claiming to be the Messiah; however, this context can't govern our own interpretation of the words themselves. Jesus is speaking to a crowd thoroughly familiar with predictions of the end of the world, but he is calling them to a deeper spiritual state, whatever the external events of the day.

This is where we can find our own meaning too. It is in being alert – not sleepwalking through our lives. It is also in a tireless search for authenticity and not being satisfied with easy answers from false saviours. This alert, awake, sensitized, attentive spiritual life is given direction and meaning by prayerful communication with God, who may call us to move on at any moment.

Lord of creation,
whose glory is around and within us:
open our eyes to your wonders,
that we may serve you with reverence
and know your peace at our lives' end,
through Jesus Christ our Lord.

COLLECT

263

Ordinary Time

Friday 25 September

Psalms **51**, 54
Ecclesiasticus 4.11-28
or Ezekiel 8
Mark 13.24-31

Mark 13.24-31

'... stars will be falling from heaven' (v.25)

With fabulous Middle Eastern hyperbole, using evocative descriptions of the darkened sun and falling stars, Jesus is trying to communicate the urgency of his message to live differently, to be attentive to the presence of God and the intolerable injustices of organized religion and politics.

It has often seemed to me that to be too literal about these pictures, and therefore to worry about whether they are 'true', is, ironically, to rob them of their beauty and power. At Advent, singing Charles Wesley's words 'Lo he comes with clouds descending', quoting directly from this passage, has often given me a greater sense of awe and expectation as the musical picture unfolds than I have received from simply reading the words. The sense of God being 'at the very gates' as Jesus says (v.29), just beyond, just out of reach, the other side of the door – all these spiritual truths are recognisable to anyone who wants to take their own spiritual lives seriously.

In the rhythm of night following day, as Spring follows Winter, we learn to expect change and movement at the heart of creation. Jesus is urging his listeners to learn from the fig tree's seasons, to be attentive to its transformation and to know the potential for transformation for us too.

COLLECT

O Lord, we beseech you mercifully to hear the prayers
    of your people who call upon you;
and grant that they may both perceive and know
    what things they ought to do,
and also may have grace and power faithfully to fulfil them;
through Jesus Christ your Son our Lord,
who is alive and reigns with you,
in the unity of the Holy Spirit,
one God, now and for ever.

Psalm **68**
Ecclesiasticus 4.29 – 6.1
or Ezekiel 9
Mark 13.32-end

Mark 13.32-end

'Keep awake ...' (v.35)

The progression in this strong language is very beautiful. Jesus has taken us from what is familiar – the built environment, the corruption of leaders, the exploitation of the poor – and developed his disciples in the process. Learn to read the signs of the times, he urges; don't be afraid when you are persecuted – what else can you expect? Be in sympathy with the rhythms of the earth, don't lose sight of the seasons, and now, finally, be aware of your life and its time. Jesus advocates *kairos* time (God's time) rather than *chronos* time (hours and minutes of our days). It has been said that living your life (as our society seems to do) according to the 24-hour news agenda is like learning to tell the time by looking only at the second hand of a clock. It's accurate, if breathless, but we will never understand the wider, longer perspective, nor the passing of the days and years of our lives.

Jesus is here saying two apparently contradictory things. Be awake and alert – live life as it were on tiptoe. At the same time, trust in God completely, because it is not for you to know the hour or the day. One seems exhausting, the other restful. It is profound teaching about an attitude to life that is summed up by St Augustine: 'Without God, we cannot. Without us, God will not.'

Lord of creation,
whose glory is around and within us:
open our eyes to your wonders,
that we may serve you with reverence
and know your peace at our lives' end,
through Jesus Christ our Lord.

COLLECT

Monday 28 September

Mark 14.1-11

'What she has done will be told ...' (v.9)

In Mark's Gospel, 'the crowd' is almost a character in itself. Jesus is often escaping from 'the crowd' or surrounded by them or overwhelmed by them. His life is portrayed as hectic, full of people, surrounded by need. Here, the crowd is given much power by the 'chief priests and the scribes', who, fearing a riot, refuse to act against Jesus during the festival of Unleavened Bread.

Once again, timing is important. Mark's Gospel gathers momentum up to the moment when the Son of Man is 'lifted up' on the cross. But, like a film script, the storytelling of Mark moves swiftly from the political plotting and hustle of the crowd to inside a house at Bethany, outside Jerusalem, where Jesus is having dinner with a friend. This poignant and beautiful story has fulfilled the prediction made about it that 'what she has done will be told in remembrance of her' (v.9), and even though history does not record her name, it is one of the most loved stories in the Gospels.

If we allow ourselves to enter the house and picture the scene, it is sensual, even overwhelming. We can imagine the woman, who appears completely grief-stricken; her crying embarrasses the others who are there, and they become angry at the intrusion and expense. Later Christian witnesses such as Margery Kempe have spoken of the 'gift of tears' that can somehow name truthful moments of pain or realization. It seems that it is from this beautiful moment, not the trial he endures before Pilate, that Jesus' body is condemned to destruction.

COLLECT

Almighty God,
you have made us for yourself,
and our hearts are restless till they find their rest in you:
pour your love into our hearts and draw us to yourself,
and so bring us at last to your heavenly city
where we shall see you face to face;
through Jesus Christ your Son our Lord,
who is alive and reigns with you,
in the unity of the Holy Spirit,
one God, now and for ever.

Psalms 34, 150
Tobit 12.6-end *or* Daniel 12.1-4
Acts 12.1-11

Tuesday 29 September

Michael and All Angels

Acts 12.1-11

'And the chains fell off ...' (v.7)

That angels are simply messengers is well documented in the Christian tradition. Angels seem to appear in two distinct ways. The first is as beings that are beyond human capacity to imagine or understand, such as the angels of Ezekiel and Revelation. In apocalyptic and prophetic literature, angels are creatures without number, indescribable, innumerable, completely overwhelming in their colossal presence, pointing to the reality beyond time and space. These are the angels with immeasurable form or power, made of light itself, capable of ethereal music and ineffable praise. They even guard, with a flaming sword, the way back to Paradise.

The second way that angels appear is as here in the book of Acts. Just as Abraham and Sarah entertained angels unawares (Genesis 18.1-8), it seems that strange visitors, recognisable and unthreatening, can come to release captives, save those condemned, bring good news from God, and be agents of connection, reminding us that there is a thin veil that separates earth and heaven. Peter's mysterious visitor brings a message of freedom to him, as he is able to walk free from prison.

Angels are big business today, with 'mind, body and spirit' sections of bookshops full of stories and testimonies about angels. In popular religion, the concept of a guardian angel has persisted over years. Without despising or rejecting this religious instinct, the biblical stories about angels don't really support that domesticated version. Angels leave us awestruck and remind us that we are never alone.

Everlasting God,
you have ordained and constituted
the ministries of angels and mortals in a wonderful order:
grant that as your holy angels always serve you in heaven,
so, at your command,
they may help and defend us on earth;
through Jesus Christ your Son our Lord,
who is alive and reigns with you,
in the unity of the Holy Spirit,
one God, now and for ever.

COLLECT

Ordinary Time

Wednesday 30 September

Psalm **77**
Ecclesiasticus 10.6-8, 12-24
or Ezekiel 12.1-16
Mark 14.26-42

Mark 14.26-42

'... the sheep will be scattered' (v.27)

This is the only explicit mention of music in Jesus' life. As an observant Jew, he sang with his friends before 'going out'. Again, Mark's Gospel reads more like a movie script as we switch scenes from the febrile Jerusalem atmosphere at the time of festival to the intimacy of dinner at home, or the astonishing preceding verses of the transformation of the Passover.

Out on the Mount of Olives, Jesus challenges his disciples and assures them that he is aware of their frailty, their capacity for desertion and betrayal. Only a few verses before he had been trying to encourage them by urging them not to worry about what they will say when they are tried. Peter, characteristically, is impulsive, passionate and, in this case, totally unrealistic. Almost in response to this reminder that he will be totally alone, Jesus 'throws himself on the ground' in prayer (v.35).

This Gethsemane conversation is the beginning of his last conversation with his Father, God. It is evident from the dramatic inevitability of the last days of his life that he is constantly talking with God, and sometimes appears to be simply on a different trajectory from the people around him. This part of the conversation begins with protest at his imminent suffering, and ends with some kind of resolution 'not my will but yours' (v.36) – an act of will that carries him through the tortuous hours to come.

COLLECT

Almighty God,
you have made us for yourself,
and our hearts are restless till they find their rest in you:
pour your love into our hearts and draw us to yourself,
and so bring us at last to your heavenly city
where we shall see you face to face;
through Jesus Christ your Son our Lord,
who is alive and reigns with you,
in the unity of the Holy Spirit,
one God, now and for ever.

268

Psalm **78.1-39***
Ecclesiasticus 11.7-28
or Ezekiel 12.17-end
Mark 14.43-52

Mark 14.43-52

'The one I will kiss…' (v.44)

Many of the sentences in Mark's Gospel begin with the Greek words *kai eutheus* – 'and immediately'. The pace of events is fast and a whirlwind story is being told. Here the scene becomes violent: clubs and sticks in the darkness of a garden where a crowd emerges from the olive trees. Mark's Gospel makes the violence real rather than threatened: an ear is cut off the slave of the high priest, and there is a cameo role for a 'young man' who runs away naked. As a literary device, this is assumed by scholars to be an indication that Mark himself was there at Gethsemane.

The events described here, committed to parchment about 60 years after the death of Jesus, have entered our culture so completely that it is hard to re-read them with fresh eyes. The deep and sinister irony of betrayal with a kiss, the reluctance even now for parents to call their child Judas, the vilification of Judas as a character in art all serve to polarize our reactions to this Gethsemane scene.

But other reflections have cast Judas much more sympathetically – as someone necessary to the redemptive arc of Christ's life, death and resurrection, and someone also who did no worse thing than the disciple who became the rock of Western Christianity, Peter. Betrayal and denial go hand in hand, and the retelling of this greatest story help us to accept our own capacity for duplicity, weakness, collaboration and shame. And not only to accept this, but to understand that somehow it is from these very painful realizations that transformation comes.

Gracious God,
you call us to fullness of life:
deliver us from unbelief
and banish our anxieties
with the liberating love of Jesus Christ our Lord.

COLLECT

Friday 2 October

Psalm **55**
Ecclesiasticus 14.20 – 15.10
or Ezekiel 13.1-16
Mark 14.53-65

Mark 14.53-65

'... their testimony did not agree' (v.56)

Muddled and contradictory testimony is often a feature of situations where the stakes are high and emotion is overriding reason in governing the actions of those in power. This interlude in the series of events is powerful as it doesn't contain the main characters, Peter, Judas, Pilate and Herod, but is illustrative of a chaotic courtroom lynching that has been a regular feature of human societies ever since. Hearing what we want to hear and making the evidence fit our preconceived prejudices are thoroughly human tendencies, and our recognition of what can happen lends weight to the necessity for the dispassionate mechanisms of prosecution and the right to a professional defence. As the nineteenth-century philosopher William James commented, 'a great many people think they are thinking when they are simply rearranging their prejudices'.

On a theological level, the story of this trial as told in Mark is evidence in itself that God in Christ is subject to human injustice and the abuse of power. Theologically this is an instance of what St Paul described as *kenosis*: God emptying himself into the life of the world and becoming willingly bound by human behaviour, boundaries, abuses and contradictions. In this kenotic life is the clue to the nature of what God does and who God is.

COLLECT

Almighty God,
you have made us for yourself,
and our hearts are restless till they find their rest in you:
pour your love into our hearts and draw us to yourself,
and so bring us at last to your heavenly city
where we shall see you face to face;
through Jesus Christ your Son our Lord,
who is alive and reigns with you,
in the unity of the Holy Spirit,
one God, now and for ever.

Psalms **76**, 79
Ecclesiasticus 15.11-end
or Ezekiel 14.1-11
Mark 14.66-end

Mark 14.66-end

'... she stared at him ... he denied it' (vv.67,68)

There is something so believable about this scene – the impulsive, enthusiastic disciple being the one who is equally emphatic about denying he was ever involved. Along with the capacity to make great commitment comes the capacity to feel great fear.

Peter the fisherman, unschooled but direct and compelling, is almost the very definition of ordinary as we watch him make his way through the three years of travelling with Jesus, the return to his nets after his crucifixion, the extraordinary encounter on the beach that restores his faith and commitment, and his life recorded in Acts, where we are told he was such a powerful orator that the crowd was 'cut to the heart' when he spoke (Acts 2.37). This man, who was so afraid here by the fire outside the house of the high priest, was, by tradition, crucified upside down, showing immense physical courage in arguing he was not worthy to die in the same way as his Lord. In the life of this ordinary man, we see a change so dramatic that it demands explanation.

Generations of Christians have found reassurance in Peter, who is by no means naturally gifted or popular, learned or eloquent. He shows that ordinary people are capable of extraordinary things, even though here he is running away as fast as he can from what he secretly knows to be true.

Gracious God,
you call us to fullness of life:
deliver us from unbelief
and banish our anxieties
with the liberating love of Jesus Christ our Lord.

COLLECT

271

Monday 5 October

Psalms **80**, 82
Ecclesiasticus 16.17-end
or Ezekiel 14.12-end
Mark 15.1-15

Mark 15.1-15

'... wishing to satisfy the crowd' (v.15)

For all the trappings of power around him, Pilate here presents a powerless figure. Indeed, the trappings themselves seem no more than a series of traps. He staggers back and forth between fearful and entangling 'what ifs' – 'What if there's a riot? What if Caesar hears? But what if giving in looks weak and I lose kudos? What if there's something in this Jesus after all?' And in all these 'what ifs', he never asks 'what is?' – What is the truth in this case? What is the just thing to do? What is my duty?'

All of us, if we are honest, must have some empathy for the vacillations of a weak man on the brink of making the wrong decision. We are all tempted to hang the principle and please the crowd. But this Gospel holds up a mirror for us: in Pilate we see something of ourselves, something of our employers, something of our politicians. Pilate is not the only mirror in the room, however. Pilate looked into the face of Jesus and looked away, but we can look into that face and see reflected back something more than our weakness and sin. We can see a depth of his love in us and for us. We can see past all our haunting 'what ifs' to the only 'what is' that counts – and that is the love of God, shining in the face of Christ.

COLLECT

Almighty and everlasting God,
increase in us your gift of faith
that, forsaking what lies behind
and reaching out to that which is before,
we may run the way of your commandments
and win the crown of everlasting joy;
through Jesus Christ your Son our Lord,
who is alive and reigns with you,
in the unity of the Holy Spirit,
one God, now and for ever.

Psalms 87, **89.1-18**
Ecclesiasticus 17.1-24
or Ezekiel 18.1-20
Mark 15.16-32

Tuesday 6 October

Mark 15.16-32

'They compelled a passer-by' (v.21)

Simon of Cyrene, himself a compelled man, is one of the most compelling figures in the gospel. We feel for him because we have all been passers-by, passing by often enough on the other side of the road, stealing guilty glances at tragedies we can't prevent and in which we are afraid to get involved.

Simon of Cyrene had no choice, and we're almost glad of that. It makes it easier to get involved and stay involved when circumstances force your hand. And if Mark's naming of Rufus and Alexander is anything to go by, it looks as if Simon and his family did get involved, however accidental the first encounter may have been. It looks as if their story, like ours, was bound up with the story of this condemned man, both in his dying and in his rising.

I ended my sonnet on Simon of Cyrene, in *Sounding the Seasons* (Canterbury Press 2012), with these words:

> *So Simon, no disciple, still fulfilled*
> *The calling 'Take the cross and follow me'.*
> *By accident his life was stalled and stilled,*
> *Becoming all he was compelled to be.*
> *Make me, like him, your pressed man and your priest,*
> *Your* alter Christus, *burdened and released.*

God, our judge and saviour,
teach us to be open to your truth
and to trust in your love,
that we may live each day
with confidence in the salvation which is given
through Jesus Christ our Lord.

COLLECT

Wednesday 7 October

Psalm 119.105-128
Ecclesiasticus 18.1-14
or Ezekiel 18.21-32
Mark 15.33-41

Mark 15.33-41

'... the curtain of the temple was torn in two' (v.38)

Traditionally we think of Christ as having made three visits to the temple, each of growing intensity and significance. We think of his coming first as a babe in arms, not in Malachi's blinding light and fire, but in innocence and frailty. Yet the light of the Christ-child was strong and clear enough for Simeon to depart in peace. We think of his coming as a boy with questions and answers that amazed his teachers, as he himself learned how to do his Father's will. We think of him coming as a man with the knotted cord, overturning the tables, unleashing the lash that drives a pathway through so that the excluded poor can find a place freely in God's house.

But surely this moment on Good Friday, when the veil in that temple is torn in two, is a fourth and final visit, the most important of all. The veil that stood between us and the holy of holies, that barrier between heaven and earth, creator and creation, which once a year the high priest passed to make atonement, that veil is torn in two. The breath of God that swept across the cosmos in the beginning, now breathed out from the cross, blows it clean away. And now the heaven of our Father lies always open to us, and we are borne there on the breath of God.

COLLECT

Almighty and everlasting God,
increase in us your gift of faith
that, forsaking what lies behind
and reaching out to that which is before,
we may run the way of your commandments
and win the crown of everlasting joy;
through Jesus Christ your Son our Lord,
who is alive and reigns with you,
in the unity of the Holy Spirit,
one God, now and for ever.

Psalms 90, **92**
Ecclesiasticus 19.4-17
or Ezekiel 20.1-20
Mark 15.42-end

Mark 15.42-end

*'Joseph of Arimathea … himself waiting expectantly
for the kingdom of God' (v.43)*

The first original engraving the young William Blake ever made, while still an apprentice, was of Joseph of Arimathea. And whether it was the Glastonbury legends enriching his imagination and ours, or something else in this liminal but luminous Gospel figure that attracted Blake, there is certainly something about Joseph of Arimathea that also draws us in.

Perhaps it is because he is a latecomer to the story, aware of Christ's claims, having been silent in the Sanhedrin trial, and only now, after Christ's death, suddenly committing himself, in this beautiful useless gesture. For every gesture of love and care for the dead, from anointing to the care and attention that goes into a funeral, is in one way useless, for the dead are past needing it.

But in another way, these gestures are beautiful for the very reason that they are useless, flowing from a pure love that cannot seek or expect reward. The love that's poured out at old graves, renewing flowers, and tending the bare earth is never lost. All these things are found in and for Christ, gathered in him and given new life, blessing those who bless in unexpected ways. And in one way at least we all stand with Joseph when we sing these lines from the hymn *My song is love unknown*: 'What may I say? Heaven was his home: but mine the tomb wherein he lay.'

God, our judge and saviour,
teach us to be open to your truth
and to trust in your love,
that we may live each day
with confidence in the salvation which is given
through Jesus Christ our Lord.

COLLECT

Friday 9 October

Psalms **88** (95)
Ecclesiasticus 19.20-end
or Ezekiel 20.21-38
Mark 16.1-8

Mark 16.1-8

'... they said nothing to anyone, for they were afraid' (v.8)

This was the original ending to Mark's Gospel, and one could almost wish it still were (though, as we shall see, there is gospel in the coda too). But this early ending has the power and mystery of a suddenly opened door. Mark had begun his Gospel with the breathless rush of his favourite adverb 'immediately'; carried us through the growing awe and power of a 'messianic secret', at once kept and always spilling out, carried us down into the darkness of Jerusalem and Good Friday, where all that immediacy of power seemed to fail, and now in these last words he brings us to another brink. Where is he?

It is as though the last page of the Gospel itself opens like the yawning emptiness of the tomb. We put down the book and glance uneasily behind us. He might be anywhere! He has sprung as easily and freely from the pages of our book as he has sprung from the tomb. Trembling and astonishment might well come upon us too as we rise from our reading, and walk away from the church knowing that the one we thought we knew, whom we had met in these familiar pages, has gone ahead of us into our unknown. Anything might happen now, and it might happen immediately.

COLLECT

Almighty and everlasting God,
increase in us your gift of faith
that, forsaking what lies behind
and reaching out to that which is before,
we may run the way of your commandments
and win the crown of everlasting joy;
through Jesus Christ your Son our Lord,
who is alive and reigns with you,
in the unity of the Holy Spirit,
one God, now and for ever.

Psalms 96, **97**, 100
Ecclesiasticus 21.1-17
or Ezekiel 24.15-end
Mark 16.9-end

Mark 16.9-end

'... while the Lord worked with them' (v.20)

So we come to this more familiar ending, and it is the last line especially that provides food for thought. I sometimes think that Christianity is not so much about propositions as it is about prepositions: we pray and worship *'through* Jesus Christ our Lord'; we know that we are in some sense *'in* Christ, and he *in* us'; we all exhort each other to do things *'for* Christ', but what are we to make of this 'with'? The Lord worked *'with'* them, and he works *'with'* us!

This is not so much mystic communion as straightforward and practical collaboration: he is already at work in the world, and we can join him! This is why 'What would Jesus do?' is such an essentially faithless question. If he is risen, the real question is not 'What would Jesus do?' but 'What is Jesus already doing'?

He is alive and at work in the world he came to save, and it is our job to get out into that world and seek for him by the signs he gave. And wherever the captives are being freed, wherever wounds are being bound up, wherever the poor are hearing good news, in any sphere, sacred or secular, we can find our hidden master and join with him in his redemptive work.

God, our judge and saviour,
teach us to be open to your truth
and to trust in your love,
that we may live each day
with confidence in the salvation which is given
through Jesus Christ our Lord.

COLLECT

Monday 12 October

Psalms **98**, 99, 101
Ecclesiasticus 22.6-22
or Ezekiel 28.1-19
John 13.1-11

John 13.1-11

'... he laid aside his garments' (v.4, KJV)

John's is at once the most cosmic and the most intimate of the gospels, and it is the intimate details that carry the cosmic implications. So here Jesus lays aside his garments and kneels at his disciples' feet, but John frames this action in the fullness of Godhead. Jesus is the one who had come from God and was going to God, and so this little laying aside becomes itself the expression of his great *kenosis*, his 'self-emptying'. For he laid aside the garment and splendour of heaven, emptied himself and took the form of a servant. So every gesture is resonant: the one who covered himself with light as with a garment (Psalm 104.2) girds himself with a towel; the one whose Spirit moved on the waters of creation pours water into a basin.

Peter, like so many of us, can cope with the cosmic but not with the intimate. He is happy with Jesus high on the mountain of transfiguration with a newly made tabernacle between the two of them (Matthew 17.4), but he shrinks from this intimate touch. But here, as in all things, Jesus stoops to conquer.

> *'And here he shows the full extent of love*
> *to us whose love is always incomplete.*
> *In vain we search the heavens high above;*
> *The God of Love is kneeling at our feet.*

(Malcolm Guite, 'Maundy Thursday'
in *Sounding the Seasons*, Canterbury Press 2012)

COLLECT

O God, forasmuch as without you
we are not able to please you;
mercifully grant that your Holy Spirit
may in all things direct and rule our hearts;
through Jesus Christ your Son our Lord,
who is alive and reigns with you,
in the unity of the Holy Spirit,
one God, now and for ever.

Psalms **106*** (*or* 103)
Ecclesiasticus 22.27 – 23.15
or Ezekiel 33.1-20
John 13.12-20

John 13.12-20

'... whoever receives me receives him who sent me' (v.20)

The final verse in this passage opens up almost vertiginous possibilities, and pictures an apostolic succession that is not so much like a chain of ordaining hands as like a richly packed nest of Russian dolls. We see the outside of whoever has been sent to us, whoever in that succession, has come to us in our lives to witness resurrection. But hidden within that person is another person, the risen Lord himself, and then hidden within him is another: 'Him who sent me'! 'Anyone who has seen me has seen the Father'. It is as though Christ's descending and self-emptying path has been reversed. He moved from the infinite to the finite, and now he invites us to move through the finite, back into the infinite!

No, this mystery is not like Russian dolls, getting smaller as you go in, for this gets infinitely larger with every unveiling. It is more an apparently ordinary door that opens into adventure – like the door in Lucy's wardrobe, that leads to the magical kingdom of Narnia in C.S. Lewis' book *The Lion, the Witch and the Wardrobe* – for what is within is not only greater than what is without, but from within comes a call into God's country, to discover that the king there has a crown also to bestow upon us. At any moment as we receive anyone whom he has sent, that door may open; at any moment we may ourselves become that door for someone else!

Faithful Lord,
whose steadfast love never ceases
and whose mercies never come to an end:
grant us the grace to trust you
and to receive the gifts of your love,
new every morning,
in Jesus Christ our Lord.

COLLECT

Wednesday 14 October

Psalms 110, **111**, 112
Ecclesiasticus 24.1-22
or Ezekiel 33.21-end
John 13.21-30

John 13.21-30

'And it was night' (v.30)

We are used to saying that night falls as Judas leaves on his fell errand, but, to be honest, this ambiguous twilight that precedes his exit is far more troubling. It is not just the horror of betrayal by someone close, the wound to which any intimacy is always vulnerable; rather it is the way John seems to emphasize Jesus' foreknowledge – indeed more than foreknowledge, as John's account shows what is almost a participation in his own betrayal. The giving of the morsel, and the chilling detail that Satan entered after the morsel, make this moment seem like a ritual 'anti-communion'; furthermore, the whispered words – a plea or a command? – 'Do it quickly' all seem to involve Jesus more actively in Judas' 'night' than we would like.

What can we make of this? Is the tragedy of Judas beyond redemption? Or is it that in some strange way, in the passion that takes in and takes on the sins of the whole world, Jesus enters into the alienation of Judas and travels with him, and, perhaps, descends to hell to find him, so that Judas too, like Peter might have the chance of a redemptive encounter, a restoration of love?

This reading would at least be consonant with the radiant love and light that begin and end this Gospel, however dark the night with which it must also deal.

COLLECT

O God, forasmuch as without you
we are not able to please you;
mercifully grant that your Holy Spirit
may in all things direct and rule our hearts;
through Jesus Christ your Son our Lord,
who is alive and reigns with you,
in the unity of the Holy Spirit,
one God, now and for ever.

Psalms 113, **115**
Ecclesiasticus 24.23-end
or Ezekiel 34.1-16
John 13.31-end

Thursday 15 October

John 13.31-end

'... love one another, even as I have loved you' (v.34, ERV)

Here is the whole Gospel concentrated into nine words. It's not simply the *novum mandatum*, the positive commandment to love, replacing all those negative 'thou shalt nots'; it's the second clause, the 'even as', that is the true foundation of this love. There is a paradox here. We cannot be commanded to love. Love does not come at command; indeed 'command' is the very thing most likely to kill it. On the contrary, only love can beget love; we can only love in response to being loved, only know what love is because we are loved.

This is self-evident at the natural level. Just as a baby learns to smile in response to the smiles of its parents and learns language by being spoken to, so the very possibility of love, let alone its vocabulary and gestures, can only be learned in response to the love that finds us first, finds us before we even know what or who it is that has loved us.

And so it is with us spiritually. We love as we are loved, and Jesus makes the new commandment possible because of the utterly new and radical way in which he has loved us: absolutely, unconditionally, without reserve and to the last drop of his heart's blood.

Faithful Lord,
whose steadfast love never ceases
and whose mercies never come to an end:
grant us the grace to trust you
and to receive the gifts of your love,
new every morning,
in Jesus Christ our Lord.

COLLECT

281

Friday 16 October

Psalm **139**
Ecclesiasticus 27.30 – 28.9
or Ezekiel 34.17-end
John 14.1-14

John 14.1-14

'Lord, we do not know where you are going. How can we know the way?' (v.5)

He may be known as 'doubting Thomas', but perhaps 'honest Thomas' or 'courageous Thomas', or even 'tenacious Thomas' would be nearer the mark!

I thank God for Saint Thomas, the one disciple who had the courage to say what everyone else was thinking but didn't dare say. He had the courage to ask the awkward questions that drew from Jesus one of the most beautiful and profoundly comforting of all his sayings. 'We don't know where you're going, how can we know the way?' asked Thomas, and because he had the courage to confess his ignorance, we were given these words of life: 'I am the way, and the truth, and the life' (v.6).

And the Thomas in me has more to ask of this passage every time I return to it. Philip may be satisfied to have seen the Father in seeing Jesus, but I wasn't there – how can I see either Jesus or the Father now? I believe in Jesus, not having seen, but still I ask how. And that last promise of 'greater works' begs as many questions as it answers. Saint Thomas puts his finger on the nub of things, and so must I, touching the wounds of one whose wounds are healing mine.

O God, forasmuch as without you
we are not able to please you;
mercifully grant that your Holy Spirit
may in all things direct and rule our hearts;
through Jesus Christ your Son our Lord,
who is alive and reigns with you,
in the unity of the Holy Spirit,
one God, now and for ever.

Psalms 120, **121**, 122
Ecclesiasticus 28.14-end
or Ezekiel 36.16-36
John 14.15-end

John 14.15-end

'Do not let your hearts be troubled, and do not let them be afraid'
(v.27)

'Noli timere' – 'Do not be afraid' – These were the first words of the angels to the shepherds announcing the Saviour's birth, and now, on the night before his passion, in this intimate gathering and parting, Jesus repeats them: 'Let not your hearts be troubled, neither let them be afraid.'

Throughout this Gospel, Jesus has proclaimed, demonstrated and embodied the love of God and taught us that 'perfect love casts out fear' (1 John 4.18). And even as he walks out into the darkness, into perhaps the most fearful situation that could ever confront us, his love is centred not on what he will face but on encouraging and comforting his disciples, lifting their eyes above and beyond Good Friday's dark horizon to the promised comforter.

Those words, 'Rise, let us be on our way' (v.31), become more than a call to leave the upper room and walk on that one night to Gethsemane. They are a call to all of us to rise from this present moment and to go on our way, girded in Christ's love, through any unknown door, even through the grave and gate of death, and not to be afraid. When the poet Seamus Heaney lay dying, his last act was to text his wife, in his beloved Latin, those two words, *'Noli timere'* – 'Do not be afraid.' No one could have better last words.

Faithful Lord,
whose steadfast love never ceases
and whose mercies never come to an end:
grant us the grace to trust you
and to receive the gifts of your love,
new every morning,
in Jesus Christ our Lord.

COLLECT

Monday 19 October

Psalms 123, 124, 125, **126**
Ecclesiasticus 31.1-11
or Ezekiel 37.1-14
John 15.1-11

John 15.1-11

'Abide in me as I abide in you' (v.4)

The Gospel of John seems to suggest that one of the key words or ideas to help us understand the ministry of Jesus and the subsequent blueprint for the Church is that of 'abiding'*. The word is linked to another English word, 'abode'. God abides with us. Christ bids us to abide in him, and he will abide in us. He bids us to make our home with him, as he has made his home with us. Christ tells us that there are many rooms in his father's house. There are many places of gathering and meeting there. And central to the notion of an abode is the concept of abiding.

To abide is to 'wait patiently with'. God has abided with us. He came to us in ordinary life, and he has sat with us, eaten with us, walked with us, and lived among us. That is why John ends his Gospel with Jesus doing ordinary things. Breaking bread, or eating breakfast on the seashore. God continues to dwell with us. He was with us at the beginning, and he is with us at the end. He will not leave us.

And he wants his Church to abide with the world – and especially to be with all those who have no one to be with them. The friendless, the forlorn, the forgotten – God wills us to abide with them, and with each other. Deep, abiding fellowship is God's will for creation, not just well-organized congregations.

*cf. Ben Quash, *Abiding,* London: Bloomsbury, 2013

COLLECT

God, the giver of life,
whose Holy Spirit wells up within your Church:
by the Spirit's gifts equip us to live the gospel of Christ
    and make us eager to do your will,
that we may share with the whole creation
    the joys of eternal life;
through Jesus Christ your Son our Lord,
who is alive and reigns with you,
in the unity of the Holy Spirit,
one God, now and for ever.

Psalms **132**, 133
Ecclesiasticus 34.9-end
or Ezekiel 37.15-end
John 15.12-17

John 15.12-17

*'This is my commandment, that you love one another
as I have loved you' (v.12)*

What might it mean to 'love one another as I have loved you?' A popular story from World War Two tells of a Romanian priest who found himself imprisoned at Belsen and deprived of all he needed to sustain his faith: no crucifix, bible, icons, devotional books, corporate worship or knotted prayer beads. So he prayed in secret – that he might respond to the call of love. He found himself spending time in the camp with the sick, the starving, the diseased, the dying and the betrayers – all those who were shunned by others. One day, as the camp drew close to liberation, someone came to see the priest and said: 'I see how you live here. Tell me about the God you worship.' And the priest replied: 'He is like me.' Few of us could ever reply: 'He is like me.'

But love is the key to this. Indeed, it is the bridge and bond between God and humanity. The call to live a life of love and character is still the deepest vocation we all share. This is why Jesus, when asked 'What is the law? What is the greatest commandment?', could reply easily that it was about loving: loving God – with all your heart, soul, mind and strength – and loving your neighbour as yourself.

This is wisdom. And the wisdom of John goes slightly further. God has befriended us, and called us. We are no longer slaves or servants but friends of God. And if friends of God, then friends of the world: 'I am giving you these commandments so that you may love one another' (v.17).

God, our light and our salvation:
illuminate our lives,
that we may see your goodness in the land of the living,
and looking on your beauty
may be changed into the likeness of Jesus Christ our Lord.

COLLECT

Wednesday 21 October

Psalm 119.153-end
Ecclesiasticus 35
or Ezekiel 39.21-end
John 15.18-end

John 15.18-end

'If they persecuted me, they will persecute you' (v.20)

For some time now, I have held that one of the wrong turns we have taken in mission and ministry is that we assume the Church is an organization, that it can be easily managed, branded and mobilized. But the Church is not an organization. It is, rather, an institution. It exists not to adapt, survive and succeed, but rather to be faithful, independent of its popularity. It may be called to martyrdom, not growth.

Of course I do think churches should be organized and well managed. True, our USP ('unique selling point') is indeed Jesus. But our KPIs ('key performance indicators'), as drawn from the Gospels, are rather mixed. It may be an abundant harvest; it may be martyrdom; it may be conversions – but it may also be being hated by our friends and family for our faith, as today's Gospel reading confirms. We are not, in other words, called to measure ourselves through metrics of popularity and growth. The only game in town is faithfulness.

It is a pity that so much of our Church-focused mission today is about getting people in, when the gospel is basically about getting people out. 'Go!' is one of the last words Jesus says to his disciples. We should focus our energies on finding our communities and loving them, not on hoping they might find us and like us long enough to stay awhile.

COLLECT

God, the giver of life,
whose Holy Spirit wells up within your Church:
by the Spirit's gifts equip us to live the gospel of Christ
    and make us eager to do your will,
that we may share with the whole creation
    the joys of eternal life;
through Jesus Christ your Son our Lord,
who is alive and reigns with you,
in the unity of the Holy Spirit,
one God, now and for ever.

Psalms **143**, 146
Ecclesiasticus 37.7-24
or Ezekiel 43.1-12
John 16.1-15

John 16.1-15

*'When the Spirit of truth comes,
he will guide you into all the truth' (v.13)*

What exactly is the work of the Spirit? One of the characteristics that marked out the early Christian saints is that they understood faith to be passion. Faith, in terms of discipleship, is often not reasoned coolness. It is passion that spills over – the love that is stronger than death. It might be thought through. It may even be willed reason. But my God, it has to be willed with very fibre of your being.

Extreme faith is not the same as passionate faith. The former can be unyielding, unforgiving and self-righteous. The latter is more like the work of the Spirit. True, it can still be intemperate and immodest, but it abounds in energy and love because it springs from the liberality of God. It is released as a kind of raw energy, precisely because it breaks the chains of inhibition, and springs forth from spiritual encounters that can border on ecstasy. But this is not, as I say, extremism. It is merely passion resulting from encounter, conversion, conviction, resurrection and transformation.

The work of the Spirit, then, is one of refinement and discernment. It is often willed acts of moderation or self-control that emerge out of passionate convictions, grace and love. That's why the list of the fruits of the Holy Spirit from Galatians 5.22 is so important. Love, joy, peace, patience, kindness, self-control, humility, gentleness and faithfulness are all rooted in the passion of Christ – a putting-to-death of our desires and seeing them reconfigured through the Holy Spirit. So excess and abundance are of God; extremism, however, is of the flesh.

God, our light and our salvation:
illuminate our lives,
that we may see your goodness in the land of the living,
and looking on your beauty
may be changed into the likeness of Jesus Christ our Lord.

COLLECT

Friday 23 October

Psalms 142, **144**
Ecclesiasticus 38.1-14
or Ezekiel 44.4-16
John 16.16-22

John 16.16-22

'... you will have pain but your pain will turn into joy' (v.20)

The striking imagery Jesus uses here is of labour pains and birth. Something new and wonderful is coming into being. But for it to happen at all, there must be some pain and loss, which in turn will give way to joy.

We can sometimes spend a lot of time in our Christian lives trying to avoid suffering and pain – attempting, so it seems, to live in the midst of an eternal late summer and an abundant harvest. But there are seasons of the Spirit. The Church – much like our own discipleship – has to learn to live through autumn and winter, if the spring and summer are to fulfil their promise. Here, Jesus offers no short-cut or diversion that bypasses pain. But God will walk with us every step of the way. We find him in pain and pleasure, in barrenness and abundance.

As Scottish philosopher, John Macmurray reminds us in his *Persons in Relation* (1970), it is important to distinguish between genuine and deceptive religion. The philosophy of deceptive religion runs something like this: 'Fear not; trust in God and he will see that none of the things you dread will ever happen to you.' But, says Macmurray, genuine faith and mature religion have a quite different starting point: 'Fear not – the things you are most frightened of may well happen to you; but they are nothing to be afraid of.'

It will turn out fine if you are turned over to God. All you need to do is give back some of the love that has already been shown to you. Love is the lesson.

COLLECT

God, the giver of life,
whose Holy Spirit wells up within your Church:
by the Spirit's gifts equip us to live the gospel of Christ
    and make us eager to do your will,
that we may share with the whole creation
    the joys of eternal life;
through Jesus Christ your Son our Lord,
who is alive and reigns with you,
in the unity of the Holy Spirit,
one God, now and for ever.

Psalm 147
Ecclesiasticus 38.24-end
or Ezekiel 47.1-12
John 16.23-end

John 16.23-end

'But take courage; I have conquered the world!' (v.33)

You can almost hear the words of Julian of Norwich speaking to us here: 'All shall be well, and all shall be well, and all manner of thing shall be well.' Jesus is clear. We cannot go far wrong if we hand our lives over to God.

The disciples are now sensing that Jesus will be leaving them. This evokes in them a searching anxiety – one that is further deepened by Jesus talking of loss and persecution. Words of consolation from Jesus are also accompanied by doses of realism: the times ahead will be tough. But I will still be with you.

To know that God is with us both in the good and the bad sometimes requires a special wisdom. To see what God can do with the dark – because it is not darkness to him. Or weakness, which of course God loves to use – to shame the wisdom of the wise. Or to see what God can do with absence – usually filling it with a different and new kind of presence. What looks like failure and loss to the world is merely an opportunity for God. He uses these hairline cracks or gaping holes in our lives, and it these through which abundant life and grace can pour. The promise of the Spirit is not that we will avoid pain or persecution – we won't. The promise is, rather, that no matter what we face, the Spirit will bring us peace.

God, our light and our salvation:
illuminate our lives,
that we may see your goodness in the land of the living,
and looking on your beauty
may be changed into the likeness of Jesus Christ our Lord.

COLLECT

Monday 26 October

Psalms 1, 2, 3
Ecclesiasticus 39.1-11
or Ecclesiastes 1
John 17.1-5

John 17.1-5

'Father, glorify me ...' (v.5)

In Saint Paul's second letter to the Corinthians, Paul talks about 'the glory of God revealed in the face of Jesus Christ' (2 Corinthians 4.6): 'For it is the God who said, "Let light shine out of darkness", who has shone in our hearts to give the light of the knowledge of the glory of God in the face of Jesus Christ.'

It is one of the boldest statements we have in scripture. Our faces smile, frown, weep, laugh, wink, puzzle, grimace, grin – and much, much more. Our faces give us the most distinctive thing about our identity. So the idea that the glory of God is revealed in just one face – that of Jesus – is remarkable. But we know, of course, that our faces change, too, as we reflect that glory and look at Christ.

It takes a lifetime of discipleship to find that our faces can 'shine' with wisdom and love. But they can. And the key to this lies in understanding 'glory'. When we glorify God, we start to see the world as God sees it: with full and deep love. God loved the world enough to send his son to abide in it, so that we might abide in him eternally.

Faces that do shine with the glory of God are seen for what they are; reflections or images of God. One of C. S. Lewis' most mature Christian reflections is *Till We Have Faces*. The theme running through the book is that of transfiguration. Our faces can 'reflect' the glory of God revealed in the face of Jesus Christ. When this correspondence occurs, we see the world differently and we can look in love, just as God gazes upon his creation.

COLLECT

Blessed Lord,
who caused all holy Scriptures to be written for our learning:
help us so to hear them,
to read, mark, learn and inwardly digest them
that, through patience, and the comfort of your holy word,
we may embrace and for ever hold fast
    the hope of everlasting life,
which you have given us in our Saviour Jesus Christ,
who is alive and reigns with you,
in the unity of the Holy Spirit,
one God, now and for ever.

Psalms **5**, 6 (8)
Ecclesiasticus 39.13-end
or Ecclesiastes 2
John 17.6-19

John 17.6-19

'As you have sent me into the world ...' (v.18)

The unknown author of the late-second-century *Epistle to Diognetus* took the view that Christians were ordinary folk going about their ordinary business. We don't have special food or modes of dress. We live where we are, and not as a separate tribal or ethnic group. But, Diognetus continued, Christians 'reside in their respective countries, but only as aliens…they take part in everything as citizens and put up with everything as foreigners…every foreign land is their home, and every home a foreign land'.

This echoes the words of Jesus. We belong here – and yet we do not. Our true home is yet to come, and our true kingdom has not arrived, but it is coming. So wherever we live, we pray 'thy kingdom come, thy will be done, on earth as it is in heaven'.

So, where do you belong? The answer from Jesus is that we are in the world, yet not of it. For some early Christians, this meant the world did not have to be taken too seriously. It was a temporary place of transit. But Jesus' words are rather more subtle – and certainly stronger. Just as he was sent into the world, so are we. And our calling and mission, like his, is one of deep abiding engagement and sanctification. We may not, ultimately, belong to the world. But we are to love, cherish and bless it without limit.

Merciful God,
teach us to be faithful in change and uncertainty,
that trusting in your word
and obeying your will
we may enter the unfailing joy of Jesus Christ our Lord.

COLLECT

Wednesday 28 October

Simon and Jude, Apostles

Psalms 116, 117
Wisdom 5.1-16
or Isaiah 45.18-end
Luke 6.12-16

Luke 6.12-16

'And when day came, he ... chose twelve of them' (v.13)

The roll call of names for the twelve apostles today singles out Simon and Jude ('Judas, son of James', v.16) for special mention. But in truth, all twelve have the same calling. What is that?

Each of the disciples is to be an ambassador of the new hope wrought in the person of Jesus. And this role is one that hinges on developing a dynamic sense of vocation. All twelve are chosen – they are called. Moreover, the kingdom of God that Jesus proclaims does not draw disciples into a new sect, so much as send them out into the world with joy, conviction and a desire to serve the world and the needs of others in the name of the living Christ. Critically, this is done in love. It is not a task or a job; it is an entire reconfiguration of our lives. You cannot really command people to love. That's the catch. Love is for falling into. It is a state of being that leads to action.

All of us who work in the Church are faced, daily, with a simple dilemma. How do we begin to complete and apply the task that the apostles bequeathed us? How do we bring resurrection and transformation to the situations and people that we are here to serve? How do we heal the sick? Comfort the lost? Bring hope, joy, peace and wisdom to those who are searching for or needing health and completeness? Be a father to the needy? Help the lame to walk? Be eyes for the blind? Or love another? Their answer, I suspect is simple. Just two words from Jesus are enough here: 'Follow me.'

COLLECT

Blessed Lord,
who caused all holy Scriptures to be written for our learning:
help us so to hear them,
to read, mark, learn and inwardly digest them
that, through patience, and the comfort of your holy word,
we may embrace and for ever hold fast
    the hope of everlasting life,
which you have given us in our Saviour Jesus Christ,
who is alive and reigns with you,
in the unity of the Holy Spirit,
one God, now and for ever.

Psalms 14, **15**, 16
Ecclesiasticus 43.1-12
or Ecclesiastes 3.16 – 4.end
John 18.1-11

John 18.1-11

'Judas … also knew the place' (v.2)

The betrayal and arrest of Jesus is told in a slightly different way in each of the four Gospels. I suspect we all harbour profound memories and wounds of betrayal. This is the focus of this story, and it is important that we understand that Jesus experienced this, as it is part of his incarnation. This includes our deepest pains, which are often not imprinted on the body but in the soul and heart.

Judas is able to find Jesus easily because they are on close and intimate terms. They are friends who have shared familiar places. Some years ago there was a radio competition to write the shortest possible sermon. The winner was called 'The kiss', and it went something like this:

'Good to have you home, son. Sorry you were in so much pain.'
'It wasn't the nails that hurt, dad. It was the kiss.'

Our attention is drawn here to the deeply physical act of kissing. The kissing of Jesus' feet by an unknown woman and the kiss of Judas in betrayal. But whatever kind of kiss it is, the point is simple. God dwelt with us, among and as one of us: the word made flesh. He even gives himself to spaces and places in which he is vulnerable. And it is Jesus who is now given, through betrayal, into the hands of his captors. They will soon become his tormentors, torturers and executioners. The body of Christ is flesh marked by pain, torment and torture. So that the flesh that Jesus eventually returns to heaven with is even more like ours, it has been loved and cherished, but also weathered, beaten and defeated. Finally, it is killed. This will be the flesh of the resurrection: one still marked with nails, but now raised by God.

Merciful God,
teach us to be faithful in change and uncertainty,
that trusting in your word
and obeying your will
we may enter the unfailing joy of Jesus Christ our Lord.

COLLECT

Friday 30 October

Psalms 17, **19**
Ecclesiasticus 43.13-end
or Ecclesiastes 5
John 18.12-27

John 18.12-27

'He denied it and said, "I am not."' (v.25)

Denial. It is one of the major themes running through the end of John's Gospel – both before the crucifixion and after the resurrection. Followers deny knowing Jesus for fear of their lives. At the resurrection, they deny what they see for fear of losing their minds.

Denial is abnegation and, interestingly, is often used as a psychological defence mechanism, in which a person is faced with a fact that is too uncomfortable to accept and so rejects it instead. They will insist that it is not true, despite all the overwhelming evidence to the contrary.

Yet the threefold denial of Jesus by Peter will, in the end, be redeemed in the resurrection story recorded by John, in which Peter is asked three times, 'Simon Peter, do you love me' (John 21.15-19). But I also like the throw-away remark made by Luke, near the end of his Gospel. After the mysterious appearance of Jesus on the road to Emmaus, the witnesses scurry back to Jerusalem breathlessly to proclaim the resurrection. They need not have hurried, for Luke tells us that Jesus has already appeared to Peter (Luke 24.34). What words were exchanged between them is not recorded by anyone. However, it is perhaps safe to assume that Peter, the man who today denies any knowledge of Jesus, could begin to understand how this same Jesus – betrayed by humanity and seemingly abandoned by God – had at the same time now become the instrument of God's blessing to humanity.

COLLECT

Blessed Lord,
who caused all holy Scriptures to be written for our learning:
help us so to hear them,
to read, mark, learn and inwardly digest them
that, through patience, and the comfort of your holy word,
we may embrace and for ever hold fast
    the hope of everlasting life,
which you have given us in our Saviour Jesus Christ,
who is alive and reigns with you,
in the unity of the Holy Spirit,
one God, now and for ever.

Psalms 20, 21, **23**
Ecclesiasticus 44.1-15
or Ecclesiastes 6
John 18.28-end

Saturday 31 October

John 18.28-end

'Then they took Jesus from Caiaphas to Pilate's headquarters' (v.28)

John's detailed account of the arrest and 'trial' of Jesus has a strangely contemporary feel to it. The men in power – political and religious – spend the best part of a couple of days passing the buck. Jesus is betrayed and arrested, and is first taken to the house of Annas. Presumably declining to take responsibility for the possible trial and execution of a popular prophet and preacher from Galilee, Annas has Jesus bound and sent to Caiaphas. But Caiaphas is no fool either. He refers Jesus on to Pilate. And Pilate – no stranger to political expediency – attempts to have Jesus released. It is only then that the will of the people begins to surface and prevail. Spare Barabbas and execute Jesus, they cry. Annas, Caiaphas and Pilate can all breathe a huge sigh of relief. Even if Jesus is to die, their involvement is only piecemeal and indirect. They don't have to take ultimate responsibility. You can wash your hands now.

The Gospel of John skilfully narrates how the political landscape works – much as it does today. No one in power wants to take responsibility for an unpopular decision. In the end then, Jesus' death becomes something of a farce. He is flogged by Pilate's people, mocked and then cynically dressed as a king. Presumably Pilate hopes that even now, this will be enough to appease the mob's fury. But it is not. They demand more blood – and death.

The train of denial and betrayal begun by Judas, and continued by Peter, continues and escalates through the political leadership. But it will end. And it ends at the cross, where Jesus absorbs the pain and death of the world, and breaks the chain of consequences we find in sin. Today is not the end; nor is it the beginning of the end. But it is the end of the beginning.

Merciful God,
teach us to be faithful in change and uncertainty,
that trusting in your word
and obeying your will
we may enter the unfailing joy of Jesus Christ our Lord.

COLLECT

Isaiah 1.1-20

'... but bruises and sores and bleeding wounds' (v.6)

No one enjoys being reminded of their faults. How many times have we heard someone – or even ourselves – say, 'well, no one is perfect'?

Those who have undergone heart surgery identify it is as a life-changing experience. Afterwards everything alters – diet, exercise, sleeping patterns, even temperament plays a role in the transition towards a healthier lifestyle. Our spiritual heart is no different. Vestiges of sin establish an ongoing need for life-changing treatments similar to medicinal therapies that cauterize, dress and repair human wounds. Warning signs of a spiritual 'stroke' or 'heart attack' are not always immediately visible; forgoing morning devotions or Bible study, empty worship or infrequent church attendance can often be rationalized with explanations of family priorities, work or sheer tiredness.

Yet, God 'waits to be gracious' (Isaiah 30.18) and eagerly extends mercy. What is the restorative cure? Grace! God's generous invitation continually beckons us to repentance, reconciliation and spiritual transformation. As divine architect, he knows what our spirits and bodies need.

The healing balm that restores broken relationships with God is Jesus Christ. As his brothers and sisters, he calls us to emulate his loving, gracious and conciliatory character. When we encounter those who bear the 'bruises and sores and bleeding wounds' of human sin and suffering, we need only apply the healing balm of Christ, that love from God that receives, heals, nurtures and restores.

COLLECT

Almighty and eternal God,
you have kindled the flame of love
    in the hearts of the saints:
grant to us the same faith and power of love,
that, as we rejoice in their triumphs,
we may be sustained by their example and fellowship;
through Jesus Christ your Son our Lord,
who is alive and reigns with you,
in the unity of the Holy Spirit,
one God, now and for ever.

Isaiah 1.21-end

*'Zion shall be redeemed by justice, and those in her who repent,
by righteousness' (v.27)*

The concept of redemption plays a prominent role in many of the prophetic writings in the Bible. Even today, God continues to inspire modern-day prophets to remind all of his people of their responsibilities to serve and safeguard others. They challenge us to exhibit God's character – modelling his righteousness, justice, fidelity – through our concern for the vulnerable, be they orphans, widows or those existing on the margins of society. When we treat others with respect, integrity and equity, we offer them a glimpse of God's mercy universally extended to all, while our actions demonstrate his plans to redeem our communities and its people.

Many churches desire spiritual revival, and many of our communities are in dire need of economic revitalization. We all long to see God's abundance poured out upon our churches, homes, schools, businesses and governing councils. As God's people, our just actions and faithful prayers positively impact on his redeeming work in our communities.

Isaiah's oracle reminds us that when a nation or community turns to God, the transformation can be miraculous. Every village and town becomes a place 'of righteousness' and our principal cities flourish. Isaiah's message encourages us to remain faithful examples of God's righteous character while continuing his work on earth. As we unite in prayer today, we ask that God's renewing presence be demonstrated throughout our nation.

God of glory,
touch our lips with the fire of your Spirit,
that we with all creation
may rejoice to sing your praise;
through Jesus Christ our Lord.

COLLECT

297

| **Wednesday 4 November** | Psalms **9**, 147.13-end *or* **34**
Isaiah 2.1-11
Matthew 2.16-end |

Isaiah 2.1-11

'Come, let us go up to the mountain of the Lord' (v.3)

In the heart of the Sinai Peninsula sits the Holy Monastery of St Catherine, from which pilgrims regularly depart in the darkness of night determined to reach Mount Sinai's summit by dawn. The desert sky intensifies the brilliance of stars, as torches and lanterns dimly illuminate the pilgrims' ascent. Guides silently direct travellers riding camels or walking the rugged route. At daybreak, once gathered around the mountain's summit, a myriad of voices in diverse languages release prayers and songs of praise as Jews, Christians and Muslims worship their God.

Isaiah foretold a time of peace and unity, when the knowledge of God will be accessible to all nations. What an incredible hope this offers us today as wars, sanctions and border disputes rage. Rarely is God trusted to resolve conflicts, as we're more prone to take matters into our own hands. This is natural; as children, we are taught to be self-reliant, independent thinkers. Yet, we cannot control every situation – events such as loss of loved ones, poor or deteriorating health, or employment redundancies often reveal our vulnerability. By drawing close to God during times of great darkness, we allow him to guide us along those treacherous mountainous paths. Relying on his faithful support revitalizes our spirits as we partake of his infinite goodness. He alone faithfully guides us during the dark times that test our human endurance.

COLLECT

Almighty and eternal God,
you have kindled the flame of love
    in the hearts of the saints:
grant to us the same faith and power of love,
that, as we rejoice in their triumphs,
we may be sustained by their example and fellowship;
through Jesus Christ your Son our Lord,
who is alive and reigns with you,
in the unity of the Holy Spirit,
one God, now and for ever.

Psalms 11, **15**, 148 *or* **37***
Isaiah 2.12-end
Matthew 3

Thursday 5 November

Isaiah 2.12-end

'...the Lord alone will be exalted on that day.' (2.17)

Who do we elevate and revere today? Do we idolize our favourite athletes? Are we zealous twitter fans scooping the latest tweet from gifted pop artists? Have we promoted our Facebook friends or social networks into the 'must do' category? Of course, our enthusiasm and passion to know more or do more isn't really idolatry. Or, is it?

Today, regular attendance at sports attractions replaces Sunday worship, along with shopping malls, nature hikes, skating rinks, bowling alleys and more. Weekly Bible study is easily supplanted by daytime television, while mid-week Holy Communion is ousted by lunch outings, the gym, or discount showings at the local theatre. The imbalance in our lives increases each day, as even life-long mature Christians express their struggle to give God total supremacy of their hearts and diaries.

It's common knowledge that activities, people and 'things' regularly vie for our time and attention. We are constantly bombarded with media messages encouraging us to do more – spend more, eat more and play more. We must not squander the rich blessings we have inherited through the faithful prayers of our Christian forebears. As we learn to prioritize how each hour of the day will be spent, Isaiah reminds us of God's heart. He desires us to discover a life-work-worship balance, whereby he alone possesses the most exalted place in our hearts.

God of glory,
touch our lips with the fire of your Spirit,
that we with all creation
may rejoice to sing your praise;
through Jesus Christ our Lord.

COLLECT

Friday 6 November

Psalms **16**, 149 *or* **31**
Isaiah 3.1-15
Matthew 4.1-11

Isaiah 3.1-15

'What do you mean by crushing my people, by grinding the face of the poor?' (3.15)

What induces divine retribution? Oppression of the weak and vulnerable! Today's reading sounds a piercing alarm as Isaiah proclaims God's love for the vulnerable. As his people, it is a love we too are called to share with those who are lost and without hope.

Many of us often cross the street to avoid someone who appears to 'live rough' or look away from those requesting a 'hand out'? Sometimes we respond out of conditioning, mistrust or fear, but, afterwards we feel ashamed and repentant. So, the affluent are not the only oppressors of the vulnerable; we also persecute them with every look of disgust or expression of 'bothersome' frustration.

As children of God, he expects us to be generous, not simply with our finances and goods, but also with our actions and gestures. A warm smile or friendly greeting to someone in need restores their humanity; they become a visible member of our society. No longer are they ignored or avoided, but one whose life has purpose and value. While we should act sensibly, our actions should yet reveal God's kindness and concern for all human life. God's blessings to us are for sharing; his message of hope and transformation extended to all. Today we ask the Holy Spirit to guide us in sharing God's love with others in visible, tangible ways.

COLLECT

Almighty and eternal God,
you have kindled the flame of love
    in the hearts of the saints:
grant to us the same faith and power of love,
that, as we rejoice in their triumphs,
we may be sustained by their example and fellowship;
through Jesus Christ your Son our Lord,
who is alive and reigns with you,
in the unity of the Holy Spirit,
one God, now and for ever.

Psalms **18.31-end**, 150 *or* 41, **42**, 43   **Saturday 7 November**
Isaiah 4.2 – 5.7
Matthew 4.12-22

Isaiah 4.2 – 5.7

'On that day the branch of the Lord shall be beautiful
and glorious ...' (4.2)

We don't often think of God's righteous judgement as an instrument of transformation. And, yet, we have heard or read numerous accounts from people who have committed appalling crimes, suffered imprisonment, turned to God and been completely changed through their personal relationship with him. This is the amazing power of grace.

God's love abounds to us in different ways. Perhaps we felt his abundance after suffering a loss, or faced a devastating 'near death' experience, or while reflecting on our sinful past deeds. Whatever the situation, we found our hearts and attention drawn to that place where hope through relationship with God was possible. Coming to God clarifies his divine love for us and opens unimaginable doors of person rediscovery, renewal, joy. We recognize that we are a branch – grafted or rooted – to reveal the beauty and glory of God.

Understanding our significance to God helps us value our relationship with him. Being overwhelmed by God's passionate love for us, like the psalmist we dare to ask, 'what are human beings that you are mindful of them, mortals that you care for them?' (Psalms 8.4) Consequently, any challenge, obstacle or righteous judgement we experience that brings us under the transforming and protective power of our redeemer, is to be celebrated. Today, we pray for God's purging, refining fire and say, 'Come.'

God of glory,
touch our lips with the fire of your Spirit,
that we with all creation
may rejoice to sing your praise;
through Jesus Christ our Lord.

COLLECT

Monday 9 November

Psalms 19, **20** *or* **44**
Isaiah 5.8-24
Matthew 4.23 – 5.12

Isaiah 5.8-24

'...the Lord of hosts is exalted by justice, and the Holy God shows himself holy by righteousness' (v.16)

Rarely do we witness the fast and concerted effort of ant colonies building the mound that will become a nest for their eggs. These insects possess an instinctive drive that prompts them to work at energetic speeds using whatever materials are available – earth, sand, pine needles, or crushed pebbles. Preservation of their vulnerable young stirs each ant to carry single specks of sand or pebbles to construct the dwelling that ultimately houses the colony.

Where are we when opportunities arise for us to work diligently on behalf of those who are most vulnerable among us? Most often, we sit silently by, awaiting God's righteous judgement. Our silence and failure to defend the needs of the vulnerable only increases their subjugation. If God has given ants the instinct to preserve their own, likewise his divine indignation empowers us to champion the needs of the weak.

Righteous justice is a divine attribute that God has graciously bestowed upon his children. This character trait compels us to work towards halting the drunken revelry prevalent in our urban towns and cities, to demand affordable housing for destitute families, and to petition for food to be made available for children, the infirm and indigent.

Today we forgive and pray God's mercy on those who exploit others for profit and ask God to give us ways actively to defend the helpless.

COLLECT

Almighty Father,
whose will is to restore all things
in your beloved Son, the King of all:
govern the hearts and minds of those in authority,
and bring the families of the nations,
divided and torn apart by the ravages of sin,
to be subject to his just and gentle rule;
who is alive and reigns with you,
in the unity of the Holy Spirit,
one God, now and for ever.

Isaiah 5.25-end

'None of them is weary, none stumbles, none slumbers or sleeps …'
(v.27)

Isaiah's imagery of the Assyrian conquest proves just as distressing today, almost as if it were being transmitted during one of our nightly newscasts. All too often our news broadcasts reveal the horrors of war, terrorist attacks and suicide bombings. Yet, Isaiah's conviction that, in the midst of it all, God's hand is yet at work, gives us hope for positive outcomes.

Many of us were mesmerized in 1996 by the televised South African amnesty hearings conducted by its Truth and Reconciliation Commission. How could any good come out of such violent, ruthless actions that displayed total disregard for human life? And yet, tears flowed as forgiveness was offered and death penalties annulled. God's message of healing compassion was visibly displayed as a gift to a grieving world.

Today, compassionate support and generosity are prevalent during national disasters and international catastrophes. Food and aid for war refugees are generously donated, collected and distributed through peace-keeping agencies. Distribution of care parcels of water, food, clothing, blankets or medical supplies is televised around the world as God's people rise to the task. When we resist evil with good deeds, we reveal God's abundant love for all nations and peoples. A God capable of humbling and chastising a nation he loved, is more than capable of exalting numerous nations to the benefit of his glory.

God, our refuge and strength,
bring near the day when wars shall cease
and poverty and pain shall end,
that earth may know the peace of heaven
through Jesus Christ our Lord.

COLLECT

Isaiah 6

'… yet my eyes have seen the King, the Lord of hosts!' (v.5)

Apocalyptic writings are full of visionary experiences that transport God's faithful seers into the divine throne room of his heavenly presence. Their narratives describe a heavenly temple full of lively worship, with angelic beings in joy-filled submission to an awe-inspiring God. Often with trembling knees, or stuttering tongue, or unabashed fear the seer humbly kneels and receive God's plan for their lives and that of God's holy people.

Each day brings fresh opportunities for God to call us, 'Whom shall I send, and who will go for us?' (v.8). How do we answer? Are we hesitant? Most leaders are; Moses acknowledged a speech impediment, Gideon laid fleece after fleece with uncertainty, and even the wise Solomon acknowledged he was a child before God. We're not all Isaiah, readily responding, 'Here am I; send me!' Even a perplexed Mary, needed a fuller explanation before replying, 'Here am I, the servant of the Lord' (Luke 1.38).

Our hesitancy when answering God is understandable. However, ultimately our response should be 'yes'. God extends a life-changing opportunity to us, to continue his work during our lifetime on earth. Regardless of the task or the odds of success, no matter how daunting the work, Isaiah's words reassure us that we will see God's power working in our midst. Today we prayerfully listen for God's life-changing call revealing possibilities of ministry to others.

COLLECT

Almighty Father,
whose will is to restore all things
in your beloved Son, the King of all:
govern the hearts and minds of those in authority,
and bring the families of the nations,
divided and torn apart by the ravages of sin,
to be subject to his just and gentle rule;
who is alive and reigns with you,
in the unity of the Holy Spirit,
one God, now and for ever.

Psalms **26**, 27 *or* 56, **57** (63*)
Isaiah 7.1-17
Matthew 5.38-end

Isaiah 7.1-17

'It shall not stand, and it shall not come to pass!' (v.7)

We can occasionally become overwhelmed by the pressures of life. We feel surrounded, powerless and incapable of responding to the burdens we carry. Fear sets in, our greatest dreads take shape, and our faith begins to falter. Then the doorbell rings or the telephone chimes, and a messenger from God speaks 'peace' over our lives. Of course, it's usually a friend, family member or neighbour, but nonetheless, God uses them at that exact moment to reassure us that our troubles will pass.

We see God's divine protection at work throughout scripture – a stream of water springs up to quench Hagar's thirst and preserve her son Ishmael, ravens feed Elijah during a national famine, and angels minister strength to Jesus in the Garden of Gethsemane. When challenges arise and appear to overtake us, we can always be assured of God's faithful presence.

Fitness trainers know that muscles have 'memory'. So, even when we're out of shape, once we resume physical activity, our muscles work hard to restore our bodies to their previous level of strength. However, once we reach that level again, we must work even harder to surpass it and gain 'new' strength. Often, life's challenges give our spiritual muscles a 'workout.' However, God sends messages of hope to inspire us and take us from strength to *new* strength.

God, our refuge and strength,
bring near the day when wars shall cease
and poverty and pain shall end,
that earth may know the peace of heaven
through Jesus Christ our Lord.

COLLECT

Friday 13 November

Isaiah 8.1-15

*'But the Lord of hosts, him you shall regard as holy ...
He will become a sanctuary ...' (vv. 13-14)*

It's unimaginable how terrified we would be if alerted 24 hours before an impending, inescapable natural disaster. We've all combed our televisions, radios, newspapers and internet for news stories about those who have survived great earthquakes, tsunamis, hurricanes or volcanic eruptions. The pictures and 'narrow escape' narratives allow us to empathize with the survivors and share in their struggle to live. But no amount of empathy can prepare us for the actual experience.

In Isaiah's prophecy, the people are warned that no amount of banding together, counsel or prophetic words will assure them of God's support. What a bleak prospect! Who do we turn to when we can't turn to God? Our government? The military? Only God has the ultimate power to save and preserve us?

Thank God for the cross! The redeeming work of Christ allows him to intercede on our behalf, averting God's righteous indignation. As mediator and redeemer, he stands alongside us, guiding us with his continual presence. Even during times of overwhelming catastrophe, the love of God and interceding petitions of Christ can be seen in the outpouring of support for those who have lost everything but their lives. 'Peace' is one of the greatest byproducts we receive from Jesus' gift of reconciliation. His peace reassures us with the knowledge of God's love and protective support.

COLLECT

Almighty Father,
whose will is to restore all things
in your beloved Son, the King of all:
govern the hearts and minds of those in authority,
and bring the families of the nations,
divided and torn apart by the ravages of sin,
to be subject to his just and gentle rule;
who is alive and reigns with you,
in the unity of the Holy Spirit,
one God, now and for ever.

Saturday 14 November

Isaiah 8.16 – 9.7

'I will wait for the Lord ... and I will hope in him' (8.17)

What legacy will we leave demonstrating our faithful witness of Christ? How many lives have we touched sharing God's word, saying a prayer, laying hands for healing, or extending God's compassion to someone from whom we have nothing to gain? A bequest can take many different forms – an endowment to a church or charity, giving a Bible, or leading someone to Christ.

In our reading today, Isaiah 'binds up' and 'seals' his prophecies, determined to 'wait for Lord'. Today, his writings represent some of the earliest surviving oracles in written form. This was Isaiah's legacy to the people of Israel, a bequest poured into gentile 'God fearers' who would later come to follow Christ – Christians. He willingly laid his writings aside for posterity, believing that God's faithful fulfillment would authenticate his calling.

It's very hard to give up our hopes and dreams, even for a small period of time and dedicate ourselves in faithful service to God. An engineer goes to build bridges and water cisterns in Equatorial New Guinea; a doctor resigns from the NHS to serve in Christian hospitals in southern Africa; an accountant leaves a post with a port authority to structure accounting systems for an international mission agency; a churchwarden takes leave to support the church during an interregnum. What bequest is God calling us to make today?

God, our refuge and strength,
bring near the day when wars shall cease
and poverty and pain shall end,
that earth may know the peace of heaven
through Jesus Christ our Lord.

COLLECT

Monday 16 November

Isaiah 9.8 – 10.4

'... his hand is stretched out still' (9.12)

Isaiah is doing what prophets were expected to do: preaching God's judgement on the nation's enemies. Not that the northern kingdom of Israel was always the enemy of southern Judah. They had, after all, briefly been one kingdom, many years before. But the complicated international politics of the Middle East even then compelled strange alliances, and Israel and Judah found themselves sometimes on opposite sides.

Israel is under a military attack that it has no chance of withstanding. Why? There is a deeper reason, says Isaiah, than simply being on the losing side. They have been faithless, godless, violent and unrepentant, we are told. One can imagine Isaiah's listeners in Judah enjoying this sermon. How comforting, to think that God's judgement falls on one's enemies. How smug one might feel by comparison, secure in the knowledge of God's favour.

But then the message changes direction. 'Ah, you,' declaims Isaiah. 'You think you are safe? Think again. Look around and see the injustice, the despicable treatment of the most vulnerable in society.' Then comes the deadly refrain, applying to Judah as to the others: 'his anger has not turned away; his hand is stretched out still.'

We may find difficult the idea of God being so involved in politics and war. Despite our discomfort, there are things we must hear. If God is against injustice, he is against injustice *everywhere*. God's own people cannot expect special treatment.

COLLECT

Heavenly Father,
whose blessed Son was revealed
    to destroy the works of the devil
and to make us the children of God and heirs of eternal life:
grant that we, having this hope,
may purify ourselves even as he is pure;
that when he shall appear in power and great glory
we may be made like him in his eternal and glorious kingdom;
where he is alive and reigns with you,
in the unity of the Holy Spirit,
one God, now and for ever.

Psalms 48, **52** *or* **73**
Isaiah 10.5-19
Matthew 7.13-end

Tuesday 17 November

Isaiah 10.5-19

'... it is in his heart to destroy' (v.7)

Isaiah provides us with a model for theological reflection on international politics. We may not like some of his conclusions, but it is worth paying attention to his methods.

The Assyrian army is rampaging around the region in which Israel and Judah are set, crushing all resistance and making slaves of the peoples. How is it possible, Isaiah wonders, for the Assyrian emperor to have so much power? The question raises doubts about the God of Israel. Is God not powerful enough to stop the Assyrians? Or is he perhaps distant and uninvolved?

Either conclusion casts doubt on the faith of the people, and the truth of their story, and neither is acceptable to God's prophet. God is fully engaged with all that is going on, says Isaiah. He allows the Assyrian emperor his victories. More than that, he encourages them. Assyria thinks it is winning all by itself, but really it is merely a temporary tool in God's hand, to be destroyed in its turn when God's purposes have been achieved. God's people have gone wrong, and God is using Assyria to put things right.

Isaiah looks at the world around him and asks the perennial question for people of faith: what is God thinking and doing? Isaiah concludes that God is not watching with remote calm, but is passionate and involved. If we ask the question about our contemporary world, where do we see God?

Heavenly Lord,
you long for the world's salvation:
stir us from apathy,
restrain us from excess
and revive in us new hope
that all creation will one day be healed
in Jesus Christ our Lord.

COLLECT

Wednesday 18 November

Psalms **56**, 57 *or* **77**
Isaiah 10.20-32
Matthew 8.1-13

Isaiah 10.20-32

'A remnant will return ...' (v.21)

Isaiah's messages of condemnation and predictions of coming judgement are interspersed in this complex book with moments of future hope. One key to this hope is the idea of a 'remnant'.

If you are lucky enough to find one of the few remaining shops that sell dressmaking fabric, you may be able to buy a remnant, a leftover bit at the end of the roll, a scrap too small to make anything with. It takes a skilled craftsperson to use the remnant to create something useful and beautiful. Isaiah imagines a remnant in the hands of God. It is an unpromising scrap, a pale shadow of the once great 'house of Jacob', but it is better than nothing. It shows that, despite everything, God's people still exist.

The composite nature of the book of Isaiah makes it difficult to know against whom God's fierce anger is being directed. What is clear is that there is a little germ of a promise here. When the Lord God of hosts, the Holy One of Israel, is in charge, the people of Jerusalem need only place their trust in the right place, and they can be certain that their story is not at an end.

When it seems that Christians are in a dwindling minority, perhaps we need to listen to Isaiah. Sometimes destruction is necessary, and in the end, a remnant is all God needs.

COLLECT

Heavenly Father,
whose blessed Son was revealed
    to destroy the works of the devil
and to make us the children of God and heirs of eternal life:
grant that we, having this hope,
may purify ourselves even as he is pure;
that when he shall appear in power and great glory
we may be made like him in his eternal and glorious kingdom;
where he is alive and reigns with you,
in the unity of the Holy Spirit,
one God, now and for ever.

Psalms 61, **62** *or* **78.1-39***
Isaiah 10.33 – 11.9
Matthew 8.14-22

Isaiah 10.33 – 11.9

'They will not hurt or destroy' (11.9)

There are chainsaws at work among God's people. As the trees hit the ground and are dragged away, it looks as though the forest has gone forever. But as woodland workers know, cutting down can lead to new growth. From a severed stump appears a slender green shoot.

We are listening to a song full of deep desire and long-held hope. One day there will be a new King David, even more perfect than before, and through him God will rule the earth.

It's easy to let the poetry carry us away. The vision of harmony throughout the whole of creation touches the deepest desires of our hearts. But let us be realistic for a moment. Wolves eat lambs, lions eat calves, and there is nothing any king can do about it. This is not a vision we can work towards. Even if people lay down their weapons, wolves will still eat lambs. This vision takes us far beyond the best we can hope for in our present reality. It invites us to imagine another world, one where there is magic and mystery, and where all cruelty and enmity is banished.

Soon Isaiah will take us back to a world where enemy armies rampage around the Middle East with God's approval. But now we have something to sustain us: an impossible dream, that one day God will come to reign over a magical world of peace and joy.

Heavenly Lord,
you long for the world's salvation:
stir us from apathy,
restrain us from excess
and revive in us new hope
that all creation will one day be healed
in Jesus Christ our Lord.

COLLECT

Friday 20 November

Psalms **63**, 65 *or* **55**
Isaiah 11.10 – 12.end
Matthew 8.23-end

Isaiah 11.10 – 12.end

'On that day ...' (11.10,11; 12.1,3)

The phrase 'on that day' features often in the prophecies of Isaiah. It seems the people of his day were longing for 'the day of the Lord', when their God would intervene on their behalf. Isaiah warns them to be careful what they wish for. Sometimes the day of the Lord is a good thing; sometimes it is dreadful, and it is always unpredictable which it will be.

Today we are still with the promise of a remnant. The day of the Lord brings a new exodus, repeating the rescue from Egypt that formed the people long ago. It is a time when songs of joy and praise will be sung, not only in Jerusalem but throughout the earth.

Isaiah will not let us pin God down. Just when we think we know what sort of God Isaiah believes in, there is something new. Isaiah's God is angry and punishing, turning on his people with the might of the Assyrian army, furious with their faithlessness and injustice. But then God sweeps around the world, gathering what is left of his people, bringing them home to live in peace.

The consistent feature of Isaiah's God is his energy. For a quiet, kind God we have to look elsewhere in the Old Testament. This God is active, engaged, on the move and unpredictable. Looking at our world, is this the kind of God we can imagine as its driving force?

COLLECT

Heavenly Father,
whose blessed Son was revealed
    to destroy the works of the devil
and to make us the children of God and heirs of eternal life:
grant that we, having this hope,
may purify ourselves even as he is pure;
that when he shall appear in power and great glory
we may be made like him in his eternal and glorious kingdom;
where he is alive and reigns with you,
in the unity of the Holy Spirit,
one God, now and for ever.

Saturday 21 November

Isaiah 13.1-13

'Listen, a tumult on the mountains ...' (v.4)

Who is in charge of the world? Well, it's obvious, is it not? The banks; the multinational companies; the superpower nations with their ferocious weapons of war.

In Isaiah's day, the answer to the question might well have been 'the Assyrians' or 'the Babylonians'. A succession of international superpowers fought for supremacy around Judah, whose only hope for survival was to appease the likely victor.

But Isaiah asserts something different. It is God who is in charge of the world, he says. We are so accustomed to hearing this from biblical writers that we perhaps forget how truly astonishing an assertion it is. Look around our world. Watch the news bulletins. Does it look as though God is in charge? It was no different in Isaiah's day. And yet Isaiah invites us to pay attention to an alternative truth. Whatever it looks like, he suggests, the truth is that God is in control. Even now, he says, God is getting ready to deal with Babylon. The mighty empire does not stand a chance in the face of the God who can make the stars go dark.

God is in charge, and it is the task of people of faith to say this, and to believe it, even in the teeth of the evidence, until one day, on 'the day of the Lord', when God comes to reign, the whole earth will see it too.

Heavenly Lord,
you long for the world's salvation:
stir us from apathy,
restrain us from excess
and revive in us new hope
that all creation will one day be healed
in Jesus Christ our Lord.

COLLECT

Monday 23 November

Psalms 92, **96** *or* **80**, 82
Isaiah 14.3-20
Matthew 9.18-34

Isaiah 14.3-20

'Is this the man who made the earth tremble?' (v.16)

What goes up must come down, the saying goes, and nowhere is it more true than of dictators who pit themselves against the very powers of heaven.

Isaiah invites his people to join with him in singing a victory song. The song taunts and belittles an emperor who has seemed to have ultimate power and authority. The poetry celebrates the fall of one who aspired to rule the known universe. He wanted to ride on the clouds, but instead is in Sheol, the dark world where the shades of the dead linger forgotten.

The poetry is shot through with the language of mythology, and, thanks largely to John Milton's *Paradise Lost*, we sometimes read here the story of a fallen angel who rules the dark kingdom. But the song has a universal application. It plays its part alongside our own mythologies such as *Doctor Who* and *Star Wars*. It says that in the elemental battle between good and evil that is fought out every day in a myriad of places around our planet, good always wins in the end. It says that anyone who thinks they can become divine is destined to fail.

Isaiah gives us a song for the oppressed. It looks at dictators and mocks them. It imagines them among the shades of the dead. It asserts that they will turn to dust. It believes that, despite appearances to the contrary, in the end good will triumph.

COLLECT

Eternal Father,
whose Son Jesus Christ ascended to the throne of heaven
    that he might rule over all things as Lord and King:
keep the Church in the unity of the Spirit
and in the bond of peace,
and bring the whole created order to worship at his feet;
who is alive and reigns with you,
in the unity of the Holy Spirit,
one God, now and for ever.

Psalms **97**, 98, 100 *or* 87, **89.1-18**
Isaiah 17
Matthew 9.35 – 10.15

Isaiah 17

'... you have forgotten the God of your salvation' (v.10)

'And for a report on the situation in Syria, it's over to our reporter in Damascus, Isaiah Amozson. Isaiah, what is happening there?'

'Well, at the moment Syria seems to be as strong as ever. But there's definitely something in the air. There's a lot of uncertainty about the future, with reports of a god called Yahweh taking control elsewhere in the region ...'

Old Testament prophets were the political commentators of their day. Here we see Isaiah fulfilling both parts of that role. First, he talks about the future fate of Syria, a feared enemy of God's people. The powerful city of Damascus will be reduced to ruins, as will Israel, Judah's other enemy to the north.

But then God's commentator turns his attention to home affairs. The future is not so good for Judah either. The problem is a failure of memory. They have ignored the old stories of the God of the desert and turned instead to the gentler agricultural gods of Canaan. They have forfeited the protection of the God whose people they truly are, and the foreign policy implications are devastating.

Among the nations of our world, in their conflicts and their alliances, can we discern what God desires? Perhaps it is up to us, who re-tell the stories of salvation, who remember where our allegiance lies, to proclaim whose world it truly is, and to get involved.

God the Father,
help us to hear the call of Christ the King
and to follow in his service,
whose kingdom has no end;
for he reigns with you and the Holy Spirit,
one God, one glory.

COLLECT

Wednesday 25 November

Isaiah 19

*'Blessed be Egypt my people, and Assyria the work of my hands,
and Israel my heritage' (v.25)*

Egypt is not only a major force in the history of the Old Testament people of God, it also has a powerful hold on their imagination. It is the place of slavery, where their ancestors were the victims of attempted genocide and where they first experienced the saving power of their God. It is a place of refuge; when Assyria and Syria to the north turn aggressive, Egypt to the south becomes somewhere to turn. It is a place of culture, assisting with establishing the early Israelite kingdom. It is a source of destruction, when Israel and Judah get in the way of its struggles with Assyria and Babylon.

But even with all this richness of meaning, Isaiah's words about Egypt are startling. The chapter begins normally enough, with talk of the destruction of the nation 'on that day'. But half way through, its tone changes. For Egypt, as for Judah, there is to be salvation after destruction. Even more surprisingly, Assyria, known for its aggression and cruelty, will be included in God's reconstruction. On the road between Egypt and Assyria, the marching soldiers will be replaced by peaceful pilgrims.

Who are God's chosen people? Here Israel loses its exclusive claim. They are not as special as they have thought themselves. They may be chosen people, but they are not alone. Every people, even their enemies – especially their enemies, it turns out – are God's chosen ones.

COLLECT

Eternal Father,
whose Son Jesus Christ ascended to the throne of heaven
that he might rule over all things as Lord and King:
keep the Church in the unity of the Spirit
and in the bond of peace,
and bring the whole created order to worship at his feet;
who is alive and reigns with you,
in the unity of the Holy Spirit,
one God, now and for ever.

Psalms **125**, 126, 127, 128 *or* 90, **92**
Isaiah 21.1-12
Matthew 10.34 – 11.1

Thursday 26 November

Isaiah 21.1-12

'A stern vision ...' (v.2)

There are times when we wish that the Old Testament prophets were a little less poetic and a little more specific. This is one of the places where commentators admit defeat. There is no way of knowing what Isaiah is talking about. What do we do with passages of the Bible like this? Perhaps the only thing we can do is go with the flow of the poetry and let our imaginations run free.

A whirlwind sweeps across the desert. The terrified watcher sees it coming, like a great hurricane, but cannot get out of the way of its destruction. People are settling down to a meal, not realizing the destruction that is about to hit. A nation is threshed like so much grain at the mercy of the spikes of the threshing machine. A sentinel sits in his tower on the city walls, waiting with dread for a message of death and defeat.

The imagery is powerful. It speaks to us of a world that is falling apart, where all is dread and danger. 'What of the night?' a voice asks the sentinel (v.11); 'what time is it?' 'Morning comes, and also the night,' is the enigmatic reply (v.12). But this phrase has been adopted as part of the Christian keeping of Advent. When the world is falling apart, and the night is all around, the only hope is that God will come to be with us.

God the Father,
help us to hear the call of Christ the King
and to follow in his service,
whose kingdom has no end;
for he reigns with you and the Holy Spirit,
one God, one glory.

COLLECT

Friday 27 November

Psalm **139** *or* **88** (95)
Isaiah 22.1-14
Matthew 11.2-19

Isaiah 22.1-14

'Let us eat and drink, for tomorrow we die' (v.13)

These chapters of Isaiah are particularly grim, full of judgement, destruction and death. Such is the picture of the inevitability of disaster that we have built up in our reading that we may well have some fellow feeling for the imagined people of Judah here. God, says Isaiah, would welcome some sign of penitence from them, some wearing of sackcloth, some weeping and wailing over their sinfulness. But they have given up. The end is inevitable, so they might as well enjoy what little time they have left.

The attitude that is condemned here is, in fact, commended by another Old Testament writer. Ecclesiastes, the Preacher, urges people to eat and drink and enjoy themselves. Life is short and nothing lasts, he says, so make the most of what God has given you.

The difference is one of timing. Isaiah's message is urgent. The day of the Lord is here. The enemy is at the gates. The judgement is imminent. This is a time to be serious. This is a time for returning to God.

The prophet's job is to interpret the signs of the times. Isaiah is a commentator on days of 'tumult and trampling and confusion'. What do we think about our own times? Is this a time for enjoying all that we have? Or is it a time for paying serious attention to the state of the world? Or both?

COLLECT

Eternal Father,
whose Son Jesus Christ ascended to the throne of heaven
    that he might rule over all things as Lord and King:
keep the Church in the unity of the Spirit
and in the bond of peace,
and bring the whole created order to worship at his feet;
who is alive and reigns with you,
in the unity of the Holy Spirit,
one God, now and for ever.

Saturday 28 November

Isaiah 24

'... the windows of heaven are opened' (v.18)

If Isaiah has frightened us in the past two weeks, today he terrifies us. His poem piles image upon image, painting a picture of utter desolation. In our minds are television pictures of the aftermath of hurricanes and earthquakes and tsunamis. Perhaps we thanked God that neither we nor our loved ones were in their path. But the trauma Isaiah describes takes in the whole earth. No one can escape. There is nowhere to run to. There is no one left to bring aid.

And perhaps the most chilling words of all are 'the windows of heaven are opened'. They take us right back to the beginning of time, to Genesis 7, when 'the windows of the heavens were opened' (Genesis 7.11), creation was undone, and the great flood destroyed almost all humanity.

God has the heavenly powers in his sights too. Even the sun and moon are to be set aside. The watery chaos is back; the heavenly bodies are covered up; the earth is breaking in pieces. The godless, exploitative, corrupt world has come to an end.

Except – there are still some who sing praises to the majesty of the Lord, the God of Israel. And there is still to be seen, in Jerusalem, the glory of the Lord of hosts. It turns out that God and his world are not quite finished yet. Even at the end of all things, the promise of God's reign ensures a future.

God the Father,
help us to hear the call of Christ the King
and to follow in his service,
whose kingdom has no end;
for he reigns with you and the Holy Spirit,
one God, one glory.

COLLECT

Seasonal Prayers of Thanksgiving

Blessed are you, Sovereign God of all,
to you be praise and glory for ever.
In your tender compassion
the dawn from on high is breaking upon us
to dispel the lingering shadows of night.
As we look for your coming among us this day,
open our eyes to behold your presence
and strengthen our hands to do your will,
that the world may rejoice and give you praise.
Blessed be God, Father, Son and Holy Spirit.
Blessed be God for ever.

Christmas Season

Blessed are you, Sovereign God,
creator of heaven and earth,
to you be praise and glory for ever.
As your living Word, eternal in heaven,
assumed the frailty of our mortal flesh,
may the light of your love be born in us
to fill our hearts with joy as we sing:
Blessed be God, Father, Son and Holy Spirit.
Blessed be God for ever.

Epiphany

Blessed are you, Sovereign God,
king of the nations,
to you be praise and glory for ever.
From the rising of the sun to its setting
your name is proclaimed in all the world.
As the Sun of Righteousness dawns in our hearts
anoint our lips with the seal of your Spirit
that we may witness to your gospel
and sing your praise in all the earth.
Blessed be God, Father, Son and Holy Spirit.
Blessed be God for ever.

Blessed are you, Lord God of our salvation,
to you be glory and praise for ever.
In the darkness of our sin you have shone in our hearts
to give the light of the knowledge of the glory of God
in the face of Jesus Christ.
Open our eyes to acknowledge your presence,
that freed from the misery of sin and shame
we may grow into your likeness from glory to glory.
Blessed be God, Father, Son and Holy Spirit.
Blessed be God for ever.

Passiontide

Blessed are you, Lord God of our salvation,
to you be praise and glory for ever.
As a man of sorrows and acquainted with grief
your only Son was lifted up
that he might draw the whole world to himself.
May we walk this day in the way of the cross
and always be ready to share its weight,
declaring your love for all the world.
Blessed be God, Father, Son and Holy Spirit.
Blessed be God for ever.

Easter Season

Blessed are you, Sovereign Lord,
the God and Father of our Lord Jesus Christ,
to you be glory and praise for ever.
From the deep waters of death
you brought your people to new birth
by raising your Son to life in triumph.
Through him dark death has been destroyed
and radiant life is everywhere restored.
As you call us out of darkness into his marvellous light
may our lives reflect his glory
and our lips repeat the endless song.
Blessed be God, Father, Son and Holy Spirit.
Blessed be God for ever.

Blessed are you, Lord of heaven and earth,
to you be glory and praise for ever.
From the darkness of death you have raised your Christ
to the right hand of your majesty on high.
The pioneer of our faith, his passion accomplished,
has opened for us the way to heaven
and sends on us the promised Spirit.
May we be ready to follow the Way
and so be brought to the glory of his presence
where songs of triumph for ever sound:
Blessed be God, Father, Son and Holy Spirit.
Blessed be God for ever.

From the day after Ascension Day
until the Day of Pentecost

Blessed are you, creator God,
to you be praise and glory for ever.
As your Spirit moved over the face of the waters
bringing light and life to your creation,
pour out your Spirit on us today
that we may walk as children of light
and by your grace reveal your presence.
Blessed be God, Father, Son and Holy Spirit.
Blessed be God for ever.

From All Saints until the day before
the First Sunday of   Advent

Blessed are you, Sovereign God,
ruler and judge of all,
to you be praise and glory for ever.
In the darkness of this age that is passing away
may the light of your presence which the saints enjoy
surround our steps as we journey on.
May we reflect your glory this day
and so be made ready to see your face
in the heavenly city where night shall be no more.
Blessed be God, Father, Son and Holy Spirit.
Blessed be God for ever.

The Lord's Prayer and The Grace

Our Father in heaven,
hallowed be your name,
your kingdom come,
your will be done,
on earth as in heaven.
Give us today our daily bread.
Forgive us our sins
as we forgive those who sin against us.
Lead us not into temptation
but deliver us from evil.
For the kingdom, the power,
and the glory are yours
now and for ever.
Amen.

(or)

Our Father, who art in heaven,
hallowed be thy name;
thy kingdom come;
thy will be done;
on earth as it is in heaven.
Give us this day our daily bread.
And forgive us our trespasses,
as we forgive those who trespass against us.
And lead us not into temptation;
but deliver us from evil.
For thine is the kingdom,
the power and the glory,
for ever and ever.
Amen.

The grace of our Lord Jesus Christ,
and the love of God,
and the fellowship of the Holy Spirit,
be with us all evermore.
Amen.

An Order for Night Prayer (Compline)

The Lord almighty grant us a quiet night and a perfect end.
Amen.

Our help is in the name of the Lord
who made heaven and earth.

A period of silence for reflection on the past day may follow.

The following or other suitable words of penitence may be used

Most merciful God,
we confess to you,
before the whole company of heaven and one another,
that we have sinned in thought, word and deed
and in what we have failed to do.
Forgive us our sins,
heal us by your Spirit
and raise us to new life in Christ. Amen.

O God, make speed to save us.
O Lord, make haste to help us.

Glory to the Father and to the Son
and to the Holy Spirit;
as it was in the beginning is now
and shall be for ever. Amen.
Alleluia.

The following or another suitable hymn may be sung

Before the ending of the day,
Creator of the world, we pray
That you, with steadfast love, would keep
Your watch around us while we sleep.

From evil dreams defend our sight,
From fears and terrors of the night;
Tread underfoot our deadly foe
That we no sinful thought may know.

O Father, that we ask be done
Through Jesus Christ, your only Son;
And Holy Spirit, by whose breath
Our souls are raised to life from death.

The Word of God

Psalmody

One or more of Psalms 4, 91 or 134 may be used.

Psalm 134

1 Come, bless the Lord, all you servants of the Lord, ◆
   you that by night stand in the house of the Lord.

2 Lift up your hands towards the sanctuary ◆
   and bless the Lord.

3 The Lord who made heaven and earth ◆
   give you blessing out of Zion.

**Glory to the Father and to the Son
and to the Holy Spirit;
as it was in the beginning is now
and shall be for ever. Amen.**

Scripture Reading

*One of the following short lessons or another suitable
passage is read*

You, O Lord, are in the midst of us and we are called by
your name; leave us not, O Lord our God.

Jeremiah 14.9

(or)

Be sober, be vigilant, because your adversary the devil is
prowling round like a roaring lion, seeking for someone
to devour. Resist him, strong in the faith.

1 Peter 5.8,9

(or)

The servants of the Lamb shall see the face of God, whose
name will be on their foreheads. There will be no more
night: they will not need the light of a lamp or the light of the
sun, for God will be their light, and they will reign for ever
and ever.

Revelation 22.4,5

Into your hands, O Lord, I commend my spirit.
Into your hands, O Lord, I commend my spirit.
For you have redeemed me, Lord God of truth.
I commend my spirit.
Glory to the Father and to the Son
and to the Holy Spirit.
Into your hands, O Lord, I commend my spirit.

Or, in Easter

Into your hands, O Lord, I commend my spirit.
Alleluia, alleluia.
Into your hands, O Lord, I commend my spirit.
Alleluia, alleluia.
For you have redeemed me, Lord God of truth.
Alleluia, alleluia.
Glory to the Father and to the Son
and to the Holy Spirit.
Into your hands, O Lord, I commend my spirit.
Alleluia, alleluia.

Keep me as the apple of your eye.
Hide me under the shadow of your wings.

Gospel Canticle

Nunc Dimittis (The Song of Simeon)

Save us, O Lord, while waking,
and guard us while sleeping,
that awake we may watch with Christ
and asleep may rest in peace.

1   Now, Lord, you let your servant go in peace:
    your word has been fulfilled.

2   My own eyes have seen the salvation
    which you have prepared in the sight of every people;

3   A light to reveal you to the nations
    and the glory of your people Israel.

Luke 2.29-32

**Glory to the Father and to the Son
and to the Holy Spirit;
as it was in the beginning is now
and shall be for ever. Amen.**

**Save us, O Lord, while waking,
and guard us while sleeping,
that awake we may watch with Christ
and asleep may rest in peace.**

Prayers

Intercessions and thanksgivings may be offered here.

The Collect

Visit this place, O Lord, we pray,
and drive far from it the snares of the enemy;
may your holy angels dwell with us and guard us in peace,
and may your blessing be always upon us;
through Jesus Christ our Lord.
Amen.

The Lord's Prayer (see p. 323) may be said.

The Conclusion

In peace we will lie down and sleep;
for you alone, Lord, make us dwell in safety.

Abide with us, Lord Jesus,
for the night is at hand and the day is now past.

As the night watch looks for the morning,
so do we look for you, O Christ.

[Come with the dawning of the day
and make yourself known in the breaking of the bread.]

The Lord bless us and watch over us;
the Lord make his face shine upon us and be gracious to us;
the Lord look kindly on us and give us peace.
Amen.

Reflections for Daily Prayer:
Advent 2015 to the eve of Advent 2016

Reflections for Daily Prayer returns
for the 2015–16 Church year with
another range of illustrious
contributors! Confirmed writers
so far include Gillian Cooper,
Steven Croft, Andrew Davison,
Maggi Dawn, Paula Gooder,
Peter Graystone, Malcolm Guite,
Emma Ineson, Mark Oakley
and Martyn Percy

£16.99 • 336 pages
ISBN 978 0 7151 4457 2
Available May 2015

> **Also available
> in Kindle and
> epub formats!**

Reflections for Daily Prayer:
Lent and Holy Week 2015

Do you enjoy reading *Reflections for Daily Prayer* and wish you
could share its benefits with others? This shortened edition of
Reflections is ideal for group or church use during Lent, or for
anyone seeking a daily devotional guide to the most holy
season of the Christian year. It is also an ideal taster for those
wanting to begin a regular pattern of prayer and reading.

Authors: Malcolm Guite,
Ben Quash, Frances Ward,
Lucy Winkett

**Please note this book
reproduces the material for Lent
and Holy Week found in the
volume you are now holding.**

£4.99 • 48 pages
ISBN 978 0 7151 4460 2
Available November 2014

Reflections for **Daily Prayer**
App

Make Bible study and reflection a part of your routine wherever you go with the Reflections for Daily Prayer App for Apple and Android devices.

Download the app for free from the App Store (Apple devices) or Google Play (Android devices) and receive a week's worth of reflections free. Then purchase a monthly, three-monthly or annual subscription to receive up-to-date content.

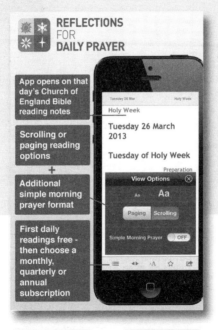

Resources for Daily Prayer

Common Worship: Daily Prayer

The official daily office of the Church of England, *Common Worship: Daily Prayer* is a rich collection of devotional material that will enable those wanting to enrich their quiet times to develop a regular pattern of prayer. It includes:

- Prayer During the Day
- Forms of Penitence
- Morning and Evening Prayer
- Night Prayer (Compline)
- Collects and Refrains
- Canticles
- Complete Psalter

896 pages • with 6 ribbons • 202 x 125mm

Hardback	978 0 7151 2199 3	**£22.50**
Soft cased	978 0 7151 2178 8	**£27.50**
Bonded leather	978 0 7151 2277 8	**£45.00**

Time to Pray

This compact, soft-case volume offers two simple, shorter offices from *Common Worship: Daily Prayer*. It is an ideal introduction to a more structured personal devotional time, or can be used as a lighter, portable daily office for those on the move.

Time to Pray includes:

- Prayer During the Day
  (for every day of the week)
- Night Prayer
- Selected Psalms

£12.99 • 112 pages • Soft case
ISBN 978 0 7151 2122 1

Order now at **www.chpublishing.co.uk**
or via **Norwich Books and Music**
Telephone **(01603) 785923**
E-mail **orders@norwichbooksandmusic.co.uk**